IN SEARCH OF THE TRUTH

A Jehovah's Witness' Quest for the Historical Church

Copyright © 2009 by St. Anthony's Greek Orthodox Monastery
4784 N. St. Joseph's Way • Florence, AZ 85232
All rights reserved
ISBN 0-9667000-6-6

Author:
Nicholas Mavromagoulos

Publisher in Greek:
The Holy Royal & Stavropegial Monastery Maheras

Translation:
Constantine Zalalas

Editing:
Mother Michaila • Christina Bourgeois
Eleftheria Kaimakliotis • Milena Mihich

Publisher in English
St. Anthony's Greek Orthodox Monastery, Florence, AZ
together with
St. Nicodemos Publications, Bethlehem, PA

Dedicated to my natural and spiritual parents, who taught me to love the Way of Life.

Contents

Foreword.. xi

Introduction...................................... xiii

1. Carriers of a new religion........................... 3
   Growing up in the Society 6

2. Flirting with the Spider 15
   The Religious Instructor.......................... 18
   Touching the Web 25

3. Preaching in Class 31

4. In the Nest of the Spider 35
   Increasing contact............................... 39
   The First Problems............................... 42

5. Luring Others to the Web 49

6. Tied on the Web................................... 57

7. Life as a Baptized Witness 63
   Foretaste of Injustice 67
   Marriage Proposal 74
   Preparing for Jail 76
   At the Disciplinary Ward 80

    At the Military Prison of Avlonas 82
    At Cassandra 90
    My Life After Jail 94
    Working the Streets 97
    The First Doubts 103

8. Persecution by the Society 113

9. Exodus.. 127
    The turning point.................................... 131
    The beginning of the end 138
    Increasing the distance 145
    My Crisis of Conscience 149
    The Letter 154
    Visiting a Foreign Denomination 157
    The District Convention............................. 162
    Inquisition 166
    Mr. Theoharakis...................................... 174
    Considering Whether to Discuss the Dogma 176
    Finally, Discussing the Dogma!..................... 180
    Committee from Bethel 183
    Using the Final Opportunity........................ 189
    Disfellowshipped 192

10. Progressing Toward the Truth 201

11. Creating a new church 205

12. Searching for THE Church 211
    Leading others to the Historical Church.............. 215

13. Leaving even this Congregation 217
    Getting used to the new Environment 227

14. In the land of the "passion-fruit eaters" 239

15. Problems and dangers 255

Small Glossary C

Bibliogragphy .... M

Index .... Q

Foreword

What was the great theological error of the Roman governor of Jerusalem, Pontius Pilate, when he asked Jesus Christ during his cross-examination, "What is truth?"[1] Theologians over the past 2,000 years, have proven that the Truth is not a specific object or an abstract idea as the question suggests, but that the truth is a person, Jesus Christ, the Son of the Living God. This is testified to with absolute clarity by Jesus Christ Himself in a conversation with the Apostle Thomas, when He says, "I am the way, the truth, and the life."[2]

Many times, however, our loving God allows a person's search for the Truth to be a painstaking and laborious struggle, lasting many years through the plethora of contemporary heresies and confessions created by the human intellect. A very moving case of such a man is the author of this book, Nicholas Mavromagoulos, who was born into and, for the first twenty-four years of his life, was raised as a Jehovah's Witness. This is the unfortunate case of a man who did not inherit his faith in Christ within the bosom of the Orthodox Church. Nevertheless, God created man with an inalienable gift, the unquenchable thirst and unconquerable drive to search for the only true God and to be in ontological communion with Him.

Nicholas Mavromagoulos not only kept this gift, he also cultivated it. The Lord, being most righteous, led Nicholas to the

---

1 John 18:38

2 John 14:6

calm port of His Church after the long-term tempestuous adventure within the embrace of this deluded totalitarian organization which calls itself Jehovah's Witnesses. Nicholas reveals towards the end of his story, "Nothing was lost all these years. These are all useful experiences in the service of the true Gospel for the deliverance of people, who are trapped in a cage and are searching for an exit."

The Holy Monastery of Maheras, wishing to help all our Christian and non-Christian brothers and sisters who may be facing the danger of getting caught in the nets of the Watchtower Society, presents this shocking and stirring biography for the proper orientation of all those who are seeking the Truth. This book is especially for those who may be searching within wide avenues which lead the soul to fossilization by human passions instead of the sanctification of the entire man, something offered only by the Orthodox Church through one's participation in its life-giving Holy Mysteries.

Abbot of the Holy Royal & Stravropegial Monastery of Maheras
Archimandrite Arsenios along with my brotherhood in Christ

29th day of February 2004
Sunday of Orthodoxy

Introduction

Dear Reader, what you are about to read in this book happens to be the fruit, the pain, and the love of its author for the millions of victims of the organization called the *Watchtower Bible & Tract Society*. The author lived through the emotions, expectations, fears, and adventures experienced by everyone belonging to this organization who searches for the truth and is greatly disappointed at some point.

These stressful experiences are more familiar than most people think; it is believed that there are now more persons who have resigned or just walked away from the Watchtower Society than active Witnesses,[3] something that former Governing Body member Raymond Franz aptly called revolving door situation.[4] It is the hope of the author that this work will provide to these disenchanted people the support and guidance they need and at the same time give some much needed information to those considering joining the Watchtower Society.

This book is a compound biography, and all references are real facts of actual people, primarily the real life experiences of the au-

---

[3] Jerry Bergman, Ph. D., *Why Jehovah's Witnesses Leave the Watchtower*, retrieved 2/1/2009 from http://www.seanet.com/~raines/leave.html)

[4] Raymond Franz, *Crisis of Conscience*, Commentary Press, 4th Edition, 2004, p. 37

thor. Some names, however, have been changed for obvious reasons: It is not the point of this book to hurt individual persons, many of whom are relatives and dear friends of mine, but to reveal the dangers and pitfalls a man-made religion can bring.

All the events have been combined into two parallel stories, following the paths of two friends, in order to enable the reader to experience an immersion into the emotions and the psychology of the members of the organization. Thus, the odd-numbered chapters describes the life, habits, and idiosyncrasies of someone who was born and raised in the Watchtower Society while the even-numbered chapters narrate the progressive subjection of his friend to this Society. The chapters in which the first man speaks have the subtitle, Nikos' story, and the chapters in which the second man speaks have the subtitle George's story. The book sees things from the perspective of these two people. The book's main goal, however, is to analyze the difficult journey of their exodus from the Watchtower and their relentless search for the Truth.

I pray to God to give to every reader that which he or she may need: understanding of and for the Witnesses; proper methodologies and techniques for all those who wish to reach them; sobriety and mental clarity to the candidate victim of the Watchtower; and a motive for research by the fossilized witness who likes to believe that he has found the ark of salvation within the Society. Finally, perseverance, courage, hope, and direction to anyone who has left the organization and who may still be in the difficult phase of restructuring his faith and his life.

I pray to God to give strength to all those who are lost in the ocean of Protestant denominations and are searching, as in a labyrinth, for the way towards God, who is His Son, Jesus Christ.

Nicholas Mavromagoulos

Some Important Dates

1975 The world fails to end as the Watchtower had prophesied. This date was based upon another erroneous assumption that Christ's invisible Kingdom started in 1914 AD. The "Armageddon debacle" brings indescribable disappointment to the Jehovah's Witnesses around the world. Many leave the Society, while countless understand that something is wrong. The Watchtower Society responds by making the disfellowshipping rules stricter.

1977 A Swiss JW Elder, Carl Olof Jonsson, sends massive evidence to the Governing Body of the Watchtower Society proving that the JW's highly important "1914 dogma" is false from a Biblical, historical and archeological perspective. His results are ignored and Jonsson is later disfellowshipped.

1980 Raymond Franz, a member of the Governing Body and a nephew of the Society's President, having examined Jonsson's evidence, gets disfellowshipped for doubting the 1914 dogma. The Watch Tower society initiates a purge in which anyone expressing doubts of the Society's beliefs gets expelled and shunned.

1983 Raymond Franz prints his *Crisis of Conscience*. The book provides a sober critique of the Society's history, teachings, and inner workings. It causes hundreds of thousands of Jehovah's Witnesses around the world to leave the Watchtower Society.

1986 George Christoula, a well known JW in Greece, gets disfellowshipped for doubting the 1914 dogma. Many Greek Witnesses disregard the Society's ban on disfellowshipped persons and flock around him for Bible study. The Greek Watchtower resorts to illegal spying and videotaping to identify them and disfellowship them as "apostates." The case is brought in the Greek civil courts and a newspaper scandal erupts. As a result, thousands of Greek JWs are either leaving the Society or get disfellowshipped.

1986 The two heroes of this book are being disfellowshipped for associating Christoula and doubting the 1914 dogma. Their search for the historical Church begins.

1995 The Watch Tower Society changes its mind about the 1914 date, shrugging off the responsibility to the individual believers!

IN SEARCH OF THE TRUTH

A Jehovah's Witness's Quest for the Historical Church

Charles Taze Russell (1852–1916)

The founder of the Jehovah's Witnesses—C. T. Russell—was raised a devout Presbyterian; at age 13 he joined the Congregational Church, and at 18, the Adventists. In 1878 he broke off and formed his own ministry and a journal: "Zion's Watch Tower and Herald of Christ's Presence." Jehovah's Witnesses believe that Russell was a profound religious leader with no respectable tradition behind him. In reality, Russell's movement had much in common with the churches he had attended—his denomination was very much a religious product of 19th century Protestant America. By the time he died in 1916, the church he had founded had already experienced many troubles and schisms.

1. Carriers of a new religion

Nikos' story

My story begins during the first half of the 20th century. As you will see, both sides of my family were fully absorbed into the Jehovah's Witnesses. Actually, my paternal grandfather was one of the first followers in our country of the organization which called itself at the time, Students of the Scriptures.[5] As a young man, my grandfather resided in one of the villages of the island of Rhodes, the largest of the cluster of the twelve islands called the Dodecanese. He was especially drawn to reading, but due to a limited Christian education and discipline, he became prey for the Society. With the aid of the organization's magazines, he spread this new faith to his island. He married my grandmother, a woman of likewise limited education, and with her they raised three children according to the principles of the organization.

---

5   In Greece, the Watchtower Society started its activities in the beginning of the 20th century. In 1912, C. T. Russell visited Greece and gave sermons in Athens and in Corinth. In 1920, the second president of the Society, J. F. Rutherford, also visited Greece and gave a lecture in Athens. Ever since, there was a slow but steady growth of the Society in Greece (according to Marley Cole, in his *Jehovah's Witnesses, the New World Society*, Vantage Press, NY, 1955, p. 223 there were twelve ministers in 1918, and 2,338 in 1948) with an all-time peak in 1985 when there were 22,466 baptized members. Following the "witch hunt" of the 90's (see ch. 9), by 2,005 some 5,000 have left the Organization!

Their son, my father, was a rare man. Although Jehovah's Witnesses claim to be pure of sin, my father really was a man of exemplary goodness and, consequently, stood apart. He was a man of deep faith and firm convictions. At the time of his youth, the Witnesses did not refuse to become soldiers, they only refused to bear arms. So when my father was drafted into the Greek army, he naturally refused to carry a weapon, which led to his incarceration. He was exiled to the remote island of Makronisos,[6] and he was tortured by people who considered themselves to be good Christians and patriots. This situation not only failed to convince him that he was in the wrong religion, it led him to conclude that he was persecuted for holding on to the true faith.

Just for the record, allow me to skip ahead a bit to state that when later the Greek government allowed the Witnesses to serve weaponless, the Society changed its position and refused the Witnesses the very identity of a soldier, a development that caused unnecessary grief to many Witnesses. In the end, the *Governing Body** finally changed its mind and now the Witnesses can exchange their active duty for some form of civil service without complications.

As a Jehovah's Witness, my father was raised to regard all religions besides the Watchtower as "Babylon the whore" and therefore to believe that Orthodox Christians were deluded.[7] Deep down, however, he must have been more reasonable, even from his childhood, com-

---

[6] Makronisos is very small, arid, rocky, uninhabited island in Greece, located close to the coast of Attica. For many years it was used as prison.

[7] "All religions," wrote the second president of the Watchtower, "properly take the name Babylon... All religious organizations on the earth are formed and carried on by men who are subjected to wrongful influence and ruled by the great enemy Satan the Devil; and this is true whether any of them know it or not... There are two great organizations in existence, to wit: the organization of the Almighty God, which is wholly righteous, pure and true, and the organization of the Devil, the mimic god, which is unholy, wicked, and entirely false." (J. F. Rutherford, *Enemies*, Watch Tower Bible and Tract Society, 1937, pp. 71-72.) For a more recent treatment on the subject see the *Watchtower* magazine of May, 15, 1989, pp. 6–9)

1. Carriers of a new religion

pared to other heterodox as I will illustrate in the following accounts.

While he was serving in the army in Athens he met my mother and they later married. Despite the negative experiences he had in the army, my father had the habit of chanting Orthodox hymns while he shaved! On one occasion, my mother overheard him and couldn't believe her ears! She asked him where he had learned these hymns, since he had never stepped foot inside an Orthodox Church. He confided in her that as a little boy he had this curiosity about the services of the Orthodox Church, and he used to sneak behind the church's windows and follow the Divine Liturgy until he memorized these hymns, all of this being done behind his father's back of course. My mother told him not to chant because it is a sin. Undaunted, my father responded, "Why is it a sin? These hymns are correct! They are in total agreement with the Bible!"

And he kept chanting. I strongly believe that if my father had been approached by even one true Christian in the course of his life, he may have taken a different path. After his death, I also discovered that he had several books from other religions, the majority were from the Students of the Scriptures. This was the name of the mother denomination of the Witnesses; after these two groups separated, the mother denomination was called the "Evil Servant," and all of its literature was banned from the circle of the Witnesses.[8]

---

8 The Jehovah's Witnesses were originally known as "Students of the Scriptures." When Russell (the founder of the Watchtower Society) died, a power struggle within the top echelon of the Society followed. Joseph F. Rutherford emerged as the strong man, but a schism quickly followed that became known in the organization as the "Watchtower Schism of 1917." Rutherford reacted swiftly, with purges in the society and calling the independent minded Bible Students "Evil Servants," "Judas Class," and the "Delilah Class". Nevertheless, for years many Watch Tower Bible Students, continued to regard the schismatics as brethren in Christ. So, to better differentiate his followers from the undisciplined Bible students, on 26 July 1931 Rutherford issued a resolution which called his followers to accept a new name: "Jehovah's Witnesses." Nowadays, worldwide, there are probably under 10,000 Bible Students outside the Watchtower Society.

On my mother's side, things were slightly different. My grandmother was a Greek from Asia Minor; she came to Greece as an illiterate refugee after the destruction of Smyrna.[9] She gave birth to many children but only three lived. My mother was born shortly after her father died, and she was baptized Orthodox a few days after her birth.

My grandmother was a rare human being. As a refuge and a widow she was alone in the world, and therefore it was very hard to provide for her children during the very difficult German occupation of Greece. Yet, during those hard years of war, she helped many people, not from her excess but by sharing what little she had.

Her firstborn son unfortunately lacked the necessary ecclesiastical experience and knowledge to see the fallacies of the Watchtower, and thus became one of the early first followers of the Society.

My grandmother and my mother, then a mere teenager, not understanding much about theology, followed her brother, not realizing they were actually falling into heresy. So it became the case that my mother was also heavily influenced by the Society from a young age. After the death of her oldest brother, she continued along with my grandmother to spread the ideas of the Society, fearlessly facing the persecutions and arrests. After my parents married, my mother became very ill, and I wasn't born until ten years later.

Growing up in the Society

When as a baby I started to talk, one of my first words was Jehovah. My parents exerted much effort to make me a model child accord-

---

9   At the end of Word War I, the Ottoman province of Smyrna (being predominantly Greek) was given by the Allies to Greece. However, skirmishes between the Greek army and Turkish irregulars under Kemal Attaturk continued unabated, culminating in the defeat of the Greek army, and the permanent destruction of the Greek population in Asia Minor. Most of the adult male civilians were sent by the Turkish government to forced labour camps (known as amele taburları) where they vanished; surviving women and children were deported to Greece.

ing to the measures of the Society. In fact, they succeeded, at least as far as theoretical knowledge was concerned; but they failed miserably as far as conduct is concerned. Naturally, they had no clue about this last detail since I always tried to present my best colors to all those outside, always striving to put my best foot forward, just like some of my fellow faithful whom I knew well. We lived *double lives*.*

Since Witnesses believe they are Jehovah's chosen people while everybody else is doomed for perdition, most of them pretend to be morally perfect and they ignore the tradition of repentance of the Orthodox Church; thus they are incapable of battling sin. Therefore, despite my very young age and my sincerity in serving God, the passions of the flesh were already developing in me and all my attempts to live up to the outward picture I was then painting were quite fruitless.

Despite these personal failures, I was making great strides in the area of academics. Even at a preschool age, I knew how to analyze in great detail the book *Paradise*,[10] a very basic supplement of the Society with many pictures. I knew almost all the stories of the Holy Scriptures better than most Witnesses and the average Orthodox Christian. This, however, did not mean that I also understood the message of the Bible as the Apostles did.

My daily concern was how I was going to guide others to my faith, believing that if they did not become Witnesses, Jehovah would annihilate them during Armageddon. Jehovah, I was taught from infancy, was a God of wrath and vengeance and He would lead everyone who failed to become a Witness to eternal destruction. But we as Witnesses were not immune to destruction either; the Watchtower quoted verse after verse from the Bible to bore into our brains that anything less than absolute compliance to their rules meant eternal annihilation. The blessed survivors, however, would

---

10 *From Paradise Lost to Paradise Regained*, Watchtower Bible & Tract Society, 1958

be rewarded for their obedience to Jehovah with the joyful occupation of cleaning the face of the earth of the slaughtered infidel carcasses.[11] I considered these frightening doctrines to be indisputable realities, especially since my parents had supplied me with dozens of Scripture verses which I had committed to memory in order to support these dogmas and to tear down any rebuttals of the opposition.

The year 1975 was near, and the dreaded Armageddon, according to the Society, was just around the corner.[12] Having a burdened conscience about my personal failures, I had nightmares about the commencement of the apocalyptic juggernaut,[13] and many a night

---

11 "After Armageddon the surviving sheep of the New World society will go forth to look upon 'the slain of Jehovah.'... To all surviving flesh the dead bodies will be disgusting, hateful things. Worms will not stop swarming over the millions of bodies until the last body is eaten up. Birds and beasts also will eat their fill of human flesh until nothing is left but white bones. Bones do not make a pretty earth. So for seven prophetic months the Armageddon survivors will gather up the bones and bury them." (*Paradise*, Watchtower Bible & Tract Society, 1958 pp. 210–211)

12 "Let it be clear from the outset that the Society in its literature *never* proclaimed flat out that 1975 would be the definite end of this world and its population. Nevertheless, the formulations 1966 onward on what *might* happen in that year, the sense of urgency on a *probable* apocalyptic event, later followed by a *possibility* of a cataclysm, had a startling impact on the proselytizing activities of the Jehovah's Witnesses. " Jon R. Stone, *Expecting Armageddon: Essential Readings in Failed Prophecy*, Routledge, 2000, p. 191

13 It is difficult to convey the excitement this prediction had on the faithful Witnesses. As Penton remarks, "Thousands of Witness young people became pioneers as did

WHY ARE YOU LOOKING FORWARD TO 1975?

WHAT about all this talk concerning the year 1975? Lively discussions, some based on speculation, have burst into flame during recent months among serious students of the Bible. Their interest has been kindled by the belief that 1975 will mark the end of 6,000 years of human history since Adam's creation. The nearness of such an important date indeed fires the imagination and presents unlimited possibilities for discussion.

² But wait! How do we know their calculations are correct? What basis is there for saying Adam was created nearly 5,993 years ago? Does the one Book that can be implicitly trusted for its truthful historical accuracy, namely, the Inspired Word of Jehovah, the Holy Bible, give support and credence to such a conclusion?

³ In the marginal references of the Protestant *Authorized* or *King James Version*, and in the footnotes of certain editions of the Catholic *Douay* version, the date of man's creation is said to be 4004 B.C.E. This marginal date, however, is no part of the inspired text of the Holy Scriptures, since it was first suggested more than fifteen centuries after the last Bible writer died, and was not added to any edition of the Bible until 1701 C.E. It is an insertion based upon the conclusions of an Irish prelate, the Anglican Archbishop James Ussher (1581-1656). Ussher's chronology was only one of the many sincere efforts made during the past centuries to determine the time of Adam's creation. A hundred years ago when a count was taken, no less than 140 different timetables had been published by se-

1, 2. (a) What has sparked special interest in the year 1975, and with what results? (b) But what questions are raised?

3. Is the date for Adam's creation as found in many copies of the Bible part of the inspired Scriptures, and do all agree on the date?

Reading between the lines
It is true that the Watchtower Society never actually "proclaimed flat out that 1975 would be the definite end of this world." However, as former Governing Body member Raymond Franz wrote, "All this steady flow of information was clearly designed to foment and build up hope, anticipation. It was not designed to calm or defuse a spirit of excited expectation... It must be remembered that the organization was not a novice in this field. Its whole history from its very inception was one of building up people's hope in certain dates." (Franz, *Conscience*, p.246). (Above: WT 08/15/1968 p. 498)

I dreamed I was dying in the midst of flames and quakes.[14] I was sincerely scared by the aspect of the upheaval that loomed just ahead of me.

---

many new converts. Businessmen sold prospering businesses. Professional men gave up their jobs. Families sold their homes and moved to serve 'where the need [for evangelists] was greater.' Young couples delayed their marriages or at least refrained from having children if they did marry. Old couples sometimes withdrew all their pension funds at once. Many, both young and old, male and female, delayed having surgery or proper medical attention (M. S. J. Penton, *Apocalypse Delayed*, University of Toronto Press, Second Edition, p. 95)

14 The drawings on page 8 and 14 are from the book *From Paradise Lost to Paradise Regained*, Watchtower Bible & Tract Society, 1958, pp. 208–209

Often my mother would take me with her for *field service**15, for the propagation of the faith. At the same time, she always took me to all the *Kingdom Hall* meetings** which were a poor substitute of Christian churching.16 She also used to take me to the *circuit assemblies**, which were biannual meetings of a large number of followers.

At that time, Greece was governed by a dictatorship, so the circuit assemblies were held in secret in the forests where we pretended to go on a field trip by bus. At different times, meetings were limited to two or three people because meetings were prohibited. All these were instrumental in teaching me to take risks or to ignore the government, thus choosing to do what I considered to be the will of Jehovah. My proselytizing activities were aimed at my age group. I remember a mother who would not permit her son to be in my company so that I would not influence him. Not only the very young, but also adults were targets of my activities. My mother used this ability of mine to let me speak instead of her, fully surprising those in our

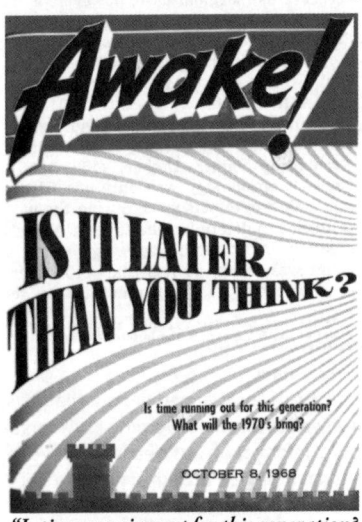

"Is time running out for this generation? What will the 1970's bring?"
Awake, October 8, 1968

---

15 JW terms that are explained in the glossary are italicized and marked with an asterisk the first time they appear in the text.

16 The Jehovah's Witnesses, being spiritual heirs of the Reformation, have a very dry worship model that usually consists of a few prayers and hymns. The guidance to *unceasing* prayer with a "contrite heart and a humble spirit" (Dan. 3:39, Psalm 50/51:19/17) that permeate the services in the Orthodox Church are markedly absent in the Kingdom Hall meetings.

1. Carriers of a new religion

audience and becoming the focus of their attention.

When I entered school, my teachers quickly realized that in religion class[17] I knew more than they did, and I could easily put them in a difficult situation if they dared to disagree with my faith. On one occasion, I happened to converse with some unfortunate adult women catechists, and the poor things did not know how to justify their faith in front of a mere child. Becoming frustrated, one of them resorted to disgraceful and unChristian behavior by losing control and using foul language and threats, telling me that my father, who had just died, was boiling in the caldrons of hell, and that I would also end up there. Of course I responded that God is not a sadist and does not torture people! After that, she left.

Growing up, I had conversations with more and more people, but I did not find anyone who could defend his faith satisfactorily. Thus, my confidence in my faith was soaring along with my arrogance! I used to challenge people, saying, "Bring on anyone you want! Your best theologian! I will show him the truth."

I also made sure to add, "If he can show me based on the Bible that I am in the wrong, I will change my faith, because I am very much interested in the truth." I was serious about this, as the future would prove.

My Junior High School Years

WHEN I ENTERED junior high school, the theologian of my religion class treated the topic of faith with much dogmatism, and he met me head-on with much obstinacy and ignorance. His manner of conduct, however, did not go unnoticed by my classmates. Every time we would disagree and have arguments in class, at recess my classmates would come to my aid, saying, "Bravo, you told him well!"

Although I was not convincing him, I was victorious in the

---

17 There is no separation of church and state in Greece; thus, religion is taught in public schools.

eyes of the class. Thus my classmates, who were all impressed by my actions, were becoming predisposed to listening to any Witness who might happen to knock at their door.

I also had a field day with the students who did not believe in God. When they listened to my arguments with the theologian, they would ask me questions about my religion, saying that all religions are fraudulent. I would then logically prove to them the existence of a single creator, and I proceeded to develop the case of my faith as the only one capable of offering true answers.

I remember at some point in high school having a very long discussion with two friends about the existence of God and questioning whether the content of the Holy Scriptures is truthful. At the time, they could not respond to my arguments, nor did they wish to be convinced, so the discussion was terminated. A number of months went by and one day they came to tell me that they believed, that they had found the truth, and that they were eager to help me to know God!

As it turned out, they had joined a Pentecostal group, convinced by the "miracles" they witnessed there. I tried to persuade them that the miracles were the work of demonic powers and not of the Holy Spirit. Of course I had no doubt about this since I had been taught from a young age that during the Judgment some will say that they did many miracles in the name of the Lord, and the Lord will answer them, "I never knew you, depart from me, you who practice lawlessness!"[18]

Since I myself did not have some miracle to display from God, I was not convinced by any miracle. This did not present any problem to me, especially since the organization had provided me with another verse against miracles: "But whether there are prophecies,

---

[18] Matt. 7:22-23

If you are a young person, you also need to face the fact that you will never grow old in this present system of things. Why not? Because all the evidence in fulfillment of Bible prophecy indicates that this corrupt system is due to end in a few years. Of the generation that observed the beginning of the "last days" in 1914, Jesus foretold: "This generation will by no means pass away until all these things occur."—Matt. 24:34.

Therefore, as a young person, you will never fulfill any career that this system offers. If you are in high school and thinking about a college education, it means at least four, perhaps even six or eight more years to graduate into a specialized career. But where will this system of things be by that time? It will be well on the way toward its finish, if not actually gone!

Should a young man purse studies? The Watchtower Society had never *clearly* stated 1975 as the end of human history, but had given plenty of hints. This 1969 article advises young Witnesses not to get a college education "because all the evidence in fulfillment of Bible prophecy indicated that this corrupt system is due to end in a few years..." (Awake 5/22/69 p.15)

---

they will fail; whether there are tongues, they will cease."[19]

Above all, however, what convinced me to disbelieve them was that those who performed these miracles believed in doctrines that I had been taught to consider demonic, such as the dogma of the Trinity and the immortality of the soul. Therefore, our discussions were not centered around miracles but on doctrine.

Although these boys were coming up with very good arguments, their limited experience with the Holy Scriptures and their having only studied for a few months made them weak opponents in a religious debate. I had the ability to throw difficult questions at them, causing them to fight against each other. At the same time, I could only see what I wanted to see. Consequently, I admired the unity and solid foundation so readily obvious to us Witnesses compared to these totally confused *goats.**

Notwithstanding all of this, I was left with some troublesome questions after hearing about their faith. Would Jehovah kill all these faithful children in Armageddon? While pondering this, I

---

19 I Cor. 13:8

found some relief remembering the answer of the Society: "If they are worthy of salvation, Jehovah will provide for them to come to the truth before Armageddon."

Strange thing, though; the year 1975 came and passed and the frightening Armageddon did not happen as foretold. In my immature teenage mind, it didn't occur to me back then to question the Society about it. This would require a few more years of growth, reading, and prayer.

As for the boys, unfortunately, a year later these boys became atheists again, in spite of all the miracles they saw saying that the miracles they had seen were caused by "unknown spiritual beings" or "undiscovered human powers of the soul." From that point on they began living as carelessly as they possibly could, enjoying the *day* or the *now* because as they claimed, "Who can really know the truth?"

Fifteen years later I met one of them who had since become a faithful child of the Orthodox faith. Back then, however, their backsliding reinforced my belief in the righteousness of my faith.

At that time, I also met George, a person who would play an important role in my life. But I will allow him to tell his story.

2. Flirting with the Spider

George's story

t was a freezing Sunday morning. Snuggled in my bed, I was enjoying the last few minutes of warmth before facing the elements and my frozen room. I loved to take it easy on Sunday mornings, especially during the winter when all of my buddies would be late to the neighborhood hangout. My father worked on Sundays, and on this particular Sunday morning my mother had gone to some memorial service, even though she very seldom attended church. I don't remember her attending church on days other than Holy Week and a few memorial services of very close relatives. Fortunately, I was still too young to have to attend to such duties. "Besides, who has the patience to endure all those endless, nonsensical chants," I thought.

With my eyes still closed, I organized my activities for the day. Sunday was the only day I could dedicate to myself. The rest of the week I worked at a jewelry design shop, and in the evenings I attended a trade high school. This was my first month in the new routine, and I was just beginning to get accustomed to the full daily schedule. Sundays, I wanted for myself.

The ring of the door bell suddenly interrupted my thoughts. I opened the door shivering. Two well-dressed men in suits and

ties were standing in front of me, sporting hearty smiles. One of them was wearing a long rain coat, a hat, and a characteristic "Hitler" mustache. They were both holding briefcases with the zippers open, to make some books visible inside. They greeted me very politely, and then the man with the mustache started the conversation.

"My name is Constantine, and I am visiting the neighborhood with my friend here to bring good news," he claimed.

"Like what?" I asked.

"Would you agree that the state of the world is getting worse and worse, and we hear on the news...," he started.

I began to lose my temper. I was still shivering with the door open, and they still had not said what they wanted.

"What exactly is it that you want?" I interrupted.

"We are advertising two magazines, *Watchtower* and *Awake*, and the current topic of interest is...," he began to explain.

I interrupted, saying, "I'm not interested, thank you."

He tried to talk me into it, "You know we also have an interesting book."

"Thank you, but I'm not interested!"

2. Flirting with the Spider

They then went on to ask if they could come inside to discuss it, and I asked them who they were. They responded, "We are Christian Witnesses of Jehovah."

Now I felt my blood boiling. "How rude!" I thought to myself. "Is it not enough that they step on the icons and the cross, that they refuse to serve our country as soldiers, and that they allow their children to die without blood transfusions, but now they are also coming to our homes!"

"Get out of here, *now*! Before I call the police," I said.

"But we are law-abiding citizens," they responded.

"That's enough! I don't want to hear anything!" I interrupted.

"But why? We are here motivated by love," they claimed.

They had now become unbearable, and I slammed the door in their faces. I heard them going down the stairs, while I was getting dressed with mixed emotions. On the one hand, I felt bad for treating them in such a way because they were so polite, but on the other hand, I needed to do my duty as a Greek Orthodox Christian. Thus, I felt proud for chasing them out since this is what they deserved, according to some adults who claimed that they knew them well.

The following evening I shared my Sunday morning success with Nikos, the fellow who sat next to me in school. Nikos and I were becoming good friends; he seemed to be a very nice guy. He did not like to curse or smoke as the other boys in school did, and he seemed to be quite satisfied with his life. He was one of the top students in school, and he seemed to have his hand in a lot of different things. He listened to my experience with the Witnesses, smiling now and then.

As the months passed by, that Sunday morning incident was all but forgotten. I was quite busy with my daily routine, so I waited for the holidays to catch up with my friends who had just about written me off. While they were out flirting at the plazas and cafés,

I was working or listening to some boring teachers. Fortunately, I had met Nikos, and we hung out together during recess.

The Religious Instructor

ONE EVENING DURING religion class, after the daily oral testing of the students, the teacher began a lesson on the topic "The Jehovah's Witnesses." I listened very carefully, much like my closest classmate who was also taking notes. I remember among other things, the teacher saying that "The Chiliasts (Jehovah's Witnesses)[20] do not accept the Panagia[21], the saints, or the Cross.[22] They defame the flag, calling it a rag.[23] They claim that the faithful who lived before Christ will resurrect and will be senators with Abraham who will be president, Jonah will be secretary of navigation, Gideon will be the secretary of defense, etc.[24] They have designated many dates

---

20 In Greece the Jehovah's Witnesses are also known called "Chiliasts," from their belief in a millennial paradise on earth.

21 "Panagia" means "Most Holy" in Greek and refers to the Virgin Mary. Contrary to the New Testament instruction (Luke 1:48), the Jehovah's Witnesses do not accept the Virgin Mary and her honorary veneration.

22 Actually, the Watchtower Society has displayed inconsistency on the subject. From 1891 to 1931 every issue of Watchtower featured a cross and a crown symbol on the front cover. Pictures of the Lord hanging from the Cross (not a stake as the Society now holds), were featured in numerous other books of the Watch Tower society as well (see, for example, Russell's *Photo Drama of Creation* (1914) p.12, and the following books of J. F. Rutherford: *The Harp of God* (1921) p.115, *Creation* (1927) p.265 & 336, *Reconciliation* (1928), p.168)

23 Not true, the Jehovah's Witnesses simply refuse saluting the flag; "we do not salute the flag of any nation… it is because we view the flag salute as an act of worship." (*School and Jehovah's Witnesses*, 1983, p 90). It does seem, though, that before Rutherford assumed the presidency of the Society, the flag was a non-issue: "…everyone in America should take pleasure in displaying the American flag… Since the Bethel Home was established, in one end of the Drawing Room there has been kept a small bust of Abraham Lincoln with two American flags displayed about the bust. This is deemed entirely proper…" (WT 5/15/1917, p. 6086).

24 It is unclear where the religious instructor got his specific information. However, the second president of the Watchtower Society, Rutherford said things in similar lines. For example, in his book, *Millions Now Living Will Never Die* (1920), wrote the following: "The Apostle Paul in the eleventh chapter of Hebrews names a long

Earth's New Rulers
"Soon you may expect to see Abraham, Enoch, Moses, David and all of these other faithful men back on earth... Being wholly devoted to the Lord and under the control and supervision of the Lord, and the visible representatives of the great King on Earth, they will do exactly which is right... Christ Jesus is the King, and his reign shall be righteous; and these faithful princes or representatives on the earth will carry out his judgments or decrees, and the entire rule or government will be righteous. Those men will be the visible governors of the nations of earth and the people will soon learn to respect, love, and obey them. (J. F. Rutherford, *What You Need*, Watch Tower Bible and Tract Society, 1932, p. 8)

---

for the end of the world, including 1924, 1925, and others, and they are constantly ridiculed. They go to homes searching for, finding, and leading astray the illiterate and old women."

Having delivered the lesson, my friend Nikos raised his hand, asking for permission to speak. The teacher gave him his consent.

"Mr. Teacher," he said, "I'm sorry, but I feel it a duty to point out the untruths written in our class textbook about the Jehovah's Witnesses. It is not true that they deny the Panagia and the saints, nor that they defame the flag, nor that they believe the ridiculous

---

list of faithful men who died before the crucifixion of the Lord and before the beginning of the selection of the church. These can never be a part of the heavenly class; they had no heavenly hopes; but God has in store something good for them. They are to be resurrected as perfect men and constitute the princes or rulers in the earth, according to his promise. Therefore we may confidently expect that 1925 will mark the return of Abraham, Isaac, Jacob, and the faithful prophets of old..." (pp. 89–90)

The Watch Tower's Forgotten Past!
The Watchtower Organization claims it is the faithful and discreet slave of Jehovah, God's visible mouthpiece that the Lord uses to issue directions to us, mortals (WT 7/1/1943 p.205). Yet, a careful examination of its brief history will demonstrate that the Jehovah's Witnesses' dogmatic theology is very unstable. Nowadays they say that "no biblical evidence even intimates that Jesus died on a cross." (WT 11/8/1972 p.28). The picture on the left, displaying the Lord hanging on the Cross, however is from one of their own publications! (J. F. Rutherford, *Children*, 1941, p98)

lie about the faithful who lived before Christ becoming senators and presidents. It is also a lie that they lead astray the illiterate and women. I'm saying this because I'm neither illiterate nor a woman, and yet I am a Jehovah's Witness."

At the sound of these last words, the class fell into a deep silence. They all waited for the teacher to respond, but he also seemed to be at a loss for words. I was shocked! My eyes popped out, and I kept staring at Nikos with my mouth wide open. How is this possible, I wondered; my best friend is a Chiliast? How did it escape me all this time? I kept asking myself these questions. The school bell rang, putting an end to the teacher's dilemma.

"Listen!" the teacher said. "I'm supposed to tell you what is written in this book. We can discuss it if you wish. We can talk about it some other time."

With these words, the teacher exited the room, while I, as though hypnotized, followed my friend outside. In the hall, some

2. Flirting with the Spider

other students were calling out to Nikos.

"Bravo! You're great! You told him off!" they cheered.

Nikos seemed very disappointed about the bell cutting him off. It seemed like he wanted to say much more.

"Another time," he said, looking at me and smiling, probably at the dumb expression stuck on my face.

"Are you really a Jehovah?" I asked.

"Witness of Jehovah," he corrected me. "Jehovah is the name of God. It is not permitted for us mere humans to be called Jehovah. There is only one Jehovah, God. We only bring witness to his name."

We were already at the front yard, and I found myself shocked and confused. My various biases were pushing me to get away from him. But since he was my friend, it would be rude to treat him this way, not to mention that my curiosity was growing by the minute. All this time we had been friends, I had told him my problems, and he had told me his. He did not show any signs of evil, as I had been forewarned concerning the people of his religion. On the contrary, he did not curse, he did not chase after girls, he did not smoke, and he treated people around him with respect. Could all of these traits be superficial?

I mobilized all of the information I had learned in school and asked him, "What relationship could you possibly have with God since you and your people hold to the heresy of Arius, that Christ is a creation? St. Athanasios proved this to be a heresy!" I wanted to corner him and also to defend my faith. Instead of stumbling on my question, he answered me with his own question.

"What is the meaning of creation?" he asked.

I kept staring at him.

"I don't know," I answered.

"Is Jesus Christ not the Son of God?" he asked me.

"Of course!" I said.

"If, in fact, He is the Son of God, at sometime He 'begot' Him in other words, 'created' Him. Is this not so?" he concluded.

"That makes sense" I replied, making my first dogmatic error.[25]

"Well then, this is exactly what we Witnesses are saying, and that's what Arius was saying. Does it seem unreasonable?" he asked.

"No, but then, what are we and St. Athanasios saying?" I asked.

"Although you should know this, I will tell you. You are claiming Christ to be without beginning—ἄναρχος—but isn't it illogical to be without beginning since He has a Father? If He always existed, then how was He born?"[26]

I was speechless.

He went on to say, "As you can see, Arius was not the heretic, but St. Athanasios, and I'm pleased that you are able to see how illogical the dogma of the Trinity is."[27]

I had never attended catechetical school, nor did my parents take any special care to teach me the Orthodox Faith. I very seldom attended church, and when I did, it was not for the sake of being churched but for the fireworks of Pascha.[28] Neither did my godfather ever teach me anything. He considered his only obligation to be a

---

25 According to the Holy Fathers of the Church, trying to comprehend God by human reasoning is condemned not only to fail but even worse: to lead us to false conclusions—i.e. heresy. It is analogous to speaking in detail about the composition of far distant stars without even knowing what a telescope is. The Church Fathers insist that the true source of divine knowledge is God Himself, who reveals Himself to those who have purified their hearts from the evil passions through keeping His commandments.

26 For an excellent and a *very* pertinent ancient treatment on the subject see St. Hilary of Poitiers' *On The Trinity, Book IV*. The ancient text is available freely online.

27 This is an over-simplified presentation of Arius' position by a person who obviously did not study the subject. Briefly, "the Arians… made a philosophical distinction between essence and energy in God and this distinction put them in the position of being compelled to teach that the Father and the Son cannot be related by essence, because a relation by essence means a relation by [Aristotelian] necessity." (see Fr. John Romanides' *Patristic Theology*, Uncut Mountain Press, p. 268–271).

28 An old custom in Greece is to set off fireworks during the Resurrection service—Pascha meaning Resurrection in Greek.

2. Flirting with the Spider 23

gift on my name-day[29] once a year and a lampada[30] during Pascha.

Thus, I grew up without anyone explaining to me the difference between the word *Son* and the word *creation*; without anyone explaining to me how the Father and the Son can exist pre-eternally, since they are found outside of the realms of time.[31] I grew up without anyone explaining to me that the sun, although it gives birth to light, did not exist before the light, but sun and sunlight exist simultaneously; and that sunlight is also *sun* and *begotten* of the sun. No one told me that the Son is the reflection of the *Light of the Father*, outside of time.[32]

I had no idea that the Father was the origin, the source of the Son. I thought He was His beginning in relation to time, being clueless about the Father creating time through the Son.[33] I now found myself weaponless in front of a man who was speaking to me about matters in which he felt expert. I was acknowledging before him not only ignorance of my Savior, but even denial of His own revelation. And while I was good at searching out exclusive social spots for dates with beautiful girls, I had never had the same appetite for searching for my God! I had never even questioned myself about Him and my faith. To me it was a given that the faith I had been born into was the one true faith, just as I would have believed it had I been born into the faith of some other religion.

And now this "given" was crumbling! I had a man in front of

---

29 In the Orthodox Church every saint has a feast day. It is a custom for Orthodox Christians when baptized to bear a name of a Saint and on his feast day to celebrate.

30 Large festal candle.

31 "God always was, and always is, and always will be. Or rather, God always is. For was and will be are fragments of our time, and of changeable nature, but He is Eternal Being... transcending all conception of time and nature... But when I say God, I mean Father, Son, and Holy Ghost. " St. Gregory the Theologian, Oration 38, *On the Theophany, or Birthday of Christ*. (New Advent, 2007, CD ROM version)

32 Heb. 1:3

33 John 1:3

me who was more than ready to demolish and knock down whatever I had held with certainty up to that point of my life. I was already greatly disturbed for having agreed to something opposed by my faith. What if Nikos was right? No! I didn't even want to think about it! The rest of the evening, in-between classes, we dedicated all of our free time to a theological discussion. What impressed me was that he had a well-tailored answer for each and every one of my questions. Many times he would even beat me to the punch, answering my question even before I had a chance to pose it. He must have had these same discussions with many others before me. He knew in advance what my answer was going to be, and in reality he steered the discussion towards the direction he wanted.

Finally, when school was over that evening, and we said our good nights, I was left in deep thought, seriously perplexed. I had always believed that discussions about God were the pointless and boring fancy of backward old men. Now, however, I had discovered for the first time in my life that underneath all this there was a fascinating charm, a thought-provoking magnificence. In full amazement, I was discovering that behind the word "religion" there was a world of enchantment, a complex and fascinating science that I wanted to get to know much better. As my train glided home through the dark, I sat engulfed in my thoughts, hardly noticing I was already at my stop.

At home, I greeted my parents and we sat at the table to eat. I did not mention anything to them about my friend, about whom I had told them many good things up until then. I felt that they would ask me to part company with him if they found out that he was a Witness. That night, even though I was exhausted, it took me a long time to fall asleep. I could not stop thinking about the discussion I had had at school.

Touching the Web

FROM THAT DAY on, my friendship with Nikos changed. At every opportunity we discussed God and His purpose for humanity. Nikos was eager to answer all of my questions to the utmost. With admiration, yet not without some skepticism, I listened to him happily talk about his expectation of eternal life. I was totally convinced that his love for God was genuine and not hypocritical. His joy when speaking about God was real.

I was truly elated to see a young man living his faith and placing it first in his life. His enthusiasm was contagious. What impressed me greatly was that Nikos never gave his own opinion. His thoughts were the opinion of all the Witnesses, and he referenced them back to the Holy Scriptures. I often wondered how he was able to find whatever he wanted so easily in the Scriptures. As for me, after our initial discussions, I looked around my house for an old copy of the Holy Scriptures, which I remembered seeing somewhere. After much searching, I discovered a small book of the New Testament in the attic under a huge dusty pile of books. I was overjoyed with my discovery because now I could check the validity of what I had heard. I would see for myself if the Holy Scriptures read by Orthodox Christians were the same as the Scriptures read by the Witnesses, since many Orthodox claimed that the two were distinctly different. That same evening I took my small New Testament with me when I went to meet Nikos.

"Now I will show you your delusion!" I said half-jokingly. "Let's see which verses you changed in the Bible."

Nikos smiled as we proceeded to compare sections of the New Testament. Although there was a slight difference in the layout, the overall meaning was the same.

"Your New Testament is the original text. My version," he said, "is a translation of the text in a more readable language. We use something more simplified than the original Greek of 2,000 years ago. The Orthodox priests, however, prefer to use the difficult ancient Greek language to keep the world in the dark."

After seeing the older form of the language in my own New Testament, I accepted his words without reservation. I did not think to look in the front of his book to see the author of his translation, Archimandrite Neophytos Vamvas.[34] Afterwards, he explained that I only had one of two books of the Holy Scriptures, the New Testament. He showed me his Bible, and referred to its sixty-six books, which he showed me in the table of contents. He told me that Christians must *only* accept the Holy Scriptures with its sixty-six books and must rely on this *only*. I accepted these last words as self-evident, assuming that this must be the common belief of all Christian confessions as professed by Nikos. Unfortunately, I had just made my second and biggest mistake to date. I failed to search and find out how many books my religion accepted as God-inspired Scripture and the reasoning behind it. I never asked for proof of the axiom *sola scriptura*[35] and why "we must *only* rely on it as the *only* God-inspired resource."[36]

---

34 Archimandrite Vamvas (1770–1855) was one of the foremost Greek scholars during the Ottoman rule. He had studied in Paris and held various teaching positions in Greece. Unfortunately, he acted without prudence in some issues. His publication of the Holy Bible to the kathareousa Greek (with the aid of British Bible Company) aroused suspicion of him being a heretic, and raised questions about the character of the modern Greek language and national identity. Fr. Neophytos' translation started a heated phase that culminated in the *Evangelika* (Gospel) riots in 1901.

35 Sola Scriptura (latin for "by Scriptures alone") is a foundational doctrine principle of the Protestant Reformation. Even though there isn't a single accepted definition in the Protestant world, it is commonly accepted that the text of the Holy Scriptures is perfect, complete, and self-explanatory to the believer. The implication being that the Bible, as understood by the individual Christian, is his ultimate source of religious authority and sole criterion of faith. Thus, Holy Tradition is regarded either as secondary or outright superfluous.

36 Actually there is not a single mention in the Bible that it alone is divinely inspired, nor that we are obliged to accept only the Bible and nothing else. Also, the New Testament canon took over three centuries to be formed and in that time the Church

> **THE WATCH TOWER**
> September 15, 1910 (298–299)
>
> We think that we get the right conception to thus view it rather than to think that we had some great power which enabled us to put together a great system of theology, more wonderful than all other systems of theology put together—a thousand times more wonderful. Therefore, the simplest way to explain the matter is to acknowledge that the Lord's due time has come and that he has guided us to the right understanding.
>
> If, then, the Lord has provided us with something in our day that other days than those of the Apostles knew nothing about, no matter how good nor how wise they were—for us to ignore the line of teaching which has been thus developed would be, in our judgment, to ignore the Lord's providences. It is for each one to think for himself, however, and to guide his conduct in every way accordingly.
>
> If the six volumes of SCRIPTURE STUDIES are practically the Bible topically arranged, with Bible proof-texts given, we might not improperly name the volumes—the Bible in an arranged form. That is to say, they are not merely commentaries on the Bible, but they are practically the Bible itself, since there is no desire to build any doctrine or thought on any individual preference or on any individual wisdom, but to present the entire matter on the lines of the Word of God. We therefore think it safe to follow this kind of reading, this kind of instruction, this kind of Bible study.
>
> Furthermore, not only do we find that people cannot see the divine plan in studying the Bible by itself, but we see, also, that if anyone lays the SCRIPTURE STUDIES aside, even after he has used them, after he has become familiar with them, after he has read them for ten years—if he then lays them aside and ignores them and goes to the Bible alone, though he has understood his Bible for ten years, our experience shows that within two years he goes into darkness. On the other hand, if he had merely read the SCRIPTURE STUDIES with their references, and had not read a page of the Bible, as such, he would be in the light at the end of the two years, because he would have the light of the Scriptures.
>
> Our thought, therefore, is that these SCRIPTURE STUDIES are a great assistance, a very valuable help, in the understand-

Sola Scriptura?
The founder of the Jehovah's Witnesses, Russell, claimed that the Scriptures are obscure; therefore, he advised, its better to read his commentaries. (*WT*, 9/15/1910). One can be hard pressed to find a louder denial of the "Sola Scriptura!"

From that day on I did not accept anything if I did not see it written in the Bible. I asked Nikos for a book of the Holy Scriptures like his, which he happily and quickly provided. I was overjoyed since now I had in my possession the "entire" Holy Scriptures with its sixty-six books.[37]

> lived and prospered without it. How? Relying on the Holy Tradition—of which the New Testament is a part. In addition, not only was the Sola Scriptura doctrine unknown to Christians until the 15th century, but it presupposes that each individual Christian had always had a full copy of the Bible; does this mean that Christians prior to the invention of the printing press were bereft spiritually? And, if the Bible is "all sufficient," then why don't Protestants all hold the same beliefs? Evangelical apologist Keith Mathison observes, "In recent years the subject has gained renewed attention due to the growing numbers of converts from Protestantism to both Roman Catholicism and Eastern Orthodoxy who claim that their conversion was due to their 'discovery' that the doctrine of sola scriptura was indefensible." (Keith Mathison, *The Shape of Sola Scriptura*, Canon Press & Book Service, 2001, p. 13)

37 In reality, Sola Scriptura does not exist; every Church and sect has its own tradition in which it understands the Scriptures. The Watchtower Society, for example, considers its periodical Watchtower to be the mouthpiece of Jehovah (*Informant*,

I believed that I had the "entire word of God" in my hands. The next few days, I began reading the book of Genesis. Although this ancient script was rather tedious, I read with much joy until I reached some difficult passages in Exodus. There, feeling tired from the plethora of names and technical descriptions, I made the mistake of discontinuing its book-by-book reading. In the years to follow, I read it selectively, like my friend.

One day my mother entered my room and asked me, "What kind of book are you always so busy reading?"

"The Holy Scriptures!" I replied. "It was given to me by a classmate who is a Jehovah's Witness."

"What! Throw it away at once! It is not the same as ours!" she yelled.

Not missing a beat, I took the small New Testament she knew, and showed her that my Holy Scripture was the same.

"Well, at least be careful not to fall into their trap because they are thrice-cursed! They are bribed as a course of their religion!" she cried.

"Don't worry! Rest assured that I won't fall away. I know what I'm doing. But, you should know that they don't get paid, because otherwise Nikos would not have to work to support himself, nor would he have to attend night school. These are ill-imagined lies!", I told my mother.

From that day on, whenever she saw me reading the Holy Scriptures, she would whisper under her breath. I considered this

---

1/1956) and it is a basic JW tenet that no one can understand the Bible except through the Watchtower. "Jehovah God caused the Bible to be written in such a way that one needs to come in touch with His human channel before one can fully and accurately understand it. True, we need the help of God's holy spirit, but its help also comes to us primarily by association with the channel Jehovah God sees fit to use." (WT 2/15/81 p.17) Furthermore, the Society considers that holding an understanding of the Bible in variance with its official position to be an *apostasy* punishable with disfellowship.

an added sign that Nikos was justified because he had made sure to forewarn me. He said that if someone is advancing in the Christian faith, his relatives and friends will oppose him and they will not want him to study Scripture. This is part of the persecution the devil will enact against him. My mother must have been greatly concerned because one day she entered the house holding a newspaper of some para-ecclesiastical organization.

"Here's proof!" she said. "Take it and read for yourself that the Chiliasts get paid off!"

I could not believe my eyes. I read a about a woman who claimed that the Witnesses offered her a significant sum of money if she would step on the icons they had placed on the floor. I pulled myself together and ran to the phone. I dialed the number of the publishing office of the paper and asked the person who answered the phone to give me the address and telephone number of the woman mentioned in the article.

"I'm sorry," they replied. "We are not permitted to give out that information."

"But if this is true, I need to know so I don't become influenced by them!" I said in desperation, but to no avail.

"You are all liars and deceivers!" I cried out, and hung up the phone.

My mother watched me in a state of hopelessness.

"See?" I snapped at her. "I don't believe everything they tell me. But you believe anything you read!"

From that moment on, I lost my trust in everything Orthodox. I considered all the Orthodox writers liars and deceivers. On a regular basis, Nikos also brought me similar "anti-chiliast" articles showing me how much "the Orthodox and the priests like to lie." Having been well-informed about the Witnesses, I was seeing the lies of some of their enemies and was outraged. I began to be ashamed of my religion. Nikos, on the other hand, reminded me of something very true. He told me, "The truth can stand by itself! It does not need the crutches of lies." He went on to conclude, "If they had the truth, they would stand by it, and they would not need to lie. They would show our mistakes from Holy Scripture. Since they don't do this, this only means that they can only resort to speaking lies."

Notwithstanding everything that was happening and everything he was telling me, what drew me towards his religion was his overall conduct. I compared Nikos' conduct with that of my other friends on a daily basis. My other friends constantly blasphemed God and His saints; they committed every kind of disgrace without any objection of conscience. Christianity meant nothing to them. On the contrary, I had someone here in front of me who lived, or at least was trying to live, the Christian faith as fully as possible.

However, I was willing to give Orthodoxy one more chance. I was waiting for the moment when Nikos would converse with the instructor of our religion class again so that I could finally determine who was in the right. But this did not happen for quite a while. The religion class was postponed. There were strikes. Feast days came and went; the weeks just passed by.

Finally, one evening when we resumed the lesson, the teacher said, "Nikos, I had promised that we would have a discussion concerning your faith. So let's begin to expand beyond the information given in our course textbook."

I rubbed my hands together with excitement as the teacher took out a book and Nikos got out the Holy Scriptures. But let me allow Nikos himself to narrate the events of that evening....

3. Preaching in Class

Nikos' story

That evening I found myself somewhat unprepared. After my experience with the theologians[38] in junior high school, I did not expect my high school teacher to confront me in front of other students. To my surprise, he kept his word. For me, this would be significant in helping me gauge him as a human being. I always carried the Bible with me since I often discussed it with George and the others, so I pulled it out and put it on my desk. The teacher opened the discussion and immediately took charge.

"Can you explain to me why your religion does not accept the Holy Tradition of the Church?" he asked.

I was speechless for a few seconds. This question had never come up. I knew nothing about Holy Tradition. I only knew how to juxtapose verses from Holy Scripture or converse about scientific matters pertaining to atheism. I was caught off guard; how would I answer now? The entire class was staring at me. Their first impression would be based solely on my answer, and this would influence

---

38 Nowadays in Greece, this term is used loosely and pertains to all religious educators in the school system. However, according to the Church Fathers, a theologian is someone who has purified his heart from the evil passions through the application of God's commandments and is granted the vision of God.

their attitude not only towards the rest of the discussion but towards all of the Witnesses. I, of course, knew some scriptural verses with the words of the Lord Jesus, which I believed befitting for the Orthodox, like the one in Mark 7:13, "Making the word of God of no effect through your tradition", but what would I come up with after that? What would I say? Here I needed to improvise and to do so quickly, so as not to appear at a loss for words.

"We don't accept Tradition because it opposes Holy Scripture!" I responded with some relief, while all eyes now turned towards the teacher. I had bought myself a little time to steer him in my direction, or so I thought.

"Where did you see this opposition?" the teacher asked quickly.

Now I was ready.

"In many areas! For example, on the subject of the Holy Trinity, tradition says that God is Trinity, the Holy Scriptures state that 'for us there is one God...'"[39] I began.

"Please do not attempt to avoid the subject!" the teacher interrupted me, catching me in my play with words.

"How am I avoiding the subject? The subject is how Holy Scripture disagrees with Tradition!" I answered using his own question.

Thus, he was compelled to close his book and continue the discussion on my grounds. Apparently, the teacher himself was not well-versed on the subject of Holy Tradition, because if he had been, he would never have accepted the dichotomy of Holy Scripture from the Tradition of the Church. He would have caused me all sorts of problems if he had told me that Holy Scripture is part of Holy Tradition.

We spent the rest of class debating the subject of the Trinity while the class followed this duel with great interest. Neither one of

---

39 1 Cor. 8:6

us, however, was convinced by the other's argument since we simply juxtaposed verses of Holy Scripture without any basis.

When the recess bell rang, in all reality, we were at a stalemate. However, I felt I was the great victor since my classmates must be thinking, "if a young Jehovah's Witness can hold his own against a high school theologian, then how much better would the higher echelon of his faith succeed in defeating the Orthodox position?"

After that discussion, the teacher and I developed a much better relationship. I really began to like him because he was the only faithful Orthodox person with whom I had ever engaged in any meaningful discussion up to that point. He did not display any dogmatism—on the contrary, recognizing my knowledge of Holy Scripture, he began to be lenient with my grades. It was such a contrast to my junior high school religion teacher who had graded me lower out of his bias against me.

I also believe that the teacher of the evening class took a liking to me because he found in me a valuable ally in his struggle with a particular atheist student. This student disagreed mostly with the narrative of Genesis. He believed that man evolved from the ape by mere chance and was not created by God. I was happy to join forces with the theology teacher to tear down the blasphemous theory of evolution. Naturally we proved him groundless at every discussion, but the atheist student still did not want to accept the existence of God.

My discussions with my teachers were not limited to religion class. Other teachers initiated discussions with me during their classes. My Modern Greek, Biology, and Electronics teachers liked to question me about my faith in the presence of my peers. Some of them were atheists or agnostics, and many times they sided with my atheist classmate, attempting to prove the unproven. Another opportunity to proselytize my religion was in my composition class. I

ΚΑΡΤΑ ΕΡΓΑΣΙΑΣ

ΕΚΘΕΣΙΣ ΕΥΑΓΓΕΛΙΖΟΜΕΝΟΥ ΓΙΑ ΕΒΔΟΜΑΔΙΑΙΑ ΥΠΗΡΕΣΙΑ ΑΓΡΟΥ ΤΟΝ ....
(Μήνας)
Όνομα.. Δευτέρα .... έως Κυριακή ....
(Ημερομηνία) (Ημερομηνία)

	Βιβλία	Βιβλιάρια	Ώρες Υπηρεσίας στόν Άγρό	Νέες Συνδρομές	Αντίτυπα Περιοδικών	Επανεπισκέψεις	Γραφικές Μελέτες
ΔΕΥΤΕΡΑ							
ΤΡΙΤΗ							
ΤΕΤΑΡΤΗ							
ΠΕΜΠΤΗ							
ΠΑΡΑΣΚΕΥΗ							
ΣΑΒΒΑΤΟΝ							
ΚΥΡΙΑΚΗ							
ΣΥΝΟΛΟ							

Service Report
In a card similar to this one, Nikos, as a Jehovah's Witness, had to report his progress in the field.

---

always made my essays very interesting, and they were always read in class without fail.

Consequently my teachers were unwittingly helping me to promote my religion to my classmates. Of course with the exception of the theology teacher, I monopolized the discussion.

With all these endeavors, in spite of investing very little time, I managed to present a rich Service Report to my organization, namely a registration of hours spent preaching and passing out pamphlets to everyone around me. Day by day, I gained their respect. I was making quite an impression, and I was winning over George, who already knew my religion better than his own!

4. In the Nest of the Spider

George's story

Time passed by, and my knowledge of the faith of the Witnesses increased on a daily basis. It is so ironic that while I never showed any interest in learning about my own faith, I was now zealously engrossed in learning about a faith foreign to me as a cradle Orthodox Christian.

I had noticed that on some evenings during the week Nikos skipped the last two hours of school. They were always the same evenings and always the same courses. He was not afraid of absenteeism because the person in charge of roll call was his friend and did not mark him absent. One day I could not hold back my curiosity, so I asked him what was going on. He told me that he left class to go to the congregation or to the church of the Witnesses. He invited me to go along with him sometime to see what takes place there. In reality I was afraid, but my curiosity got the best of me. So that very same evening, after we worked things out with the person who called roll, we gathered our schoolbooks and left. We walked for a few minutes discussing, as always, various religious matters. Although I did not show it, I felt very anxious. I was feeling uneasy because I did not know what I would run into, and because I was also feeling like a traitor to my faith, a faith which considered these people heretics.

We came to a building which housed a manufacturing plant on its lower level. It was barely visible in the dark. There was a balcony with a glass patio, covered with red curtains. After climbing the exterior concrete staircase, we came to a painted glass door with a scratched-out space for a peephole. My heart was pounding as we entered the half-opened door that led into a small reception area. The man on the other side of the peephole met us with a big smile. His name was John, and he was a very likeable young man with a wide mustache. He quickly approached us and greeted us with a very powerful and heartfelt handshake. We introduced ourselves and then climbed up the circular concrete staircase. I tried to walk as quietly as I could, even though John had helped to dispel much of my initial anxiety. At the top of the staircase, inside the open door, about twenty to thirty well-dressed people were seated in neatly arranged rows of chairs.

I stared at the floor of wood-patterned linoleum. I immediately thought of all the things I had heard in the past about such meetings of the Witnesses, and I leaned over to Nikos and whispered in a joking manner, "I hope there are no icons underneath this floor!"

He burst out laughing and then ran inside, leaving me there at the door. He said something to someone, and then in front of my astonished eyes, Nikos and two or three others lifted up the vinyl flooring for me to check if there were any icons underneath.

In spite of the embarrassment I felt for causing this scene, I looked from the corner of my eye to see if what I had heard was true. Soon after, everyone came over to introduce themselves, still laughing. I felt comfortable since they had not gotten upset about lifting up the vinyl flooring. In fact, they were rather amused by it. They were people of all ages, from the very old to young children. There were men and women, of varying education, and a few were illiterate.

"If we stepped on icons, we would be ascribing some worth to

7. (a) What makes the Bible prophecies regarding Christ's presence and the "last days" so remarkable? (b) In contrast with what the Bible foretold, what were world leaders forecasting just prior to 1914?
8. (a) Which generation did Jesus indicate would see the end of this system of things? (b) So of what can we be certain?

ARMAGEDDON

Some of the generation living in 1914 will see the end of the system of things and survive it

Can You Really Live For Ever on Earth?
For many decades the Jehovah's Witnesses lived with the promise that the 1914 generation will never die but "will live to see the end of the system of things." The above picture is taken from the book *You Can Live Forever in Paradise on Earth*, (1981, p. 154). The book was printed twice, in over 30 million copies, but became obsolete only 13 years later when the Society methodically retracted the "1914 dogma."

---

them! For us, icons have no worth whatsoever and it would be a total waste of time to deal with them!" someone said.

I sat down, and in a few minutes the teaching began. John, the likeable young man we met at the entrance, was the teacher. After a prayer, everyone opened a red book which had recently been published. The book was titled, *You Can Live Forever in Paradise on Earth* and the Witnesses referred to it as the "Red Bomb."[40] It was a very colorful book, full of pictures presenting the entire basic teaching of the Witnesses in a concise format. As someone read, I took in the meeting room.

The chairs were positioned in rows, and the room could accommodate about seventy people. In the front was a raised, carpeted, wooden stage and on the center of this stage was a podium with a microphone. Behind the podium was a large red curtain and di-

---

40 Watchtower Bible & Tract Society, 1981. It was published twice in 71 languages and in over 30 million copies. It had a red cover (hence the nickname) and it relied more on its colorful pictures than the depth of its articles. The book became outdated as the Society quietly retracted the "1914 dogma" and it is now out of circulation.

rectly above it was a plaque with a verse from the Holy Scriptures. Directly across the room were more red curtains and I realized that these were the ones I saw from the outside as we entered the building. On two sides of the room were four air fans placed on shelves, and throughout the room were picture frames on the walls, depicting events of the Holy Scriptures, and handicrafts of the tetragram "yhwh" or the *Watchtower*.

When the reading ended, John began to ask questions and the rest raised their hands to answer. I lowered myself into my chair, somewhat terrified, and whispered in Nikos' ear, "If he calls on me, what do I say?"

"He won't call on you if you don't raise your hand!" he answered laughing.

Then he showed me the questions at the bottom of the page in the red book and explained how to find the answers in each corresponding section of the book.

"If you want, you can answer, too," he told me. But I did not feel courageous enough until the very end of the first hour of our study. When the last paragraph had been read, I nervously raised my hand and offered a brief answer to a question.

The lecture ended with one more spontaneous prayer from a member. Then we remained for another hour to socialize[41] and I

---

41 Unknown to the first time visitor, the cordiality displayed by the Jehovah's Witnesses to the newcomer is not spontaneous and unstudied. Quite the contrary, there are specific directions in the secret manual for the Elders (*Pay Attention to Yourselves and All the Flock*," Watch Tower Bible and Tract Society, 1991, p. 22–23"): "Newly associated ones are especially in need of attention. When they first come to the Kingdom Hall, new ones may feel like strangers; we want to change that feeling to one of warm friendship. If you notice a new one standing by himself or talking only with the one who studies with him, take the initiative to approach and greet him and introduce him to others. Teach attendants to greet new ones, and occasionally remind them to do this…" However, once a newcomer gets baptized he will soon discover that "this special kindness is often extended to those studying with the Witnesses which is not necessarily shown to baptized Witnesses." (Dianne Wilson, *Awakening of a Jehovah's Witness*, Prometheus Books,

questioned them constantly. The discussion was centered on icons, traditions and priests. The Witnesses were quick to inform me that the veneration of icons amounts to worship, for icons are idols, and there are plenty of Old Testament passages against idols, and how Jesus Christ had condemned the Jewish traditions and consequently we must only accept the Bible. At the time I didn't have the foggiest notion about any differences between *worship* and *veneration*, or *icons* and *idols*, or the Jewish and the Christian tradition. Thus, I accepted all the inaccuracies they were telling me without protest.

Being influenced by the prevailing judgmental anti-Orthodox sentiment of the group, I then began slandering the priests of every known and unknown scandal, of every sort of rumor that had reached my ears without having any proof or direct experience of what I was saying. As I spoke to the crowd of Witnesses, I noticed that I had become the center of attention. Everyone listened to me, nodding their heads with satisfaction. I was feeling very good because I had people around me eager to listen, discuss, and share my views. As we parted, I was confident that these meetings were very edifying. In reality, I confused "cult acceptance" with "spirituality."

Increasing contact

AS TIME PASSED, I became more and more involved with the faith of the Witnesses. Each week on a regular basis, I left school and went with Nikos to their meetings. Even on Sunday evenings, I avoided the company of my friends and attended the meetings. Even though I was an Orthodox Christian, I had not yet spent even one hour a week in my church, and now I was spending at least five hours a week attending the meetings of a religion unknown to me only a few weeks earlier.

2002, p. 45) As a matter of fact, cordiality can change to ostracism quite abruptly when the Society so decides.

And I also made one of the most basic of mistakes: while I was absorbing all of the basic tenets of the Watchtower faith, it didn't occur to me to examine the history of this religious organization which claimed to be "the truth." Not a smart thing on my part.

One day Nikos took me to his home and introduced me to his family. His mother was disabled so she could not attend meetings regularly, as was also the case with his elderly grandmother. This explained why I had never met them before. They were two very hospitable women, taking great joy in offering all they could to welcome me as a visitor, while talking constantly about God. It seemed natural for Nikos to acquire a love for God, living in this type of environment.

My visits to their home increased, and each time I felt I came away knowing more about God and His will. In the beginning, I listened with much skepticism to what Nikos said and demanded proof. Now, however, I accepted everything he was saying without any hesitation. My skepticism was now turned toward every other source of information other than the Watchtower.

Nikos' method of teaching was also instrumental in this. When I asked him something, he replied promptly, but he did not stop there. Immediately he brought up the arguments used by various Orthodox Christians on whatever topic we were discussing, and proceeded to refute them. Thus, he gave me the impression that he had a complete picture of the subject from both sides of the coin, while solidifying in my mind his own personal point of view.

One day he suggested that we start a systematic Scripture study at his house. I accepted with much joy, and from then on, on non-school days or during breaks, we went to his home and studied.

In reality, however, our study was not directly from the Holy Scriptures but from some Watchtower literature. Being an immature teenager, I failed to grasp that this contradicted the "Sola Scriptura" principle. Why weren't we just reading the Bible?

INFORMANT

JANUARY, 1956   "Prove me now herewith, saith Jehovah of hosts, if I will not open you the windows of heaven, and pour you out a blessing."—Malachi 3: 10, AS.   BROOKLYN, N. Y.

SERVING WITH JEHOVAH'S CHANNEL OF COMMUNICATION
18th Annual *Watchtower* Campaign Gets Under Way

Let All Share Fully

¹ Jehovah is the source of all knowledge. When he speaks, all should listen and learn. And how does he speak? Through his appointed channel of communication—his collective congregation of anointed ones. By this means we learn of the diversified wisdom of God, as demonstrated in his marvelous creative acts and the irresistible outworking of his grand and thrilling purposes. What a joy it is to have this grand information communicated to us by Jehovah "through the congregation," as year after year we continue our happy association with it!—Eph. 3: 10, NW.

² As servants of Jehovah we desire to serve along with this channel of communication and aid in dispensing this information to others. During January we shall do this by extending to all the opportunity to subscribe for the *Watchtower* magazine, the main instrument used by the congregation to dispense Jehovah's communications. Good-will persons with whom Bible studies are being held should be invited to subscribe, as well as friends, relatives and others that we have the privilege of contacting.

³ The first day of the 18th annual four-month *Watchtower* campaign is on Sunday. On Monday, the second day, almost everyone will be free from his secular work, so all congregations will arrange for a special day of service. Let all of us help to get this campaign off to a good start by spending these first two days in intensive door-to-door preaching, presenting a year's subscription for the *Watchtower* magazine and three booklets (including *"This Good News of the Kingdom"*) on a contribution of $1. Publishers may offer both subscriptions—*The Watchtower* and *Awake!*—on a contribution of $2 with six booklets given to subscribers. If one already subscribes for *The Watchtower*, then offer the *Awake!* subscription. If the subscription is not taken, then endeavor to leave individual copies of *The Watchtower* and *Awake!* on a 10c contribution and be sure to call back on prospective subscribers and all who show interest.

⁴ By diligent effort and with Jehovah's blessing upon our activity, undoubtedly all congregation publishers will be privileged to obtain at least two new subscriptions for the campaign, pioneers twenty and special pioneers thirty. As all serve zealously with Jehovah's channel of communication the way will be opened for many more good-will persons to learn, through the pages of *The Watchtower*, Jehovah's grand and thrilling purposes now in course of fulfillment.

How Does Jehovah, Speak? Through the Watchtower Magazine.
"Jehovah is the source of all knowledge. When he speaks, all should listen and learn. And how does he speak? Through his appointed channel of communication—his collective congregation of anointed ones… the Watchtower magazine [is] the main instrument used by the congregation to dispense Jehovah's communications." (*Informant*, January, 1956)

Nikos was excited about my steady progress in the truth (as the Witnesses referred to their faith). Over time, I began to abandon all of my hobbies, except for chess. Nikos and I played chess equally well, and we played quite often. The rest of the time, however, was devoted to studying the books and the magazines of the Watchtower.[42] I considered them spiritual nourishment from God through the "faithful and discreet slave," in other words those "anointed" of the Society.[43]

---

42 According to the Watchtower Society "The Watchtower [magazine] is the principal means of dispensing spiritual food at the proper time." (*Pay Attention to Yourselves and All the Flock*" 1991, p. 38)

43 The Watchtower Society has made repeated claims that they are Jehovah's official mouthpiece and channel (see, for example, WT 7-1-1943 p.205). But, actually,

They had me convinced that the international publishing and evangelistic crusade of the Witnesses, along with its "good fruit," served as the infallible proof that it was the "organization of God" since "God always carried out His plan through an organization."

Little by little, I began to adopt and use all the terminology used by the Witnesses. I called their faith *the* truth. I referred to them as brothers although they did not consider me a brother yet. I referred to all those who were not Witnesses as *worldly** or goats. Consequently, I felt that I already belonged to a special elitist group of privileged elect who would survive the "destruction of Armageddon."

One day, I joined Nikos' family as they attended a meeting at a private estate in Malakasa. Thousands of Witnesses flooded the estate, and the entire day passed with compunction as I listened to an endless number of homilies, demonstrations and theatrical plays. That evening I returned home feeling "well fed." This was how I always felt when I heard the homilies of a Witness *Circuit Overseer**. Inside of me, the decision was already at hand. Once I overcame my fears and weaknesses, I would become a Witness of Jehovah.

The First Problems

THE WITNESSES ADVISED me to keep our contact secret until I became "sure-footed in the faith,"[44] and until "the seed of truth took root in my heart." Otherwise, "the Devil would take the seed, and I would be lost." They had forewarned me that "a man's enemies

---

the first use of the title was ascribed to Russell himself: "Thousands of readers of Pastor Russell's writings believe that he filled the office of the 'faithful and wise servant,' and that his great work was giving to the household of faith meat in due season. His modesty and humility precluded him from openly claiming the title, but he admitted as much in private." (WT 12/1/1916; See also A. H. Macmillan, *Faith on the March*, Prentice-Hall, inc., NJ, 1957, pp. 126-127).

44 See 1 Cor. 16:13

"There may be opposition to your continued study of the bible." (You Can Live Forever, p24)

will be those of his own household,"[45] and how at some point I would "suffer persecution" for the sake of my faith. In the beginning, I did not say anything to others (i.e., non-Witnesses), mostly because I was ashamed. What would people say if they found out that I was keeping company with Witnesses? However, I remembered the words of the Lord: "But whoever denies Me before men, him I will also deny before My Father Who is in heaven."[46]

This led me to slowly change my opinion, until the time came when this shame and cowardice gave way to boldness, and boldness turned to enthusiasm. The belief that they are being persecuted for following Christ is what keeps many people in the Watchtower early on. And if someone says anything against the JWs, they think the Lord's words are being fulfilled which "proves" to them that they are in the true religion. This is a self-fulfilled prophecy but before I realized it, I jumped in and did not turn back. The more I learned, the more enthusiastic I became, and the more I wanted to share my new views with my own people. Now I finally understood how Nikos felt and why he undertook such a great struggle for his faith.

---

45 Mat. 10:36
46 Matt. 10:33

One evening, after spending a number of hours in the teachings of the Witnesses (an evening full of blessings I used to say), I returned home full of enthusiasm. It was an exceptionally rainy night, but I felt such euphoria that I barely noticed the weather. As I entered the house, I sang one of the hymns of the Witnesses in a low voice and, ignoring the forewarnings, began to speak to my mother.

"Today was a wonderful day!" I said to my mother as I was taking off my leather jacket. "I did not have school, and went with Nikos!"

"Why didn't you have school?" she asked.

"The teachers were on strike," I answered.

"And where did you go with Nikos?" she asked again.

"To the church of the Jehovah's Witnesses," I answered in a most natural manner. "If you only knew how much I have learned there!"

"What! You have been there before?" she cried.

"Yes! Many times! Come and you'll see how good it feels!"

These last words I said amidst a pandemonium of screams and incomprehensible sounds coming out of her mouth. I was trying to speak to her rationally but to no avail. She was beside herself.

"You will never step foot there ever again!" I distinctly heard her say among other things.

"I've already made up my mind! I will become a Jehovah's Witness. We ought to obey God rather than people," I argued.

"You were born Orthodox, and you'll die Orthodox!" she shouted.

"Precisely because I don't want to die, I will stop being Orthodox! *Now* you remember your Orthodoxy? What did you teach me about God all these years! Nothing! And now that I've found the truth, you want to hold me back?!" At that point my father walked in.

"Why are you yelling?" he asked.

"He wants to become a Jehovite!" my mother tearfully replied.

"What! It would be better for you to become a transvestite! If you dare become a Chiliast, I will disown you!" he added in outrage.

4. In the Nest of the Spider

"I have no interest in your money! I have already chosen my path!" I said forcefully.

"If you become a Chiliast, you must leave my home!" he shouted to intimidate me.

I felt my blood boiling. This was the moment of trial, the moment of decision. Just then the words of the Lord echoed in my ears: "There is no one who has left house or brothers or sisters or father or mother or wife or children or lands, for My sake and the gospel's, who shall not receive a hundredfold now in this time, houses and brothers and sisters and mothers and children and lands with persecutions-and in the age to come, eternal life."[47]

With tears in my eyes, I put on my leather jacket; I bade them farewell, and though my mother was crying, I left. Deep in thought, I walked through the torrential rain without an umbrella. Maybe the Witnesses were right. They had told me not to speak openly yet, but I didn't listen. They had told me that members of my household would go against the "truth," but I didn't expect it. I thought I knew better than them. Now I was suddenly kicked out by my own parents! After walking in the rain for a long time, I sat on a plaza bench, exhausted and wet. I sat there all night, worrying about how my mother and my father were feeling, seeking God's help.

I wasn't the only one who worried that evening. When my mother overcame her initial anger and realized her mistake, she began wondering where I could have gone in the middle of the night in the rain. Her first impulse was to locate Nikos' phone number in the telephone book, and she called his home. His mother picked up the telephone and asked who was calling. She heard a distressed voice.

"This is George's mother! Where is my son? Where are you keeping him?"

---

[47] Mark 10:29-30

"I don't understand what you are saying!" Nikos' mother answered.

My mother explained what had happened, and after she complained and threatened, she finished with these words:

"My child used to be good! Now, because of you people, he left home. I expect you to find him!"

Nikos' mother, after reassuring her that I was not there, attempted to calm my mother down, promising that the minute they saw me, they would send me home.

However, I did not return home that night, and they were all concerned. In the morning, I decided to go see how my mother was. My father was already at work. The minute she laid eyes on me she hugged me, crying, and told me what had happened. I immediately called Nikos to put him and his family at ease. Afterwards, I made my position clear, telling my mother that I was an adult and free to choose my life's path. I told her never to bring up the subject of religion again. She replied by asking me for a favor. She told me that she wanted to invite over an archimandrite[48] relative of ours to help me see my mistake, and if he could not convince me, then I would be free to do whatever I considered to be the right thing. This was a fair and reasonable request, so I accepted it willingly. My father did not seem opposed to this either. I continued my Christian activities, being relatively free, sensing a deep joy at being tried for the sake of Christ and for successfully overcoming this very first trial.

The day of the archimandrite's visit drew near. I waited for him with the Holy Scriptures on the table, while my mother, hardly able to contain her joy, felt certain that at the end of this visit I would cease all contact with the Witnesses.

When the archimandrite arrived, he sat and socialized with my

---

48 Literally "the leader of the flock;" originally it signified a Monastery Abbot, nowadays it can also signify a celibate Orthodox priest.

4. In the Nest of the Spider

parents, something very natural since they hadn't seen each other in years. He asked me about my school, my work, and everything else—except the subject of faith! I was desperately searching to find some opportune moment to start a spiritual discussion with him; however, he did not give me a chance. After several minutes had passed and he had already discussed at length various family matters with my parents, I found the courage to intervene.

"Father, what's your opinion of the Holy Scriptures?" I asked.

"Why are you bringing this up now, especially since we haven't seen each other for so long! If you want to hear the Gospel, go to church," he replied, leaving all of us flabbergasted!

I could not believe my ears! Nikos, a man my parents considered to be a heretic, could not stop speaking about God, and his faith affected all of his actions. Yet right here in front of me, I had someone considered to be a liturgist of God, and he viewed the Holy Scriptures as a subject not worthy of discussion. In spite of his answer, a few minutes later I took courage and asked him another question about the Orthodox faith. His answer froze any further desire within me to converse with him.

"Why do you want to bring this up? My son, why don't you forget about the Holy Scriptures for now, we're discussing something more interesting here." he replied.

This time I saw my mother and my father sink into a state of gloom. They began to understand that someone can be a priest, but this alone does not guarantee his love for God. When the archimandrite left, my mother was left staring at me in a desperate sort of way, since I had not managed to extract even one word out of him about God.

"Evidently he doesn't want to take any of his work home," I said ironically. "It seems that he considers Christianity a career, an occupation."

This was the most opportune time to begin speaking to my mother about the faith of the Watchtower. I spoke to her about those people who took joy in listening to questions about God and who use the Holy Scriptures during every one of their discussions. I asked her to study the Holy Scriptures with me so I could show her why it was not to the archimandrite's advantage to discuss the Holy Scriptures. She accepted, more so to see what I had gotten myself into and to learn what they were telling me. From that day on, I began to pass on to my mother everything I had learned from Nikos. Nikos' family did not stay idle either. His mother would often phone my mother. Nikos was coming over to our house more often, and Nikos would speak with my mother about his religion. Occasionally my mother would say, "Nikos is such a good boy! The only bad thing is that he is a Witness."

She used to repeat this up until the time she stopped considering the Witnesses heretics.

As far as I was concerned, there was nothing holding me back. I had embraced my new faith with great fervor. I eagerly participated in every activity of the Witnesses. Outside of their meetings, which I very seldom missed, I began to go out to work the street. I would go from door-to-door and declare the good news of the Witnesses. Nikos managed to teach me what I needed to know, following the school directives of the organization, along with the example and the mannerisms of those who had taught him.

5. Luring Others to the Web

Nikos' story

From a very young age, I followed those who worked the street door-to-door. This is something I never questioned; I just took it for granted. All Witnesses are made to feel that working in the Organization's program will have a determining effect in their salvation and their children are to follow after their parents. In the beginning, I only observed others as they began a discussion with the homeowner, and I spoke only when spoken to. Of course, I had observed many demonstrations and practice sessions at the *Theocratic Ministry School*,* and I had participated in a number of them, but in reality I did not have the courage to initiate a conversation with a stranger all by myself.

This changed, however, one Sunday when I was assigned to collaborate with the Circuit Overseer of the Witnesses. The overseer would come at different intervals to evaluate and bolster the activities of the local congregation. He had about twenty such congregations which he visited consistently, since he received a nominal fee from the Society for his living expenses and travel, being allowed to be the house guest of the local Witnesses. These overseers were replaced at different intervals, and they usually had their wives with them who were also quite knowledgeable in the faith. I developed

"A Deacon (now Publisher) in Motion"
Greek *Watchtower* 8/1/1959 (p.349)

a special liking for this particular overseer because he was one of our distant relatives, and my mother constantly referred to him as a great role model, someone worth imitating. I admired him and was also jealous of him in the good sense of the word. I thought of him as a true spiritual brother. The word "spiritual" I understood to mean a man who knew a lot and who possessed the ability to influence others, as most Protestants do (this is totally unrelated to the Orthodox meaning of the term, which we will see later.)

As I said before, prior to this one Sunday when I began collaborating with the overseer, I had been reluctant to go door-to-door on my own. On this day, we studied the verse of the day, and then we were instructed about what to present to each of the households we visited. I was not aware of it back then, but these were studied lessons of marketing and were presented to us every Thursday as the lessons of the Ministry School. Finally we set out to distribute our products in our sectors. The sector was the section of our territory which we were assigned to and which we were responsible for evangelizing.

5. Luring Others to the Web

As we walked the streets, we discussed many things. We never missed an opportunity to speak to someone at the beginning of our journey because the walk could be considered as work, and this all needed to be recorded in our monthly bulletin. When we drew near the large multi-housing complex of local workers assigned to me, we stood outside of the locked exterior door and pretended that we were ringing one of the bells. We repeated this several times, until someone coming out of the building opened the door. We entered the elevator, and on our way up to the tenth and last floor, we quickly sketched on a pad the position of the twenty apartments of the high-rise. In every box we would keep track of our progress by marking whether or not the man was home; if we had opened a discussion with him; if he had accepted a pamphlet, book, or periodical; if he was friendly or polemic; his name or any other information we could gather about him and so forth.[49]

Subsequently, we would transfer a tabulated summary of this information to the secretary of our congregation; he, in turn, would tabulate everyone's information into a monthly summary and would forward it to Brooklyn headquarters.[50] This reporting system was a great way for the elders to monitor our "spirituality" and exert more

---

[49] This is actually a mandatory practice. "Train publishers," the Society admonishes the elders, "to keep an accurate house-to-house record so they can call back on interested people. Make arrangements for calling again where no one was at home." (*Pay Attention to Yourselves and All the Flock*," 1991, p. 60)

[50] "The importance given to these reports is undeniable. Every Witness reports to the congregation, every congregation reports to the Branch Office of their country, every Branch Office sends a detailed monthly report to the international headquarters where these monthly reports are compiled, averages are figured, percentages of increase are noted. They are studied with the same avid interest that a large corporation would study the figures of its production records, its business growth; any fluctuations or downward trends in the number of Witnesses reporting time, the hours reported or the distribution of literature, become causes for concern. Branch representatives become uneasy if the monthly reports for their country fail to show increase, or worse, show a decrease." (Franz, *Crisis of Conscience*, p.281)

THE 1948 FIELD SERVICE REPORT OF JEHOVAH'S WITNESSES WORLD-WIDE

Country	1917 Av. Pubs.	1948 Av Pubs	Per-cent Incr.	Peak Pubs.	No. Com-panies	Total Literature	Total Hours	New Subs.	Individual Magazines	Back-Calls	Av Book Studies
U. S. of America	67,630	72,945	7%	78,566	2,901	8,383,231	16,964,919	230,378	6,486,766	4,550,198	51,023
Alaska	17	30	80%	43		8,066	11,361	325	6,661	3,630	34
Bahamas	17	32	84%	44	1	8,356	13,969	257	2,304	6,123	134
Bermuda	4	6	50%	7	1	2,448	4,858	206	804	3,054	42
Cameroun		60	New	81	1	95	6,854	3	214	1,177	4
Ecuador	14	29	110%	42	1	3,328	14,047	43	1,637	4,404	42
Fr. Equ. Africa		2	New	2			20			21	
Guadeloupe	13	28	120%	46	2	435	7,797	13	256	1,373	31
Iceland	3	3		6	1	3,107	1,628	114	1,003	651	5
Liberia		9	200%	15	1	2,236	5,629	31	395	1,935	17
Neth W Ind.	28	36	30%	43	2	15,321	12,591	712	8,273	4,514	42
Palestine	8	22	175%	30	6	1,774	5,398	14	346	345	7
Peru	22	40	85%	51	2	19,642	22,494	339	1,854	8,175	106
Portugal		10	New	14	1	2,351	1,180	14	118	237	
Sierra Leone	22	24	10%	33	1	1,899	4,162	41	843	1,183	10
Spain		24	New	43	7	782	4,916	42	169	1,407	6
Syria-Lebanon	99	109	10%	129	8	8,981	26,856	165	4,462	7,481	82
Virgin Islands	17	32	90%	47	1	8,358	8,363	496	2,326	4,580	79
Argentina	679	927	35%	1,012	45	135,672	224,369	1,992	44,054	64,701	551
Australia	3,234	3,503	6%	3,722	201	240,881	728,440	6,162	321,328	202,689	2,041
Fiji	9	10	11%	14	1	7,471	5,619	107	2,189	1,902	13
Java	11	9		10	1	1,182	812	19	23	227	3
Singapore	6	10	66%	14	1	1,352	3,817	106	595	1,397	18
Austria	751	1,286	71%	1,552	129	247,312	281,000	4,394	106,021	126,706	606
Belgium	876	1,177	34%	1,357	43	184,757	295,585	1,693	54,225	60,434	592
Luxembourg	47	47		59	3	2,776	12,366	52	10,040	4,153	46
Bolivia	16	36	125%	46	2	9,263	25,493	302	2,492	8,184	74
Brazil	648	1,077	66%	1,319	57	391,400	397,325	3,601	68,300	58,555	832
British Guiana	134	174	30%	220	10	19,298	63,650	383	20,978	16,914	257
British Honduras	38	38		49	5	2,309	11,907	38	3,911	3,886	55
British Isles	12,149	14,676	20%	15,555	612	2,039,777	3,886,753	58,387	351,586	1,241,320	8,104
Eire	37	52	40%	62	4	15,022	45,206	535	1,194	11,735	43
Malta	6			8		39	3,032		37	421	9
British West Indies	700	980	40%	1,071	37	54,281	254,073	1,501	79,638	70,941	959
Burma	19	36	90%	52	2	20,714	16,727	912	3,372	6,619	82
Canada	11,224	12,603	12%	14,219	561	658,229	2,315,951	23,087	840,003	524,593	5,209
Chile	137	191	40%	231	11	43,177	69,425	820	13,828	19,583	272
China		8	New	28	3	12,619	9,353	99	1,428	2,479	30
Colombia	29	28		37	4	21,752	19,608	879	2,856	7,064	80
Costa Rica	449	637	41%	915	21	27,713	150,935	795	21,463	37,346	579

The 1948 Field Service Report of the Watchtower Society World Wide
The "field reports" handed by the individual Jehovah's Witnesses, like Nikos, to their congregations are reported to the central offices in Brooklyn, NY. Above: part of the annual field service report of the Watchtower Society worldwide (WT 1/1/1949, p.9)

---

pressure on us.[51] Yet, from the basis of these records it can be easily demonstrated that the door-to-door ministry just doesn't work to convert people. For example, statistics for 1986 indicate that it took a tad over 3,000 hours of service to make a new convert. This means I needed to bang on doors 8 hours a day, 5 days a week, for a full year and a half before I could convince anybody to become a Witness. Of course, the Governing Body is fully aware of this, but still doesn't change methods! Why? Because door-to-door is the best method to sell their literature.[52]

---

51 Wilson, Dianne. *Awakening of a Jehovah's Witness—Escape from the Watchtower Society*, Prometheus Books, 2002, p. 53

52 Leonard & Marjorie Chretien. *Witnesses of Jehovah,* Harvest House Publishers, 1988, p. 52. Raymond Franz notes, " In reality, there is strong evidence that only a minority of Witnesses became such as the result of a visit to their doors. I have asked groups of persons by what means they became Witnesses and, in each case, out of perhaps a dozen persons only one or two had first been interested through that means. The majority were interested by family members, workmates, ac-

5. Luring Others to the Web

As a matter of fact, as early as in 1934, some brothers protested to Rutherford that, "this carrying books about is merely a book-selling scheme."[53] The successor of Russell, however, thundered a tirade, blasting verse after verse from the Scriptures, why the brothers should go on the streets to sell his books![54] Rutherford was instrumental into shaping the Watchtower Society into the door-to-door book-selling business we know. But as the Organization discourages its members from learning too much of its history, these controversies were unknown to me when I was working the streets.

As we were knocking on the doors of the upper floors, we found that quite a few people were not home and the rest were totally indifferent. However, my partner had one more problem besides knocking on doors. He was instructed to convince me to also speak to the residents. I wanted this, but I was timid. At one door, when the resident came out, I just stood there looking at him without saying a word even after we had agreed that I would start up the conversation. Fortunately, my partner intervened and spoke. At the next door, he tried another technique. He would speak first, and then I would take over. And this is what we did. When a woman opened her door, he introduced himself and after a brief prologue he said, "My friend here has something to show you."

I proceeded to display the magazines at hand, and I did rather well. We tried the same technique with other residents as we made our way through the building.

In the high-rises, we always started our work at the top, working our way down, so that if some antagonistic resident came out with hostile intentions, we would have an exit open in front of us.

---

quaintances and similar contacts. Reports by circuit overseers have presented similar evidence. (Franz, *In Search*, p. 221)

53 WT 1/1/1937 p.5
54 Ibid.

> "Chess has been a game of war ever since it was originated 1,400 years ago. The chessboard has been an arena for battles between royal courts, between armies, between all sorts of conflicting ideologies. The most familiar opposition has been the one created in the Middle Age with one set of king, queen, knights, bishops, rooks and pawns against another.
>
> "Other conflicts depicted have been between Christians against barbarians, Americans against British, cowboys against Indians and capitalists against Communists. ... It is reported that one American designer is now creating a set illustrating the war in Vietnam."
>
> Probably most modern chess players do not think of themselves as maneuvering an army in battle. Yet are not the game's connections with war obvious? The word for pawn is derived from a Medieval Latin word meaning "foot soldier." A knight was a mounted man-at-arms of the European feudal period. Bishops took an active part in supporting their side's military efforts. And rooks, or castles, places of protection, were important in medieval warfare.
>
> Thus Reuben Fine, a chess player of international stature, wrote in his book *The Psychology of the Chess Player*: "Quite obviously, chess is a play-substitute for the art of war." And *Time* magazine reported: "Chess originated as a war game. It is an adult, intellectualized equivalent of the maneuvers enacted by little boys with toy soldiers."
>
> While some chess players may object to making such a comparison, others will readily acknowledge the similarity. In fact, in an article about one expert chess player, the New York *Times* noted: "When Mr. Lyman looks at a chessboard, its squared outlines dissolve at times into the hills and valleys and secret paths of a woodland chase, or the scarred ground of an English battlefield."
>
> When one considers the complex movements, as opposing chessboard armies vie with each other for position, one may wonder whether chess has been a factor in the development of military strategy. According to V. R. Ramachandra Dikshitar, it has. In his book *War in Ancient India* he examined this matter at length, and concluded: "The principles of chess supplied ideas to the progressive development of the modes and constituents of the army."
>
> *The Need for Caution*
>
> Some chess players have recognized the harm that can result from playing the game. According to *The Encyclopædia Britannica*, the religious reformer "John Huss, . . . when in prison, deplored his having played at chess, whereby he had lost time and run the risk of being subject to violent passions."
>
> The extreme fascination of chess can result in its consuming large amounts of one's time and attention to the exclusion of more important matters, apparently a reason Huss regretted having played the game. Also, in playing it there is the danger of "stirring up competition with one another," even developing hostility toward another, something the Bible warns Christians to avoid doing.
>
> Then, too, grown-ups may not consider it proper for children to play with war toys, or at games of a military nature. Is it consistent, then, that they play a game noted to be, in the opinion of some, an "intellectualized equivalent of the maneuvers enacted by little boys with toy soldiers"? What effect does playing chess really have upon one? Is it a wholesome effect?
>
> Surely chess is a fascinating game. But there are questions regarding it that are good for each one who plays chess to consider.

Should a Jehovah Witness Play Chess?
Was Niko's decision to quit playing chess entirely out of his own volition? Actually the Awake magazine had said: "The extreme fascination of chess can result in its consuming large amounts of one's time and attention to the exclusion of more important matters..." (Awake, 3/22/1975).

If we started from the bottom, we might have been trapped on one of the upper floors by those below who had already seen us. Besides, it was less tiring to descend than to ascend. By the time we made it to the lower floors, I had already become very self-confident and was engaging in conversation all by myself. I remember feeling very gratified because I had given away many magazines and one book. My partner, however, seemed to be even more satisfied because he was observing one more of the *publishers** becoming independent enough to knock on doors. From that time on, I went out more often for field service. I would bring others along less experienced than me, and for whom I was responsible, to teach them presentation skills. Soon enough I taught my friend George how to make presentations.

At the same time that I began knocking on doors, I was also a member of an amateur chess team, and I would go and play ev-

5. Luring Others to the Web

ery so often in the small neighborhood tournaments. That year my team advanced to the semi-finals and organized ten matches every Sunday. So I also began to officially participate in these organized matches. Half of the month, when the matches took place away from home, I did field service work, and the other half of the month, when we played at home, I went to the chess club. One Sunday my mother asked, "How can you abandon the work of Jehovah and spend your Sundays at the chess club?"

I justified myself saying that I also needed some recreation, and I was already dedicating two Sundays a month to the work of God.

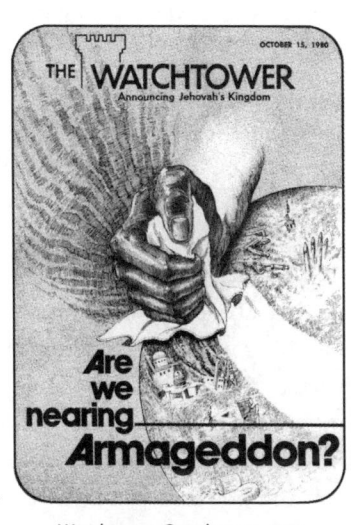

Watchtower, October 15, 1980

Inside, however, I felt a real struggle. I did not feel good knowing that so many people around me would perish in Armageddon, and instead of warning them, I was playing chess. Therefore, I made a big decision: I walked away from the team. From then on, every Saturday and Sunday morning I went to the start-up meetings and then to the work of God.

With this maneuver, my mother succeeded in isolating me from *bad associations** I might encounter at the chess club and to steer me towards spiritual activities. As all non-Witnesses were "of the world," I had to stay as far away as I could from them, which included just about everyone around me. I was warned: "The worldly people may seem nice, but their hearts are evil because they don't love Jehovah."

Little by little, all of my other activities ceased and I was dedicating all of my free time to the Society. The only hobby I held on to was the study of scientific journals, something that proved to be very helpful later on in my search for the true God. I remember some of the people we called on asking me, "If someone could prove to you that your religion is false, what would you do?"

"Of course I would abandon it," I said with confidence; and I continued, "Do you have any proof of this sort?"

The man had no clue even about his own religion, so I challenged him, "If I prove that you have a false religion, would you abandon it?"

"I really don't care about these things." he replied.

So we left him. Honestly, though, I was willing to research anything without fear if someone asserted that he could prove me wrong. Yet no such person materialized, not then nor in the following years, and I interpreted this as proof that I had the true faith. Another time, someone came back with, "Why should we listen to you and not have you listen to us?"

"Great! I'm ready to hear you. What do you have to say?" I asked.

But these people remained speechless for an entire minute while I waited for their answer. They obviously had nothing to say. This, along with some hotheaded reactions at a few homes, convinced me that there was no other correct religion but mine. I believed that I was "persecuted" for the name of Jehovah just because these "persecutors" did not have any serious arguments and they reacted vehemently. If they had had the truth, I was thinking, the best approach would have been to try to convince me of it. In all the years of my membership in the Society, I knocked on thousands of doors, and I met all different types of people. However, I did not meet one person who could respond to my challenges and give me lessons of truth and spirituality. Those people would come much later…

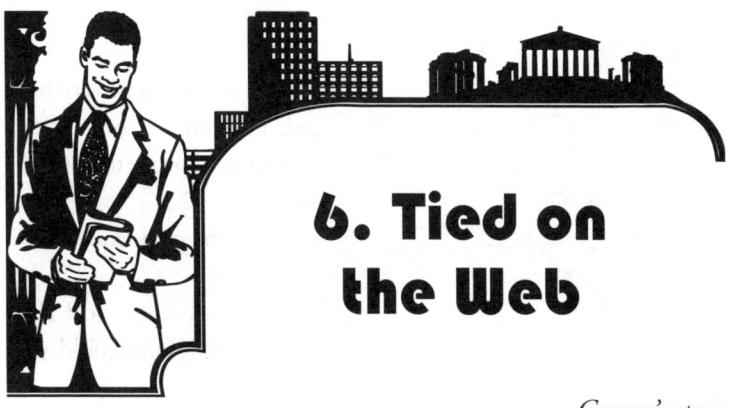

6. Tied on the Web

George's story

In those days when I first began knocking on doors, Nikos explained the method used by the International Watchtower Society to direct the work. He explained that the Society closely followed the work and progress of those sent out to evangelize by keeping track of monthly statistical data which showed any weak points. He showed me a report that needed to be filled out by every Witness, showing specific elements of his monthly activities. If I wanted to, I could also report the statistics I gathered to the Society, thereby contributing to the international data. Nikos also explained that by reporting my activities, I would officially be included among the publishers.

What he failed to tell me, however (something that he was not very conscious about either), was that by filling out the report, the person evangelizing was acknowledging his full submission to the Watchtower Society. It was no longer permissible for him to have his own opinion or any opinions different from the organization in matters of faith, nor could he act independently or use methods not approved by the organization. If he showed any disregard for these bylaws and acted or believed differently, the sword of disfellowship hung over his head.

«Μηδέ νά συντρώγητε» μέ ἕνα ἀποκομμένο ἄτομο

"You should not even eat" with a disfellowshipped peson. (Greek Watchtower 01/15/82)

Disfellowship, or expulsion, is the worst possible punishment for a Witness. It is decided after one or more court hearings by a *Judicial Committee** of elders convening behind closed doors,[55] thus excluding the presence of any spectators. Once a Witness has been disfellowshipped, the Elders would simply announce to the congregation that so-and-so has been disfellowshipped.[56] No more details

---

55 "During Russell's day and even during much of Rutherford's presidency, Bible Students or Witnesses were tried before the whole 'Church' or local congregation in an attempt to follow Jesus's command at Matthew 18:17. Under the new arrangement that custom was abolished. The Watchtower of 15 May 1944 (p. 151) stated: 'The offended one may tell the Church.' According to theocratic order this would not mean a congregational meeting with all present, but telling it to those charged with the cares of the congregations and representing it in special capacities. What this meant was that the Watch Tower Society had really established a clergy class, in spite of denials to the contrary, and church courts which were inquisitions in the dictionary and legal sense of the term. They were to fulfill 'the role of judge, jury and prosecutor of the accused.'" (Penton, *Apocalypse*, p.88)

56 "Excommunications are announced to the congregation, but elders never say why a person was expelled. Witnesses can only guess from a long list of offenses

are said, for legal reasons, as many Witnesses sued the Watchtower for libel.[57] After his disfellowship (for whatever reason) from the Society, this person would be an outcast. Not even a simple greeting is permitted from the rest of the Witnesses[58] who would also be penalized with disfellowship![59] Hence, a disfellowshipped Witness would suddenly lose all friends and relatives that were Witnesses, even his parents and children, who might then live in a different house. His marriage could possibly receive a deadly blow, and he could even lose his employment if his employer was a Witness. Only a future re-enrollment in the ranks of the organization could restore the relationship of all other Witnesses with him. Reinstatement, however, is a lengthy, lonely, and humiliating procedure.[60]

All of this was possible for a Witness after he handed in even

---

that range from smoking cigarettes to manslaughter. Homosexuality, fornication, drunkenness, slander, fraud, gambling, apostasy, fits of anger and violence, and adultery are others. The excommunication announcement tells members to begin shunning that person. If they don't, they, too, risk being disfellowshipped. Fear of being disfellowshipped is gripping for many Witnesses. Because they believe that only Witnesses will be saved from death, many don't associate with non-Witnesses. Being disfellowshipped, then, means losing your circle of friends, not to mention family members who remain in the faith. Elders disfellowship 50,000 to 60,000 Witnesses around the world each year, [Witnesses' national spokesman J.R.] Brown said. 'It's not an unusual occurrence, as far as we're concerned,' he said (See *Spiritual Shunning*, on St. Petersburg Times, 8-22-2002)

57 Jay Walter, *My 6-Year Journey Out of the Watchtower*, (retrieved 11/24/2008 from http://www.exjws.net/pioneers/part18.htm)

58 See WT 9/15/1981, p. 25.

59 These "disfellowship policies," comments Presiding Overseer Anthony Crispin, "were enacted when Ray Franz, a member of the Governing Body, left the Organization. It seems that the Watchtower Policy changes when circumstances serves the interest of the Governing Body in getting rid of someone they want to railroad. This is what happened to Ray Franz and his friend Gregerson." (Anthony Crispin, *A Guide to Reinstatement for Those Disfellowshipped from the Watchtower*, Lulu.com, 2008, p. 40)

60 "A possibility of reinstatement to repentant excommunicants was held out. But often that entailed sitting silently in meeting without having anyone speak to the penitent from one to three years; and when he was restored to fellowship, he would usually still be kept on "probation" and denied certain congregational privileges. For years, when one was disfellowshipped, he was told that never

a single report with his personal statistics for the Society. Being ignorant of all these, I began to hand in my report. At that time, I regarded the Society as the "loving" organization of God. This was my honeymoon period in the Society, when I was treated as a newcomer. Later on, with the play-acting done, I would see its true face.

Enrolling in Ministry School

AT ONE OF the Society's meetings, I was approached by an *elder** and asked if I wished to enroll in the Theocratic Ministry School. I accepted and immediately I was notified to present a short lecture and interpret a passage from the Holy Scriptures. This is a course of study that never really ends and from which nobody ever graduates and the only goal is to train preachers and evangelists for the Society. The students practiced giving small lectures, then corrections and suggestions would be offered by one of the elders. The meetings were held every Thursday and lasted two hours, in conjunction with another meeting on the examination of ministry, a small internal booklet given only to publishers. On Sundays, there was a common gathering for everyone to study the *Watchtower*, the most basic periodical of the organization, and to hear the public lecture of the week. On Tuesdays, there was a study of some designated book where only a few people would gather in a family environment. This series of meetings took place in three separate homes because the local Witnesses were divided into three groups.

The day for my talk came. For the talk I had prepared some notes taken from the *Watchtower* magazines pertaining to the text I was assigned to read. But as I took my stand in front of the microphone with sixty pairs of eyes staring at me, I was overcome with fear. Fortunately, except for a few mistakes in reading, everything went well. I finished one minute before my allotted time. After-

---

again would he hold an appointed position under the society's direction." (Penton, *Apocalypse*, p.90) wards, my examiner came to the speaker's stand and marked my report in the "advice" section with a "G" for "good" in one part of my examination, and with a "W," meaning "more work is needed" in another area of my examination. After the initial homilies I was assigned to read, things became more difficult because I needed to expand on the subject quickly and from memory, without reading the homilies from my notes, with the exception of the Holy Scripture verses. In a short while, I overcame my initial stage fright and delivered my homilies with confidence and without notes.

My Parents and I Become Baptized

THROUGHOUT THIS PERIOD I continued to teach my mother about the Society by exposing her to some of the books of the Witnesses. She had already espoused everything I believed, and urged me to progress in the Society. As far as my father was concerned, he also began to display some interest, influenced by the change in my mother. In the beginning, they attended the meetings to see me offer a talk. Later on, they started coming to the weekly meetings. In a short period of time, they developed friendships and their interest was intensified. Soon, they, too began to fill out the evangelizing report and to witness to others.

In the second year of our involvement with the Witnesses, all three of us participated in the baptism of dedication. Although we had been baptized by the Orthodox Church, we believed that baptism to be invalid because we received it when we were infants and lacked understanding. "An infant does not possess knowledge of its 'dedication,'" they had told us, and they pointed out the verse in Matthew 28:19-20: "Go therefore and make disciples of all the nations, baptizing them in the name of the Father and of the Son and of the Holy Spirit, teaching them to observe all things that I have commanded you." They emphasized, "You first become a disciple and then you are baptized!"

And we, like total fools, never took the time to analyze this verse grammatically. This would have to wait a number of years to come to fruition; we were all made to feel confident that we would survive Armageddon, and that we would progress toward human perfection in a period of a thousand years, before the final tribulation. For us, this was a tremendous hope since we had never heard the true Christian Gospel.

Much like the merchant in the Lord's parable, we were searching for pearls without yet having discovered the most "precious pearl."

We believed that the only things needed for our salvation were adherence to the Society as the *ark** of salvation, and to preach to others about all of these things. Woe to anyone who found himself in the world and outside of the Society during Armageddon. Jehovah himself would kill this person without any hope of resurrection.

This instilled a deep sadness in us and we agonized for our friends, our relatives, and for everyone around us in general. This compelled us to speak "in season and out of season" for what we firmly believed, in order to have these people saved along with us.

We were deeply saddened by the malice and bad attitude of certain individuals who accused us, claiming that somehow we were bribed or that we stepped on holy icons, while we were sacrificing much of our energy and time for their sake. Rather quickly, our relatives and friends began to avoid us. They asked us not to speak to them about our newly found faith; however, we insisted on speaking to them about it.

When informed about my mother's change in faith, her godfather and uncle stopped speaking to us for years, up until his dying moments. We had almost succeeded in proselytizing him but he died Orthodox. He never came to understand that he was partly responsible for our ordeal because he never took care to teach my mother the Orthodox faith as a godfather should.

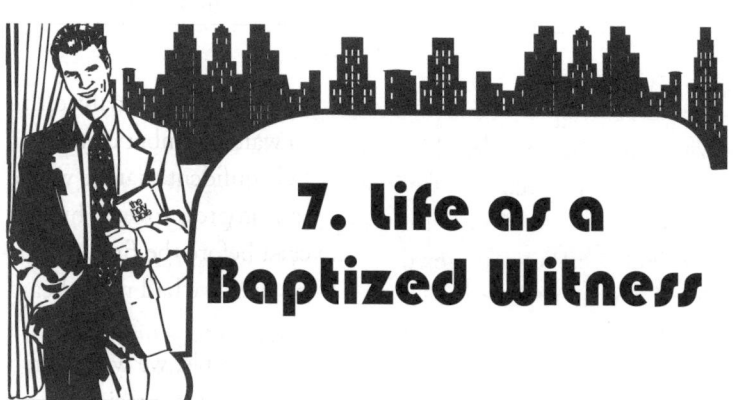

7. Life as a Baptized Witness

Nikos' story

n spite of my success in the work of Jehovah, I had not been baptized as of yet. Since my friend George was baptized before me, he kept asking me, "When will you be baptized? I came to the 'truth' through you, and yet I was baptized before you?!"

"I'm not ready!" I answered. "But I won't take much longer."

The reason for the postponement was that I was still drowning in sin. I was constantly postponing my baptism, with the expectation of first cleaning up my lifestyle. This was the same reason dozens of other witnesses had also postponed their baptism.

At the time, I was teaching four different Bible study groups, yet, I dared not to proceed with baptism because I still struggled with some bad habits that I had developed in my youth. Being ignorant of the real meaning of baptism, I believed that I first needed to stop sinning, then, in a state of purity, I would enter the pure organization of God.

In reality, I lived a double life. I was one person when preaching and someone totally different when I was flirting with my old girlfriends in secret. I felt terribly guilty every time I went out on a date, thinking that this would be my last time, but I kept doing it over and over again. Naturally, George had no idea about these activities since he considered me such a bright example.

Besides my shame in front of God, I was also feeling ashamed for something else. I kept thinking, what if I ran into one of my girlfriends while ministering door to door! I would ridicule not only myself but the Society as well!

Actually, one morning as I was about to enter a high-rise with my partner, I saw one of my old girlfriends sitting on the balcony and I panicked! I blurted out an excuse to my partner and we left, heading toward another section. I escaped being ridiculed but this close call did some good. I became determined to avoid flirting publicly and yet to continue other secret sins in private. "At least," I thought, "if only Jehovah sees me, He will understand my struggle." However, to make my life even more difficult, members of the Society asked me to hold a Bible study with a teen-aged male Witness who happened to have an older sister. It did not take me long to realize that this young lady was flirting with me very provocatively and with immoral intentions. First, I couldn't understand how it was possible for a Jehovah's Witness to behave in such a way. Later however, I thought that because she was also unbaptized, she might fall by making the same mistakes as I. Amazingly, in the face of so much seduction, I controlled myself with much effort and prayer so as to keep myself from backsliding into my old evil habits. She harassed me to the point of the Bible study becoming a nightmare. I was truly afraid that one day she would manage to get me alone, and I was afraid of how I would respond.

Fortunately, nothing ever came of it. However, all of these incidents still prevented me from being baptized. Deep inside, I knew that some day it would come to fruition. But that didn't stop my mother from constantly questioning me as to why I was still unbaptized. I kept answering her that I first wished to complete some

7. Life as a Baptized Witness

more studies so that the dedication of baptism would find me totally ready and well established in the truth.

A First, if Small, Independent Study

ABOUT THIS TIME, I had come across an interesting book called *An Encyclopedia of World Religions*. It summarized the most basic religions of the world, and examined one hundred heresies. The book described the origins and beliefs of each religion, but failed to explain why they believe in such a way. Even though I thought that my study of world religions was fairly complete, I was unaware of the most basic tenets. I was searching this book to find religions that shared similarities with my own. Then I would consider them worthy of more research. The fact that I failed to find anything close further convinced me that I was on the right path. As I finished reading the book, I promised Jehovah that I would not repeat the sins that I kept doing up to that point, and announced to my mother that I would be baptized at the upcoming gathering.

Baptized in the Watchtower Society

THE NEXT DAY an elder began to pre-qualify me with the pertinent questioning, in order to be convinced that I would prove to be a suitable candidate for baptism. Due to the great number of questions he needed to ask me, he came to my house every day. Although I was found suitable, based on my ability to answer his questions, in reality I continued sinning, transgressing my promise to God up to the day of my baptism.

From that day on and for quite a few months I stayed clean, keeping my promise to God. I was baptized along with hundreds of others in the swimming pool of the Malakasa Estate of the Jehovah's Witnesses. I will never forget the emotional charge of that day. From the moment I found myself under water up until the time I fell asleep late that night, I felt that I had an "open line" with God. I prayed incessantly, and for the first time in my life, I kept all my senses and movements in check, fearing to sadden Jehovah. Unfortunately, I did not manage to keep this "guarding of the senses" for very long. Little by little I began to return to my old agonizing struggle with sin.

Zealous in the Society

MY BAPTISM OF dedication was reason for much promotion in the Society. In other words, I was given more responsibilities within the congregation. I was now able to lead everyone in prayer during the opening and closing of the meetings, I could read the paragraphs of the quiz pamphlets, and I was able to participate in the different works of maintenance needed in the Kingdom Hall. I was made a *microphone man** and could also serve as a doorkeeper or pass out different publications to those present. Besides all this, I was also advancing in the knowledge of the dogmas of the Society. Even though Witnesses who read all the current publications were few and far between, I not only read all of them but even the older ones—*a fact that helped me later in my exodus from the Society.* Thus, I progressed very quickly, and surpassed in knowledge those much older than I.

Since I had covered most of the sectors in working my territory, almost everyone knew that I was a Witness. I remember many times when walking on the street, I would hear from behind closed windows, "Look, the Chiliast[61] is passing by!" This made me feel proud because I believed that I was being recognized as a servant of Jehovah. Consequently, I was also progressing in arrogance, judgmental criticism, and fanaticism. I looked at my countrymen who did not belong to my religion as a multitude worthy of destruction as "children of perdition." I was feeling a certain sense of superiority about my religious knowledge, but did not cease to be very concerned about non-Witnesses.

---

61 Chiliast is a prevalent term in Greece for the Witnesses. It is derived from the number 1,000, or "chilia" in Greek, and denotes JW's expectation of Christ's earthly reign for a thousand years.

7. Life as a Baptized Witness

Characteristic of my fanaticism was the following incident. One day my mother opened a discussion with an Evangelical Christian who told her that our faith was false, and that in reality all Christians will go to heaven, not just the 144,000 as we believed. He also proceeded to show her some verses which she found very problematic. When she returned home, she told me what happened and expressed some doubts about the doctrine of our faith. My reaction was immediate and explosive.

"Aren't you ashamed?" I exploded. "Instead of convincing him of the truth, he convinced you?"

"But he showed me some verses from the Bible," she protested.

"If you ever tell me again that you disagree with the Society of God, I will turn you in to the elder to cut you off for apostasy!" I interrupted her. She was shocked at my words. Immediately she began to tremble and cry.

"You would turn in your own mother?" she said, weeping. I was unyielding. I did not pardon anyone who doubted the Society, the conduit of God, as I believed. I was relentless in this regard, even toward my own mother and myself. After that, my mother never dared to express any doubt of the Society so I did not need to turn her in. However, as it turned out, it became necessary to turn myself in! I will give an account of that ordeal, in the belief that it will offer much useful insight into my overall psychology of that time.

Foretaste of Injustice

A NUMBER OF months passed by since the time of my baptism. It was summertime now, and we had moved to our vacation home in Salamina where we generally spent our summers. Feeling weary from summer temptation and from the pressures of being young, I began to develop a strong desire for a particular girl; and, according to the Holy Scriptures, desire conceives sin. Blinded by this desire, I began to actively pursue different methods to develop a relationship with her. In fact, after applying these schemes and silencing the voice of my conscience, I succeeded in going out with her, ready to fulfill my plan. We were finally all alone, and I needed to make the first move. She consented immediately, and then all of a sudden I was inundated with guilt. I felt that I was betraying Him Who died on the cross for me, He Who left His glory to die for my sins. And I, the "baptized", the "Christian", was ready to throw away His sacrifice like a piece of dirt! I got up immediately, asked forgiveness from the astonished young lady, and disappeared.

Months passed by, and by then we had moved to our winter residence. I continued to live as I had previously, without confiding in anyone about my summer sins. I saw myself as a violator of the promise I had given to God at my baptism. It was only a matter of time before these pangs of guilt would find an outlet.

The Confession

ONE SUNDAY EVENING we were participating in the study of the Watchtower; and, as always, I paid close attention to every detail of the lesson. At some point during the duration of this lesson, a section of the article was interpreted which dealt with hidden sins. Based on the logic of the Society, I was somehow convinced from this article that in order to be forgiven by God, I needed to reveal my deeds to the elders who would treat me, the fallen brother, "with understanding and care."

It did not occur to me back then, but this was strange advice for an organization totally opposed to confession. Up until the end of that meeting I wrestled with my shame since I was not accustomed to confessions. After the closing prayer, however, I came to the big decision. I drew near to my favorite elder and expressed to him that in obedience to the advice of the Watchtower I would like to speak to him about a certain sin I had fallen into after my baptism. I briefly described what had taken place and bade him goodnight. He told me that we would discuss it again at another time.

The next day he came to my house with another elder asking me to attend a special meeting with them the following day. However, I was extremely disappointed. I had confided in one elder, now a second one knew of my situation, and the following day a third one would get involved. If this was not enough, they told me that they would require the presence of yet another Witness who had been teaching me the Holy Scriptures. When I originally revealed my sin, I did so for the sake of advice and for forgiveness from God. I did not expect to find myself as a defendant in the presence of a judiciary committee! I didn't realize it at the time (nor did I have any knowledge of these matters) but the Witnesses confused advice and reformation with trial and punishment.[62] Given no other alternative, I went to this trial hoping that my sin would not be publicized.

The elders' visit to my home compelled my mother to constantly question me to the point where, out of sheer frustration, I told her not only the reason for the visit but also exactly what I had done. After recovering from her initial shock, she said that I had made a mistake in revealing this to them because it would invite trouble.

I answered her, "Since the Watchtower writes and confirms confessing these things, it is the right thing to do. Do you remember how upset you were when I told you of my intentions to turn you into the elder? As you can see, sin is something that I don't forgive very easily, not even for myself. So don't take these words as lacking in love but as words of real concern."

"Very well, but you will see that the confession with which you

---

62 In the Watchtower's Organization, the admission of certain sins—especially of the flesh—warrants a "behind-the-doors" investigation by a judicial committee; this can mean grievous repercussions for the accused, even to disfellowship.

entrusted the elders yesterday is something you will surely regret someday," she replied.

From that day on and for many months after, I was ashamed to face not only the four men on the committee but my own mother as well. The next day my stress level was at its highest when it came time to face the committee. This stress was much worse than the anxiety I had felt during final exams because now I had feelings of shame. In the afternoon, I took my Holy Scriptures and went to the Hall. As I entered, I noticed all four of them sitting and waiting for me with the Scriptures opened in front of them. Their big smiles did not manage to put me at ease. I sat across from them trembling. I was constantly thinking of what I would say to them if they asked me details about my "adventure." The presiding elder (the one I had confided in initially) broke the silence. He congratulated me for having the courage to admit my sin to them and then asked me to describe what happened. With difficulty I briefly related the incident to them, all the while being very concerned that my voice would soon begin to tremble. As I was speaking, every so often they would interrupt with supplementary questions, compelling me to describe even the smallest of details. When they seemed to be satisfied, they asked me why I did this.

I made a huge mistake by saying, "I imagine that since before being baptized these things were part of my former lifestyle and had become very powerful habits for me, I therefore succumbed to them again for a short while."

"Please explain to us, what were you doing before you were baptized?" they quickly asked.

"What does it matter? Especially since I had not dedicated my life to God yet?" I protested.

"From the moment you were evangelizing, your conduct is of great importance to us," they answered.

7. Life as a Baptized Witness

Not having much choice, I began to give an account of the beginning and the continuation of my struggles with sin. I was totally red from shame. They did not seem satisfied with my general references, however. Surpassing every boundary of indiscretion, they were seeking to hear details of how I did everything! My situation was dramatic. I spoke with great difficulty and got the impression that one of them found great satisfaction in what he was hearing as he pressed on with his insatiable questioning. I had difficulty controlling the muscles of my lower lip as I felt the ends of my lips pull downward. I had difficulty articulating words, a feeling similar to when one is exposed to extremely cold conditions, and the chin becomes paralyzed and numb.

Across from me, I saw the fourth elder (the one who assisted me with biblical studies) lower his head, apparently feeling embarrassed by everything he was hearing.

Suddenly, I came to the realization that the shame I was feeling was not towards God (knowing that He already had forgiven me), but I was ashamed before people. My fear of punishment or not being understood was not the fear of God, but the fear of men. I sensed that the people across from me were not only being arbitrary in their approach, but worse yet, that they considered themselves judges not only of the "Christian" period of my life, but of the period before my baptism as well! This last realization was something I was never able to come to terms with.

When I had completed my narration, I felt totally humiliated because of the exhaustive indiscrete interrogation. I felt some relief from having been able to sense their arbitrary attitude early on, and thus was able to conceal much more and even worse deeds than the ones they managed to get out of me. All these past events and actions were of an unbeliever without any real relationship or dedication to God, and they were things I wanted to forget.

My judges asked me to step outside for a moment so they could decide my fate. Alone outside in the hallway, I tried to understand how I had managed to fall into their trap. After a few minutes, they called me back inside and informed me that for a designated period of time, I would be *marked**. In other words, I would be deprived of certain privileges held by the rest of the Witnesses. More specifically, I would no longer be able to participate in the functions of the Hall; I would no longer be a reader nor a microphone man; I would not lead the congregation in prayer or give talks; and I would not be allowed to answer questions at the meetings.

Usually when someone is marked, it is forbidden for the other Witnesses to keep company with him; he is shunned almost as if disfellowshipped. However, they did not bring this up in my case, simply because I did not socialize with the other youth of the congregation. A group of about ten young Witnesses had already ceased identifying with the local congregation, choosing instead to enjoy the mundane pleasures of this world. I had avoided their company even before, since their conduct was very unappealing to me.

My four judges asked me what I thought about this punishment. "I believe I deserve it since I transgressed the oath of my dedication," I said.

"Not quite!" they replied. "We are not punishing you for what you've done after your baptism. We are punishing you for what you did *before!*"

I was flabbergasted! These people could not distinguish between being baptized or unbaptized! I did not say anything. It would have done no good anyway.

What's more they could not understand—and neither could I at the time—that for the person who repents there is no need for punishment, simply advice. In all reality, my judges saw the penance not as a helpful or therapeutic aid, but as a sort of revengeful punishment in the name of God for the sin committed. Before I left, I begged them to keep what I had said confidential, and then I bade them goodnight.

Struggling to Come in Terms

ON THE WAY home, I was struggling to come to terms with the event. The whole thing was absurd; I could see that. Yet I was trying to justify the event in my mind for the sake of the Society.

"It seems that this punishment is Jehovah's will, so that I won't repeat this offense!" I thought. "The elders may have punished me for wrongfully, but I will humbly accept this as punishment for my sin. After all, the elders are human beings and certainly are not infallible. The Society should not be blamed for this."

At that time, I believed so much that the Society was God's channel on earth, that I had made it a habit for whatever deficiencies I saw to pass the blame onto its members and not on the Society.

After all, this was the policy of the Watchtower Society: to take credit for every positive element and for everything bad or negative to shift the blame onto its members as individuals. As a good student I had learned to use this double standard and in this way I always found the Watchtower Society perfect. The imperfections I pushed onto the individual Witnesses.

Strange thing, though, but at that time I did not keep the same measure for other religions. As I think back, I realize that I demanded perfection from the members of other faiths, and in the absence of it, I placed the responsibility on their religions. When I would hear something scandalous about a Greek priest, I did not accuse the priest but the Orthodox Church. On the contrary, when I noticed any good qualities in an Orthodox Christian, I did not ascribe it to his faith but to his personal talent.

Yet that evening everything was confused in my mind; I was trying to justify both the interrogation and the punishment for a sin *before* my baptism. Subconsciously, I did not want to believe that this indicated a problem inherent in the Society's theology.

"Even the elders are not perfect!" I thought. "If I can go directly to the perfect God, why should I reveal my sins to imperfect people? My sins are against Him, I ask forgiveness from Him and He understands me. Since the judicial committee would rather punish than advise, there is no clear reason for me to ever be in their presence again if I have repented about a certain sin. Since there are no perfect elders, I will never go back to them."

Thus, the words of my mother came true. She had told me that I would regret this confession. I remembered her words yet again when I discovered that everything I had told them leaked out!

Marriage Proposal

I GRADUATED FROM the night high school at last, and finally had much more free time at my disposal to do the urgent work of the harvest, which was working the Gospel door-to-door. I no longer saw George, my classmate, after graduation. There were more important priorities than social contacts. The important thing for him was that he was already in the truth, and I was informed that he was progressing well. Besides, I needed to evangelize others. My status in the Society had been improved and the Bible studies that I conducted for people interested in the Society were constantly increasing.

Externally, I gave the impression of being the perfect Witness. Yet the temptations of the world were many and my struggle to bridle my passion became harder. Toward the end of my adolescent years I felt ready to start a family. The only obstacle was the mandatory army service I needed to face in about a year (after the expiration of my postponement). I had but one or two summers free, and then I needed to face the consequences of my denial to carry arms.

As we did every year, that summer we went with my mother

and my grandmother to live in our vacation home in Salamina. This area was known for its high percentage of faithful Witnesses. Fifteen years ago in our neighborhood there was only one woman Witness. Now we had grown to five families. But since we were quite a distance from the major local congregation, we used to organize some independent meetings in our neighborhood. That year, however, the Society announced that these types of private meetings would be discontinued, and we needed to go to the official meetings only. Thus we needed to find a local Hall and attend its meetings.

With the help of a local Witness woman who came to our door to preach out of mere chance, we were led to one of the three local congregations rather quickly. They were all strangers to me, and despite the repeated introductions, I could not remember anyone's name. However, towards the end of the meeting, a certain well-dressed young lady wearing all white caught my attention. Although she seemed not to notice me, I very much noticed her, and I kept looking towards her as she was conversing with her girlfriends. Up to that point, several matchmakers had introduced me to a number of young girls, but in this woman I saw the person with whom I could spend my life. I learned rather quickly that she was available, that her name was Roula, and that she was the daughter of the *Presiding Overseer** of the Hall. I was not concerned about much else. The fact that she was a Jehovah's Witness and the daughter of an *overseer** served as a guarantee of her overall conduct and personality.

From that moment on, I began to turn on the charm around Roula. I flirted with her at every meeting and every opportunity I had. I was present at the start of every meeting and talk, and I accepted every invitation for volunteer work at the local Hall. Despite this intense siege, however, the "city" was not falling. Worse yet, I sensed that she was beginning to avoid me. Toward the end of the summer, I tried a different approach. I asked my mother to intervene and discuss the matter with her mother. Although Roula's answer was negative, her mother presented it very politely, stating that her refusal was temporary mainly because of her young age. I still had hope. Working methodically, I slowly began to earn Roula's affection, and by the end of the following summer, the "city" fell.

We announced our intentions and celebrated the joyous event with our very close relatives. After a brief talk and a blessing given by one of the elders, we were officially spoken for. The few invited relatives who were not Witnesses observed with obvious indifference. For the next ten days, Roula and I had a wonderful period of getting to know each other. We both knew that we did not have much time ahead of us because on the eleventh day I needed to sign in at the army barracks in Corinth.

Preparing for Jail

IN GREECE, THERE is mandatory military service for all males upon reaching adulthood; yet if the enlistee is a student, the draft can be postponed so he can complete his studies. In 1983, I had finished school and the prospect of serving my country lay ahead of me. As most people know, Witnesses are to refuse military service.[63] The good news was that in 1977 the Greek government had made provisions for objectors of conscience to opt out from bearing arms by

---

63 Actually, the Society's founder, Russell, did not see anything conflicting to Holy Scripture with the draft: "Obedience to the laws of the land might at some time oblige us to bear arms, and in such event it would be our duty to go into the army, if unable in any legal and proper manner to obtain exemption…There could be nothing against our conscience in going into the army. Wherever we would go we could take the Lord with us, the Captain of our salvation, and wherever we would go we could find opportunities to serve him and his cause" (WT, 5/15/1903, p. 121). Yet, his successors, had "newer lights" on the subject. Even so, the Watchtower Society at times had double standards. For example, in 1960 Mexican witnesses of draft age were allowed by the Governing Body to bribe military officials to obtain their military fulfilment certification. (Franz, *Conscience*, pp. 132–144)

> *Question.* I was surprised to note your advice to any who might be drafted into the army. Would not your advice seem like *compromising* to avoid trouble?
>
> *Answer.* It is proper to avoid trouble in a proper manner. It is proper to compromise when no *principle* is involved, as in the case mentioned. <u>Notice that there is no command in the Scriptures against military service.</u> Obedience to a draft would remind us of our Lord's words, "If any man compel thee to go a mile, go with him twain." The government may compel marching or drilling, but cannot compel you to kill the foe. You need not be a good marksman.

Can Witnesses Go to the Army? Pastor Russell Replies:
"Notice that there is no command in the Scripture against military service" (*Watchtower*, August 1, 1898, p. 231). His successors, though, would receive "new lights."

---

choosing four years of unarmed duty. These provisions would have made many generations of Witnesses, including my own father, very happy. Unfortunately, three years prior to that, in 1974, the Governing Body had received *new light** on the subject that since alternative service work was a substitute for military service, it was impermissible for Christians to accept it.[64] Therefore, as a faithful Witness, I really had only one choice: to refuse military identity altogether and go to jail.[65]

In past years, the men of my religion were treated very brutally in jail for refusing to serve. My father, for example, was incarcerated at the rocky island of Makronisos and was subjected to many tortures. These tortures left indelible marks on him up to his death, and perhaps may have led to it. During the years of my youth, how-

---

[64] "Therefore, any work that is merely a substitute for military service would be unacceptable to Jehovah's Witnesses… Civilian servitude as a substitute for military service would be just as objectionable for a Christian." (AW 12/8/74, p.23)

[65] "The official position of the Watch Tower Society… was that because this [alternative] service was a "substitute" [for military service] it therefore *took the place of* what it substituted for and… came to stand for the same thing… Thousands of Witnesses, mainly young men, spent time in prison for refusing to accept… alternative military service… the result of an unscriptural position, imposed by organizational authority." However, "The May 1, 1996, Watchtower reversed this policy. In an article titled 'Paying Back Caesar's Things to Caesar," [the Society] gave the readers none of the history of the policy that existed for more than 50 years" (Franz, *Conscience*, pp. 121–122)

ever, conditions were better, almost rosy in comparison. Aside from the isolation and separation from our loved ones, jail was less painful than the military itself!

Before my registration in Corinth, we called one of our friends named Stamatis, who had just finished his jail term, in order to get a better understanding of what life in jail was all about. He was serving as an elder while in jail. We met face-to-face, and he explained that in jail all the Witnesses are not necessarily well-behaved. Some of them are immature, and they annoy and scandalize the rest. Thus, I needed to be very careful in my choice of friends and to remember that I'm being imprisoned for Jehovah and not for people.

After preparing me for what I might encounter in jail and advising me on how to deal with these different circumstances, Stamatis shook my hand and wished me well. Five years later, when we would meet again, we would both be disfellowshipped and outside of the Society.

Before my registration, I also made it a point to visit *Bethel**, the central office of the Society in Marousi, for further advice. During my visit, I met a young man whom I would soon join at the Disciplinary Ward in Corinth. The office worker in charge of military matters briefly repeated what Stamatis had already told me, and forewarned, "From the moment you pass through the door of the army camp, you will be on your own: you and God. To anyone who asks, you will reply that your refusal of military duty is clearly your personal choice and not your duty as a Witness. You must not give the impression that the Society has an anti-nationalist agenda. They must understand that your choice to refuse the military is clearly your own."

As for me, this was true. Although the Society had led me to espouse this line, this was also my own belief, and I preferred to die rather than to transgress my conscience on this matter.

This, however, was not the case with all the imprisoned Wit-

7. Life as a Baptized Witness

nesses. Some went to jail not to disappoint their families; others went out of fear of being disfellowshipped by the Society. For these last ones, their imprisonment was not the result of their own free choice, it was mainly due to coercion from the Society. They did not necessarily find anything wrong with serving their country bearing arms or in functions where weapons would be excluded as provided by law. Yet they were compelled to undergo imprisonment because disfellowship from the Society was something far worse.[66]

To gain a better perspective of what disfellowship means for a Witness, I will relate one specific incident. When I was in jail in Avlonas, they brought in a very nice, polite young man for refusal of military service. We shared a cell for a few months, and I observed how terribly he was affected by this jail sentence. I had seen him during visiting hours crying continuously while holding his wife in his arms. One day, quite unexpectedly, we learned that this Witness signed himself out of jail to join his army rank. We were all very surprised and considered him a traitor of the faith, immature and a coward. I especially harbored some feelings of anger against him. A brief time later we were informed that he was disfellowshipped, and that his own wife wanted nothing to do with him! I never learned what became of him. However, only now do I understand what he went through. I pray that God may protect him and strengthen him, wherever he may be.

---

[66] According to Raymond Franz, in a survey taken by the Governing Body among all the Branch Committees in the world, asking whether the Witnesses in their countries understood the policy of objecting military and alternative service. "What do the facts show? …It… graphically demonstrates the power of indoctrination to cause people to sacrifice liberty, years of life and livelihood and family association, in order to obey something that they do not understand or really believe—doing this purely out of a sense of loyalty to an organization." (Franz, *In Search of Christian Liberty*, pp. 258–260)

At the Disciplinary Ward

ELEVEN DAYS AFTER my wedding proposal, I traveled with my fiancée and our families to Corinth. I was feeling lost, unable to adapt to so many abrupt changes in my life. Almost two weeks earlier, I promised to share my life with this young woman, and in just a few hours I would encounter the loss of my very freedom. I was no longer in charge of my destiny.

I showed up for enlistment at the last possible moment, striving to enjoy every last minute of my freedom. Finally, we entered the Camp at Corinth. I embraced everyone who escorted me, and after hugging and kissing my fiancée, I handed her a letter. Then I took my suitcase and walked toward the guard. I told him that I was here for enlistment, and he directed me where to go. As I walked away, I glanced back at my fiancée who was busy reading my letter.

I asked a soldier for the whereabouts of the Commanding Officer, and he pointed to a building. I wanted to see him first, being uncertain of his personal reaction toward my refusal of service. As I walked along, I prayed to God to provide me with the strength and wisdom to act according to His will. However, I had already been informed by the Witnesses at Corinth that the Commanding Officer was a man of understanding, and this put me at ease.

Suddenly a very stern voice interrupted my thoughts: "Hey! Where do you think you are going?"

I turned and saw a soldier. "I would like to speak to the Commander!" I answered.

"It is forbidden! Go back with the others and wait for enlistment!" He told me abruptly.

"But I have something personal to tell him!" I insisted.

"Do what I tell you, unless you want problems," he said.

I returned and sat on a bench across from the entrance, feeling discouraged. I was relieved to see that my relatives were still wait-

7. Life as a Baptized Witness

ing outside. I waited a few more minutes until the soldier stepped away. During this interval, while all my relatives were looking towards me, I observed that my fiancée had turned her back. From afar, I sensed that she was crying and did not want me to see her, to spare me additional pain. I stood up again and carefully walked toward the direction of the Commanding Officer's quarters. I was stopped at the door by someone dressed in civilian clothing who asked where I was going. When I said that I was seeking the Commanding Officer, the man said, "That's me."

"I came for enlistment, but I need to tell you that for reasons of conscience, I must deny military identity."

"That's okay, son. Go with the others and they will tell you what to do. We have others like you."

I thanked him but left puzzled. I couldn't imagine that this would be so easy! I was happy to learn that in addition to the young man I had met in Bethel, there would be others like me. After the registration proceedings were completed, I advanced toward a table where they were handing out army uniforms. Naturally I refused, and they called a Corporal who was serving as a warden to escort me to the Disciplinary Ward.

The Ward was an old building, well maintained on the outside but the interior left much to be desired. When I first saw my new room in the ward, especially the bed, I wondered how I could possibly sleep there. The mattress and the blanket were full of all sorts of stains. But I adapted rather quickly to these conditions, and chose the cleanest military blanket to be found in the ward. In this place, the only consolations were the friendly warden, the visitations, and the generous portions of food.

As every trained Witness should do, I immediately began to promote my faith to all those around me: the prison guards, the wardens, the drug addicts and the deserters. During the month that I stayed there, I began two Bible studies, one with the warden and a second one with a drug addict. The study with the warden was so successful that one evening he summoned the soldiers at the Unit Recreation Center and began relating everything he learned about the future of the world as imagined by the Witnesses.

The month went by very slowly for me, so slow that it left me with as many memories as the entire year at the Military Prison of Avlonas did. I passed my days reading my new Bible, which I had bought a few months prior, and writing letters to my fiancée. I even kept to a daily schedule for my spiritual progress, to take advantage of every minute spent in jail. I had developed what the people of the Watchtower Society called a deep sense of the urgency of time.

Finally, the time came to go to Avlonas. They took me in the police wagon, and after two stops, I saw the walls of the prison.

At the Military Prison of Avlonas

THE MILITARY PRISON of Avlonas (MPA) was a palace compared to the miserable disciplinary ward of Corinth. As we entered the outer yard, I was glad to see so many Witnesses waving at us. I stepped out of the police wagon with my suitcase, and was directed toward the prison offices. Two men dressed as civilians inspected my folder and then asked me in a serious tone, "Why are you refusing to join the army? Don't you want to serve our homeland?"

"No, that's not it. It's because my *Bible-trained** conscience doesn't allow me to," I answered, a response I had rehearsed a thousand times.

"Are you saying that we have no conscience?" they asked.

It was precisely what I was expecting to hear.

"No, I did not say that. You have trained your conscience differently!" I replied.

Of course, I was simply attempting to avoid the issue. In reality, as a Witness, I believed that this was not an issue of different con-

Η προσεκτική μελέτη της Βίβλου αποκαλύπτει οτι ο Βασιλιάς Ιησούς Χριστός 'θα συντρίψει τα έθνη με σιδηρένιο σκήπτρο'

"The careful study of the Bible reveals that the King Jesus Christ will crush the nations with an iron scepter." (Greek Watchtower *1/15/1988*)

---

sciences as I told them, but of different camps. You see, Witnesses do not object military service because they are pacifists but because they pledge their allegiance to Jehovah.[67] It follows that all soldiers belong to the opposing camp of Satan, and therefore are to be destroyed at Armageddon. Thus, I considered those fellow teenagers, who safeguarded the freedom of my country, worthy of eternal death!

They continued to question me, and I responded as a well-trained student. At some point one of them stood up and welcomed me with a broad smile and a handshake.

"Welcome, brother! We are the elders of the prison's church!" he said, and introduced himself.

The other one did the same, while I was laughing in disbelief. I entered my new environment accompanied by Nikos, one of the elders. I had imagined the interior of the jail to be gloomier. I had imagined a very narrow hallway with cells on either side. Instead,

---

67 "While not pacifists (they preach "the mightiest of wars, Jehovah's war, fought by the greatest warrior Christ Jesus at Armageddon"), the Witnesses do conscientiously object to participating in the wars of Christendom and Pagandom." (Cole Marly, *Triumphant Kingdom*, Criterion Books, 1957, p. 212)

there was a huge, open space with three-story-high ceilings. The first two stories were lined with doors on both sides. Dozens of inmates were roaming freely in this entire space and in its yards. Only the ubiquitous iron bars were as I had imagined.

While walking along the staircase, I could tell the Witnesses apart from the criminals by their clothing. The criminals wore uniforms, while the Witnesses were dressed in civilian clothes.

I followed Nikos to the second level to see my new cell. It was numbered Z7. It was one of the larger cells and housed seven other brothers. I was later informed that just about all the new inmates started their sentences in large cells, but eventually they would be transferred to smaller and quieter ones. Nikos showed me a bunk bed and told me that I would be sleeping on the top bunk.

"Do you fall out of your bed at night?" he asked.

"I don't know, I've never slept on a high bunk bed," I said.

"Would you like to switch? My bed is at the bottom," he said. I gladly accepted, not realizing that this was a sacrifice on his part; as I found out, the lower beds were the more privileged.

Cleaning Up Earth   Page 55

"The Scriptures then further show that for a long period of time after the battle of Armageddon is over companies of survivors will be sent over through the land to clean it up and to destroy these bleached bones." (*His Vengeance*, 1934, pp. 54–55)

7. Life as a Baptized Witness

Maturing in the spirit

THE ONE YEAR I spent at the MPA was a year of social maturity and growth for me. I had the opportunity to meet all sorts of people from all over the country. In a short span of time, I met young men of my faith at all ranges of the spectrum of faith and behavior.

Of course, for an Organization that makes such exalted claims about its morality, it was such a discredit for of its members to be seen publicly cursing, reading filthy magazines, and falling into sins of the flesh like the worst of the wordlies. So, ten years later, the Society created committees which would not allow the "immature" brothers to be imprisoned together with the rest of the Witnesses, disregarding the dangers of forced living conditions with common criminals. Thus, the Society indirectly compelled them to enlist in the army and pushed them into disfellowship.

Time passed very slowly, miserably slow; my only consolation was the monthly visit by my fiancée and the weekly visits by my mother. Luckily, being the first-born son in my family, I only had to serve one half of the sentence, compared to the full sentence served by others.

In the beginning, I tried with much zeal to take advantage of every moment in jail by devoting my time to studying. As time went on, however, I became weary. Despite this, I managed to read for several hours each day. My Bible was full of notes on the sides of its pages. My goal was to record all the interpretations of the verses, as published in the magazines of the Society. This was a common practice among the Witnesses.

During my stay there, the jail administration demanded that we use the military blankets to make our beds. Since, as objectors of conscience we were wearing our civilian clothing, certain of us felt that accepting these blankets was tantamount to accepting the military identity, so we refused them. But the *Governing Body** approved their use and the issue of preserving one's conscience was to be tested now from our own Organization! There was indeed tremendous pressure from own elders to accept these blankets. Yet we held our position, presenting them articles from the *Watchtower*, claiming that "in matters of conscience, no one can intervene, and the decision ultimately remains in the hands of the conscience-challenged individual." Finally, the administration moved us objectors to the recovery ward where we did not have to use military blankets. I stayed there until my transfer to the jail of Cassandra.

The recovery ward was the quietest section of jail. The permanent noise prevalent in the regular cells was gone. We also had other advantages in this facility. We had three recreational rooms: one for our meetings, one for ping-pong and one for television. But most importantly we had private, clean bathrooms with a toilet, the lack of which was a real problem in the previous cells.

The First Questions

BY DOING VOLUNTEER work, I was earning days off my sentence so I could be released from jail earlier. In the beginning my job was to mop; later on, I was peeling potatoes for the common meals. Still I had plenty of free time and the recovery ward was quiet and conducive to reading. It housed a library and the religious section had some Orthodox anti-heretical books. One day I decided to read an Orthodox book pertaining to my religion. Through this book, the Holy Spirit carefully began to prepare my future exodus from the Witnesses. The book included correspondence of the Orthodox in charge of the anti-heretical struggle alongside correspondence of the people of my faith. The Orthodox responses humiliated the Witness writers and I was so much scandalized that I assumed the Witnesses' letters were mere forgeries, especially since I had no trust in the Orthodox writers whatsoever; I considered them all liars.

However, I kept reading the book and couldn't reject one verse pertaining to II Corinthians 6:6-7. This verse stated "…by purity,

7. Life as a Baptized Witness

by knowledge, by long-suffering, by kindness, by the Holy Spirit, by sincere love, by the word of the truth, by the power of God…"

If the Holy Spirit was the power of God, as I believed as a Witness, then this verse would not be written this way! In a summary of dissimilar characteristics, the verse differentiates very clearly between the Holy Spirit and the power of God. This verse showed very clearly that the Holy Spirit was definitely not a power of God. I searched all issues of the *Watchtower* but did not find an answer. Thus, I kept this verse in my mind, waiting for the day when God would give me a satisfactory answer.

One of my hobbies from a young age was to read scientific journals. One of my favorite subjects was Einstein's *Theory of Relativity*. So one day while lying in bed in the recovery ward, I was reading about the essence of space and time. I was intrigued by the fact that space and time are expandable elements, much like a rubber band, and they are dependent on the matter they enclose. However, I was even more intrigued by the belief that space and time were created simultaneously with the universe.

I remembered that at some point when I was younger I had asked one of the elders the following childish question: "Where was God before the creation of the Universe?"

He gave such a ridiculous answer that even as a child I considered it foolish. I had placed this question on the back burner all these years without discovering a satisfying answer.

On this particular day, however, my question returned more forcefully: "Where and when was God before He created the Universe? And did 'where' and 'when' even exist?" But now, for the first time, I felt that I had the background to give an answer. I began to delve mentally into the concept of God's pre-eternity. Immediately I thought, since space and time are dependent on the material make-up of the world, and they have their beginning from the creation of the universe, then God is 'outside' of space and time and space and time are His creation. Before the creation of the universe, 'where' and 'when' simply did not exist. Only God existed.

My mind (guided by the grace of God) followed this train of thought, shocking my innermost being: "But then, if God made everything through Jesus Christ His Word, then space and time as well were made through Jesus Christ!" I ran and opened the Holy Scriptures to John 1:3, where it says about Jesus Christ: "All things were made through Him, and without Him nothing was made that was made."

I panicked! But then, I thought, Jesus Christ is also the Creator of time! This means that He has no beginning!

Now I understood why non-Witnesses believe in the Trinity! I thought, There must be some mistake in this conclusion, because if He had no beginning, He would not be a Son! Every son has his beginning from his parents! But if the Logos (Word) has a beginning, then it is not possible for Him to have created time!

I thought about this for a long time, unable to find an explanation. Unfortunately, at the time, I did not know that the Son had His beginning from the Father, in terms of the cause! I was also further confused because of the verse that I had been taught, which stated that Christ is "the beginning of the creation of God,"[68] and I interpreted this as "the first creation."[69] I did not realize that the

---

68 He refers to Rev. 3:14 ("ἡ ἀρχὴ (arche) τῆς κτίσεως τοῦ Θεοῦ").

69 Actually, it is a teaching of the Watchtower society; "the Bible plainly states that in his prehuman existence, Jesus was a created spirit being, just as angels were spirits beings created by God. Neither the angels nor Jesus had existed before their creation... Jesus, in his prehuman existence, was... 'the beginning of creation.' (Revelation 3:14)... Yes, Jesus was created by God as the beginning of God's invisible creations." (*Should You Believe in the Trinity?*, 1989, p. 14). Yet, the word rendered as "beginning" (arche) has more than one lexical definitions, and the Watchtower fails to see its usage in the Scripture as a whole and in the context of the statement in particular. Most importantly, the Society fails to take into consideration the witness of the ancient Christian literature.

word "arche" in this context means "authority".[70]

So, at the time, I improvised a certain theory to satisfy the impasse at which I had found myself. Deep inside me, however, I knew that my "makeshift exegesis" could not stand up to serious critical thought. This discovery tormented me so much that it "switched on" some subconscious self-defense mechanism; somehow the whole matter was removed from my thought for many years. So I continued my studies and daily activities without losing any sleep over whether the Lord Jesus Christ had a beginning or not.

The Effects of Imprisonment

UNFORTUNATELY, JUST A few weeks before I got word of a new transfer to the agricultural prison in Cassandra, jail got the best of me, and I began to have a variety of psychological problems. Day by day my depression was escalating to the point that I began to understand the phrase, "I'm about to lose my mind." If my transfer to Cassandra had been delayed any longer, the damage could have been irreparable. Although Cassandra was much farther from my house, I wanted to go there because my life would not be in danger. In case of war, we would be called to serve if we were found in the military prison. This meant certain death for anyone who refused to fight. All of us at the military prison of Avlonas anxiously listened to the daily news to hear if there was

---

70 The Greek word that most English translations render as "beginning" is "arche" (ἀρχή). As it is known, many words start with an absolute meaning (in this case "arche" means "beginning") and later on can acquire a metaphorical meaning as well. Thus the word "arche" came also to signify "the person or thing that commences, the first person or thing in a series, the leader." (see Col. 1:18; Rev. 21:6, 22:13) Our English prefix "arch-" (=chief, principal) comes from this word. Finally, in the 8th century B.C. Greek philosophy attached a philosophical meaning to the word, and "arche" also came to signify "first cause, origin." The last sense of the word was used repeatedly in the Greek Old Testament (see Wisdom 14:27; Sirach 37:16; 10:13; Psalm 110:10) and most likely this is the correct meaning of Rev. 3:14. For example, St. Clement of Alexandria, in his 2nd century *Stromata*, says "The Son, looking at the benevolence of the Father, acts, being called thus Savior God, the beginning (arche) of everything." (St. Clement, *Stromata*, Book 5, ch. 6).

any imminent crisis in the relations between Greece and neighboring Turkey. All this changed, however, when we entered Cassandra. There we escaped that danger.

At the necessary time, God's providence worked in such a way that I soon found myself in a new environment, which quickly cured my psychological problems. Now, after all these years, those unpleasant events have been erased from my mind and only the good memories remain. The only exception is the lingering image of my disabled mother as she limped away from jail, permanently tired and grief-stricken.

At Cassandra

WE WERE TRANSFERRED to Cassandra by a public bus. We made a rest stop twice and the guards left us free to walk around the nearby residential areas. I had not been free like this for a long time, so it was a real treat to see the country setting for a span as far as the eye could see. The guards knew that none of us would escape, so they sat and relaxed at a small bar-restaurant. There was definitely no comparison between this trip and the short distance transfers in the police wagon between the MPA and the court sessions.

My first impression upon seeing the dilapidated buildings of Cassandra was one of disappointment. I was assigned to the Xenophon wing, which had four cells. Each cell had about twenty beds, (if they could be called that), full of fleas. The food was almost always nasty and insufficient. That's why we would often shop from a "roach-coach" green-grocer who came by. The standard work here was harder compared to Avlonas. It was farm work which lasted four hours compared to only one hour of mandatory work at Avlonas. Visits from Attica (the county of Athens) were scheduled once a month, at which time I got to see my family members. Visits were better than in Avlonas because they lasted longer, and they allowed us more privacy. Another pleasant surprise was that we met up with many of our friends who had been sent to Cassandra during previous transfers and whom we hadn't seen for a long time.

The Power of Christian Humility

THERE WAS A fully organized congregation with elders and a meeting hall in that prison. We often had a visiting religious official of our faith provide us with homilies. There was even a courtroom for the spiritual committee and since the elders were very strict even the most unruly behaved themselves. Yet a friend of mine demanded scrupulous adherence to the cell rules, and his insistence created a strong sense of animosity among some of the cell residents so they decided to make his life miserable. They purposely walked with wooden shoes on the hollow floor when he was trying to sleep; they left him insulting notes; and they opposed all of his requests.

The situation became explosive when his adversaries accused him to the elders, piling up groundless charges against him. He came to me in a state of despair and said, "My accusers are many! The elders will never listen to me! I'll try to explain all the things they'll bring up against me, but they'll never believe me!"

"If you want my advice" I said, "do as I say, and you will win. When the elders comes, do not accuse your adversaries at all. Ask for forgiveness, and tell them that you are at fault for everything, even though this is not the case. Use the example of Christ who taught us to overcome evil with good."[71]

He disagreed at first, but soon realized that he had no other choice. When the elders arrived, my friend requested to be the last one to speak. His adversaries began to pile up a heap of accusations against him. He listened with exemplary patience. At the end, he was given the opportunity to speak.

---

71 Rom. 12:21

"I ask forgiveness from everyone. I am to blame for everything! I will try to become better from this point on."

A deep silence overtook the entire cell. This most unexpected answer froze them in their tracks. However, his most outspoken adversary became red as a tomato and began to go into a howling, trembling craze: "Now what do I saaay!" and he continued to howl inconceivable words.

"All right! I understand who is at fault!" said the elder, and turned towards the accusers warning them, "Be very careful not to create another incident because you will have major problems!" Then he walked out, leaving the entire cell speechless.

That elder was one of the best young men I had met in my life. No one inside the walls of the jail would sacrifice their time and effort for the sake of others. But he was eager to give up his own work days in order to help others get out of prison early, with the full knowledge that every missed day of work would keep him one extra day in jail. We all loved him and respected him.

Working Towards my Release

ACCORDING TO A particular rule, someone could ask to be released early "under terms," but he needed to count his days very carefully to avoid falling short of the absolute minimum, in which case they would call him back for military service, and he would be jailed all over again if he refused to serve. This happened to "rank 12-40," they were released much earlier under this grace period. Since they had not fulfilled the minimum days called for by the law, they were re-called and re-sentenced, thus spending more time in jail than the rest of us.

In Cassandra, I managed to become in charge of the dining hall where three work days counted as two. While I estimated that it would take longer for me to be released, I was fortunate to escape the harsh work at the jail farms. When the response to my request

7. Life as a Baptized Witness 93

to be released "under terms" came back positive, I still needed a few days to complete the number of days demanded by law. Thus, I risked being put out too early, something that could backfire as it did for those in group 12-40. Fortunately, they allowed me to stay in jail a little while longer with the understanding that I would work in the farms in order to catch up my workdays much faster.

This took place in the middle of the winter, and not being conditioned to outdoor work, I became ill. During my final days, I was obliged to work with a fever to keep them from releasing me prematurely. Finally, the day of my release came, but it was much different than what I had been expecting....

All those months, I had been dreaming of my release day, the day that I would be free to live in the outside world again. That day was upon me, but I found myself begging the guard to let me sleep there one more night. I had a very high fever and my head pounded unbearably. I only wanted a place to lie down and get some sleep, even in a jail cell.

"I don't have the right to keep you any longer!" the guard responded with his usual indifference. "You must leave!"

I pulled myself together and started off. I could hardly believe that I was leaving all by myself. Subconsciously, I looked around expecting to see some prison guard. I took a bus to the airport of Thessaloniki and a few hours later, I landed at the Hellenic Airport in Athens where I was greeted by my fiancée.

I did not tell her that I was ill, and pretended to be healthy. Even though I enjoyed seeing her after all this time, I could not wait to crash in my bed. A few days later, I went to Avlonas to receive my prison release certificate. Upon entering, I rejoiced at seeing many of my old friends. I was received in the elder's office. Bethel made sure to always have a elder in the prison, someone specifically sent by them, to provide immediate orientation to those incarcerated. They gave me a form that I needed to sign in order to validate my release. I took the paper and proceeded to read it but they interrupted me.

"It's okay! Everyone signs this or else they can't get released!"

By now I had read half of the form, and as I placed it on the table, I quickly read the other half. I was in shock! This paper referred to me as a soldier! And it was written in such a manner that by my mere signature, it would mean that I fully accepted that identity. My mind worked very quickly.

"So, let me get this straight! Everything was a sham? I sat in jail for a year and a half, only to accept that I'm a soldier by signing this paper?"

I remembered how much I fought not to accept the military blankets in Avlonas and really did not want to sign the form. Yet at that very moment I thought of my mother, my fiancée, and all those who had signed before me, and I considered it rather foolish for me to sacrifice my freedom and my life plans for a small compromise. I signed it. I was now free from jail, but not from guilt.

As a postscript to this whole painful farce, let me add that in 1996 the Governing Body proclaimed "newer light" that alternative service work in lieu of military service is once again permissible for Witnesses![72]

My Life After Jail

I ADJUSTED FAIRLY well to my new state of freedom. The only remnant from my jail term was my duty to report once a month for three years to the police station in my area. While I was in jail, my father-

---

[72] "Many of these lands make provision for such conscientious individuals not to be forced into military service. In some places a required civilian service, such as a useful work in the community, is regarded as nonmilitary national service. Could a dedicated Christian undertake such a service? Here again, a dedicated, baptized Christian would have to make his own decision on the basis of his Bible-trained conscience." (WT 5/1/96 p.19)

7. Life as a Baptized Witness

in-law had opened a business in Salamina (a suburb of Athens) and we agreed that after my wedding I would work there. However, my mother and my grandmother were not in a position to stay by themselves. We searched and by the grace of God found two homes in the same neighborhood so that we could be near each other.

Finally, our special day arrived. The pastor who married us was an elder who had been authorized by the state to conduct marriage ceremonies. He was also married, but I detected some sadness in his eyes when he told us that his wife was one of the *remnant** and that she would go to heaven.[73] Therefore, after the Armageddon, she would not be next to him because he belonged to the *great crowd**, and he would remain on earth. Fortunately, my wife and I were both of the great multitude and of the earthly hope, and we would live together eternally. The marriage concluded with a talk about our duties and our responsibilities as a married couple. The pastor also took this opportunity to say a number of things in hopes of proselytizing some of the dozens of Orthodox Christians who had been invited. Then we departed for the customary celebration.

When I was about to transfer my church membership to Salamina, I kindly asked my new elders not to publicize that I had been marked. They explained that since I was no longer in that state I did not have any restrictions.

So I quickly assumed various tasks such as assisting in the congregation hall, and shortly thereafter, I became a *ministerial servant**. This meant that I needed to teach from the pulpit from time to time,

---

73 The Society teaches that in 1914 Christ was enthroned as King invisibly, the Heavenly Kingdom took effect (again invisibly) and a little flock or anointed class of 144,000 people were selected to occupy it. These people were chosen from a period of Christ's ascension at Pentecost to 1935 ad. According to the Society, some 8,700 are still living with us on earth. This "anointed class" will spend eternity as spirit creatures in heaven with God, while the rest of the JWs (the "Great Crowd") will be on earth. So how does a JW knows whether he belongs to the elite "little flock" or to the plebeian "great crowd?" Here the Society usually keeps tightlipped.

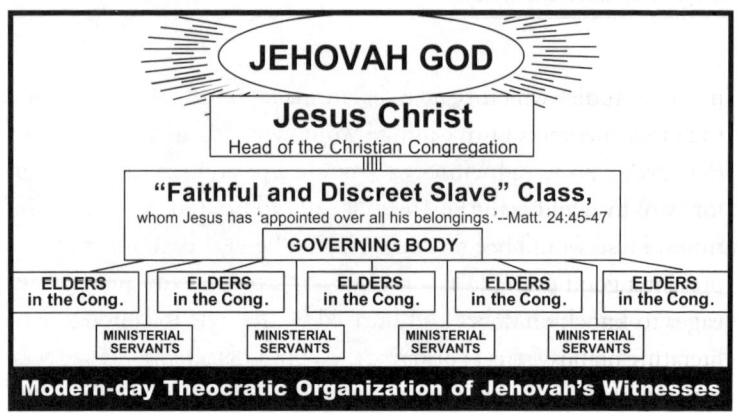

Chart based in the Watchtower *December 15, 1971, p. 749*
Note: the chart does not clearly indicate the position of the circuit and district overseers that stand between the Governing Body and the Elders of the Congregation.

or give public homilies wherever they sent me to preach. The Watchtower Society provided me with talk outline formats; I only had to expand and build up these outlined talks to an approximate length of forty-five minutes under the absolute censorship of the Society.

I also led one of the book studies, served as the treasurer of the congregation, and was responsible for providing and making copies of profit-and-loss statements. I was also responsible for the distribution of periodicals to the congregation, and I often participated in the theocratic meeting for the purpose of interpreting verses of the Holy Scriptures or analyzing sections from a book entitled *All Scripture is inspired of God and Beneficial*.[74] Sometimes I participated in conventions and often attended the Theocratic Ministry School.

I was progressively becoming adept at whatever service the Society asked of me, and I often took part in organizing the behind-the-scenes work for the *district conventions.** My presence was never lacking when the Society asked for volunteer work, whenever time and my life circumstances permitted. The hours and the time spent

---

74 Watchtower Bible & Tract Society, second edition, 1983

in Bible studies which I entered in my weekly report far exceeded the other members of my congregation, with the exception of the *Pioneers**, who were members that made a commitment to preach for two, five, and eight hours per day for one or more months. At times, I also would become an *auxiliary Pioneer** since I needed to present a good example as a ministerial servant. I was always very eager to knock on doors and to work the streets (sell Watchtower literature on busy street corners). However, a special event that took place while I was working the streets proved to be a turning point in my journey toward Orthodoxy.

Working the Streets

SHORTLY BEFORE MY incarceration, democracy in Greece was restored and so we were free to advertise the magazines on the streets.[75] When I was released and moved to Salamina, however, I ran into a zealous priest who caused us severe problems. Every time we stepped foot on the street,[76] within a few minutes we were surrounded by a multitude of Orthodox who prevented us from making any progress. Several large signs displayed slogans against us, and the priest was preaching through a megaphone, attempting to expose the heretical teachings of the Watchtower Society.

As a Jehovah's Witness I was taught to consider all clergy "as the most reprehensible of all God's enemies"[77] because while "they

---

[75] "The new Constitution... recognized Chiliasm as a 'known religion' and placed it under the protection of the Constitution, giving it thus freedom of movement and action." (Arch. Panteleimon Benezitis, *Η Ποιμαντική Αντιμετώπισης του Χιλιασμού*, Apostoliki Diakonia, 1976, p. 12)

[76] Note that "street witnessing" is a relatively recent practice. "In February, 1940, the street-corner witnessing with the Watchtower and Consolation magazines was inaugurated as a regular service assignment. Thereafter street gospel preaching was undertaken regularly by all companies of Jehovah's witnesses and has borne rich fruits." (*Theocratic Aid to Kingdom Publisher*, Watch Tower Bible and Tract Society, 1945, p. 194)

[77] For a historical presentation of the Watchtower's attitude towards the clergy, see Penton's, *Apocalypse Delayed*, p.127–130.

Typical anti-clerical propaganda in the Watchtower literature
From the book *You Can Live For Ever*, p. 25, 1981

pose before the people as preachers… yet they are diligent in keeping the people away from the Bible."[78] Watchtower literature made me very biased against all clergy and therefore I very much misunderstood the priest and got very irritated with his actions.

Today I understand that he was trying to protect his flock. This was the first time in Greece that the constitution provided us legal backing for public missionary activity,[79] and the Greek people were unaccustomed seeing Jehovah's Witnesses openly in the streets selling "Christian" literature from… America! After all, Greece was not Brooklyn but the same country where apostles Paul and Andrew had evangelized long before Russell or Rutherford were born. The people's mistake, however, was in their overall approach. Instead of looking at us as lost sheep, they looked upon us as ravenous wolves. It appeared as they were not concerned about our salvation but only for the salvation of the Orthodox.

Unfortunately, there were also a few over-zealots that did not

---

78 J. F. Rutherford, *Prosperity Sure*, Watch Tower Bible and Tract Society, 1928, p. 13

79 See Arch. Panteleimon Benezitis, *Η Ποιμαντική Αντιμετώπισης του Χιλιασμού*, Apostoliki Diakonia, 1976, p. 12)

behave as Christians; they made us feel like heros, further cementing our delusion that we were in the true faith. These people would make all kinds of inaccurate remarks saying that we stepped on holy icons, calling us "employed agents of America," "Jews," anti-Christs and so forth. They tried to lynch us on three separate occasions. One day while advertising magazines, we encountered two Orthodox people who annoyed us. One of them began to insult us with obscenities, cursing even Jesus Christ and the Panagia![80]

On another occasion, when my wife was pregnant with our first son, we went out with two others to work the street. Not before long, we were surrounded by our opponents, including the priest with the megaphone. All of a sudden, someone from the rooftop of a high-rise threw a large glass soda container full of water which landed next to my wife. If this had fallen on her head, she would have been dead! A little later, another person lit some fireworks and tossed it at her feet. She could have been killed or have had a miscarriage.

On many occasions, our adversaries would come up to us and read excerpts from anti-chiliast books (apologetics) about the changes the Society had made to some of its basic doctrines. We were not too concerned about this, however, because we had been instructed that this was new light and that God revealed the truth to His people progressively.[81] The Orthodox could have been much

---

80 Witnesses in America did not fare any better. "As a result of all the various merchandising methods employed by the Watch Tower during [Rutherford's] time, many clergymen, journalists, and others referred to it as a racket. Even some of Rutherford's followers became disenchanted, complaining, 'This carrying books about is merely a book-selling scheme.' Not to be outdone, the Judge turned the tables and had Jehovah's Witnesses parade in front of churches on Sundays with placards bearing the slogan "RELIGION IS A SNARE AND A RACKET." This outraged the sensitivities of the public, and as a result persecution came upon the Jehovah's Witnesses. On several occasions Witnesses were attacked by mobs and beaten or tarred and feathered." (Chretien, *Witnesses of Jehovah*, p. 47)

81 "...Adjustments become necessary from time to time," says the Society, "for Prov. 4:18 tells us that "the path of righteous ones is like the bright light that is getting lighter and lighter until the day is firmly established." Oh, apostate opposers of truth

more effective if they had shown us some of the thousands of verses in Scripture that escaped our attention, this would have been far more problematic and thought provoking to us at the time.

The reference to the doctrinal changes of the Society are effective when they are revealed to newcomers, to people who have not suffered destruction of their critical thought by the methodologies of the Society, to people who still use their discernment, or to people who have once again begun to think freely without blinders.

The "old-timers," though, are not troubled in the least when someone points out to them the theological mistakes of Russell or Rutherford or Franz. They believe that men could hardly be expected to absorb the full truth all at once. It is simply beyond the powers of finite men, as Jehovah knows only too well. So, having regard for human limitations, Jehovah has chosen to reveal His truth progressively, little by little. In view of this there is little point to be bothered with the half-truths of Russell when one can read the fuller truths in the Society's current publications. With this sophism the Society covers its past blunders and retains the confidence of the Witnesses as Jehovah's channel of communication to mankind.

"Triple contradictions," therefore, can be especially effective, where the Society changes some dogma and then regresses to its previous views, which it previously considered Satanic.[82] Based on this, the intelligent seeker understands that such a journey cannot be labeled progressive when it goes back-and-forth showing that

---

'gnash their teeth' at such progressive revelations, but this does not disturb us. (Acts 7:54) Rather, we thank Jehovah that 'light itself has flashed up for the righteous one, and rejoicing even for the ones upright in heart.' (Psalm 97:11)." (WT 2/15/84 p. 11).

82 "The Watchtower of December 1, 1981, carried an article attempting to justify all this shifting back and forth on various doctrinal points on the Society's part. It used the analogy of a boat tacking against the wind. The problem is that the shifting of teaching often brings them back virtually to the point where they began." (Franz, *Crisis of Conscience*, p. 347)

7. Life as a Baptized Witness　　　　　　　　　　　　101

its new light turned to darkness again![83] Hopefully, a sincere Witness will understand that this overstrained verse (Prov. 4:18) about bright light refers to the progressively bright journey of each individual of faith, and not to the dogmatic alchemies and immaturities of a religious organization.

Our opposition, however, did not understand all of this. In reality, neither do most Witnesses; they are programmed to see only what the Governing Body tells them! In the end, lack of understanding from both sides scuttled the effort of outreach to the Witnesses, making it impossible for us to be helped by them. Their activities made us even more fanatical, and we returned each time even more obstinate. We were organized and highly coordinated in our missionary efforts. Along with those of us standing on the streets, we usually had others following at a distance so in the event of an incident they would serve as eyewitnesses. In fact, many times we ended up pressing charges to the local authorities, complaining of some type of impropriety enacted against us.

Usually, when someone would purchase a magazine from us, members of the opposition would run and take it out of his hands. If this was done with the consent of the man involved, it did not present a problem. At times, however, when they took it from him without asking, he would get angry. We accused them of being afraid that people might learn the real truth, and we struggled with more zeal.

On one occasion, a Witness from my previous congregation

---

[83] "There are very few Watch Tower publications that were published during the first 80 years of the organization's 110-year history that are not today considered 'out of date.' (They are also almost without exception 'out of print' and unavailable.) Rather than being recognized as a sign of unstable research and of hastily devised teachings, this is actually presented as evidence of 'advancing light'! The problem is that, in quite a number of cases, the pretended 'advancement' has simply taken the organization backward to teachings it earlier discarded as in error and replaced by what was claimed to be more 'advanced' truth. In such cases, what was once "advanced truth" now becomes error, and what was once error now becomes 'advanced truth.'" (Franz, *Christian Freedom*, 2004 ed. p. 482)

The photocopy at left is a prepared legal guide on the appropriate charges a Witness can use in counter-attack if arrested in Greece.

came up and bought a magazine, pretending to be Orthodox just to fake them out. When they went to take it from him, he yelled and chased them away, treating them as pests.

I often challenged them to a discussion. Yet, no one ever seemed willing to discuss anything without the presence of their priest, whom I despised and had no desire to speak with because I considered him an ill-disposed enemy of God. Yet, at length someone accepted my challenge, and I joyfully set up a meeting with him. When the rest of the Witnesses found out about the meeting, they tried to convince me to cancel.

"He has talked to us a number of times," they argued, "but he doesn't want to accept the truth."

"You never know! Maybe Jehovah will help him this time around!" I said and went to meet him.

The First Doubts

I TOOK THE Bible, a New Testament concordance, and some books of the Society with me. Primarily, however, I would rely on a small booklet briefly presenting the history of the Church in negative, scandalizing accounts. Since it had the approval stamp of the Holy Synod of the Orthodox Church of Greece on the first page, I believed that whatever I would show to my challenger would be irrefutable. I was not aware that the Holy Synod approves books without always reading them, and that the approvals of the Synod are not always accepted by the Church.[84]

"Before we begin our discussion," my challenger said, "we need to establish our sources of truth. The Orthodox accept the Holy Scriptures, the Ecumenical Councils, and in short, the entire Holy Tradition of the Church. At this point I will agree to base our discussion solely on the Holy Scriptures out of concession, in order to help you. Do you accept all the books of your organization in addition to the Holy Scriptures?"

"Only those which were not reevaluated based on a newer and better understanding by the Society," I answered, to block him from bringing up all kinds of "new light" changes of the Society over the years. However, I already had a problem. With his initial comments, he already rendered useless my little booklet against the Church because it wasn't approved by an Ecumenical Council! I preferred to begin first so that I could always keep him on the defensive and he would not have any opportunity to structure an attack.

After I exhausted my time referring to all the negativities in the small book, he commented that while this particular author may

---

[84] "As the Orthodox Patriarchs of the East responded to Pope Pius IX, in 1848, 'in our Church neither Patriarchs, nor Synods were able to introduce novelties, because the defender of the faith is the body of the Church, the people, who wants his religion eternally unchanged and exactly the same as their fathers.'" Panagiotis Trembelas, *Dogmatiki tis Orthodoxou Ekklisias*, vol. 2, page 404)

be a theologian,[85] he is not truly Orthodox but of a very Protestant mindset. Consequently the book is seriously flawed and inappropriate for this discussion. After this, he began to answer every one of my arguments with very simple answers, often with one phrase, to the point where he refuted my entire case within a few minutes.

I was looking at him expressionless and he must have sensed this because he told me, "I'm sorry that I've destroyed your arguments so quickly, but these things are very simple!"

Being that we had divided our discussion period into equal segments and his time was already finished, it was my turn to talk again and keep him on the defensive. So I began the attack, followed again by his defense. This went on for six hours! Since I kept him continuously defending his position, he did not have the time nor the opportunity to begin dissecting some serious issues on my side.[86] Right before the end of our discussion, and while accusing St. Constantine of a number of things I had heard and read, I took out a volume of an encyclopedia. This volume was full of accusations against the saint. "Do you believe everything you read in encyclopedias?" he asked me.

"Yes, except about evolution," I replied.

"Then you must also believe this" he said, and took a photocopy out of his briefcase from some encyclopedia.

---

85 i.e. He had a diploma from the University of Theology of Greece; getting the diploma doesn't automatically mean acquiring the Orthodox mindset.

86 "In most cases you could go on endlessly discussing scriptures and doctrines with a Jehovah's Witness, without converting him or causing him to leave the sect… The Organization's stranglehold on the individual's mind must first be broken before effective teaching can be done from the Bible… Because the Witness had come to view the organization as God's spokesman, the interpretations of Scripture that it offers must be correct, and yours must be wrong. You need to undermine the organization's perceived authority before you can get a JW to reason from the Bible. It usually takes a lot of solid evidence of false prophecies, back-and-forth doctrinal deception flip-flops, and outright deception on the part of the Watchtower Society before a JW can even begin to think about Scripture and what it really says." (David A. Reed, *Jehovah-Talk: The Mind Control Language of Jehovah's Witnesses*, Baker House, 1997, p. 139)

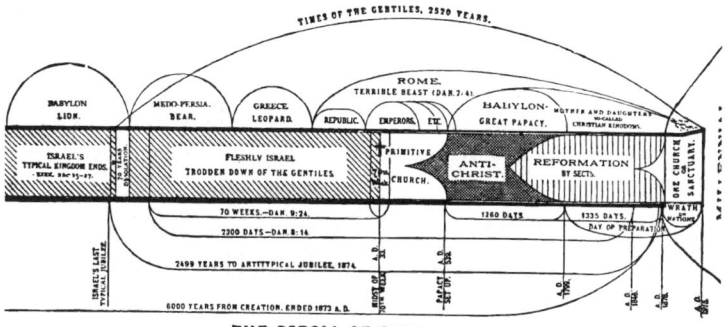

In 1878 C. T. Russell, the founder of the Watchtower Society, published his *Thy Kingdom Come*, in which he claimed that the "Times of the Gentiles" would *end* in 1914 and that the Second Coming of Christ would come the same year. Above a timetable from the said book (1898 edition, p. 131)

The subject was about Jerusalem. Among other things, it said that the destruction of Jerusalem took place in 587 B.C., not in 607 B.C. as I was taught by the Watchtower Society. This has great ramifications on all the doctrines of the Adventist organization,[87] because this date serves as the foundation of its central dogma, holding that the Second Coming of Christ took place in 1914.

Almost all the doctrines of the Society—even its claim after 1919 of being the "Society of God"[88]—are based on the dogma of

---

[87] The founder of the Watchtower Society, C. T. Russell, had been an Adventist and many of the Society's central teachings can actually be traced to Adventism. "A religious movement culminated in 1844," wrote Russell, "the participants in which were then, and since, generally known as 'Second Adventists' and 'Millerites,' because they expected the second advent of the Lord to occur at that date, and because a Mr. William Miller was the leader and prime mover... The Miller Movement was the beginning of the right understanding of Daniel's visions, and at the right time to fit the prophecy. Mr. Miller's application of the three and a half times (1260 years) was practically the same as that we have just given..." (*Thy Kingdom Come*, 1880 edition, pp. 84–86). What this admission means is that "Sola Scriptura" is simply a myth—the Watchtower Society, like every other denomination, follows a tradition; in this case the Adventist tradition.

[88] "The Watch Tower Society claims to be God's "sole channel" and "mouthpiece" on earth. In short, its message implies that the kingdom of God was established in heaven in 1914, that the "time of the end" began that year, that Christ returned invisibly at that time to "inspect" the Christian denominations, and that he finally rejected all of them except for the Watch Tower Society and its associates, which

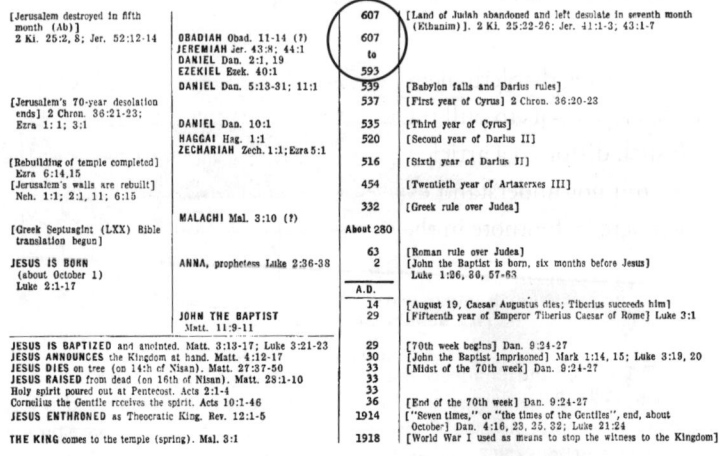

The World History according to the Watchtower
(This Kingdom is at Hand, **1944, p. 175**)

1914.[89] At the time, of course, the significance of this had not yet struck me, so I looked at the dogma of 1914 as a date without any special importance. This was also true for my challenger, who simply looked at this as an unorthodox dogma that needed to be refuted.

Therefore, when I presented, *Thy Kingdom Come*,[90] with the pur-

---

he in 1919 appointed as his sole "instrument" on earth. The Society teaches that the generation of 1914 will not pass away until the final end comes at the "battle of Armageddon," when all who have not joined the Watch Tower organization at that time will be destroyed forever. Jehovah's Witnesses expect to survive this doomsday to live forever in paradise on earth. The year 1914, then, plays a crucial role in the teaching of the Watch Tower Society." (Carl Olof Jonsson, *The So-Called "Bible Chronology" of the Watch Tower Society*, 1993)

89 The Society held on to the "1914 dogma" until 1994! "…Today, most of the generation of 1914 has passed away… Jesus' words will come true, 'this generation will certainly not pass away until all these things have happened.' This is yet another reason for believing that Jehovah's thief-like day is imminent." (Awake!, 4/8/1988, p. 14)

90 The book was first printed by C. T. Russell in 1891. Besides a very amusing section on the great pyramid, most of the book's interest comes from his understanding on the Bibles' prophecies. Russell had taken his timeline from the Adventists, but he came to a different date—the Gentiles' times would end in 1914, and the millenial kingdom would immediately follow. Or, as he wrote in his *The Time is at Hand*, "True, it is expecting great things to claim, as we do, that within the coming

7. Life as a Baptized Witness

pose of proving that Jerusalem was destroyed in 607 B.C., he only said, "The Society wants to pull the wool over our eyes and lead us astray with such distorted a article to keep us from discovering the truth."

I did not understand exactly what the book was about, but I remembered a footnote in the book. What I did not know was that the author of this footnote, Raymond Franz, a member of the Governing Body and a nephew of President Franz, had been accused of apostasy and expelled because he no longer believed in that date![91] While still in jail, I had heard that Raymond Franz was in apostasy and had left the Governing Body, but at the time I did not pay any special attention to this fact, nor was I aware that this was connected to the dogma of 1914. However the fact that I was not very well versed on this topic was very upsetting to me. If I would have studied the foot-

Raymond Franz

---

twenty-six years all present governments will be overthrown and dissolved... In view of this strong Bible evidence concerning the Times of the Gentiles, we consider it an established truth that the final end of the kingdoms of this world, and the full establishment of the Kingdom of God, will be accomplished by the end of AD 1914." (1902 edition, pp. 98–99)

91 Raymond Franz was an eminent Jehovah's Witness. He had been a full time missionary from 1944 to 1965; served at the organization's headquarters for 15 years (1965–1980); and had been a member of the Governing Body of Jehovah's Witnesses for seven years (1971–1980). Four years after the 1975 debacle (when the Society's Armageddon failed to happen) allegations were made against him regarding "heretical beliefs." In May 1980, he was forced to resign and on 31 December 1981, he was disfellowshipped. Franz wrote two books (*Crisis of Conscience* and *In Search of Christian Freedom*) in which he provides a well documented critique of the organization, in a calm and objective tone, that helped countless Jehovah's Witnesses to leave the Society.

CAN IT BE DELAYED UNTIL 1914?

Seventeen years ago people said, concerning the time features presented in MILLENNIAL DAWN, They seem reasonable in many respects, but surely no such radical changes could occur between now and the close of 1914: if you had proved that they would come about in a century or two, it would seem much more probable.

What changes have since occurred, and what velocity is gained daily!

"The old is quickly passing and the new is coming in."

Now, in view of recent labor troubles and threatened anarchy, our readers are writing to know if there may not be a mistake in the 1914 date. They say that they do not see how present conditions can hold out so long under the strain.

We see no reason for changing the figures—nor could we change them if we would. They are, we believe, God's dates, not ours. But bear in mind that the end of 1914 is not the date for the *beginning*, but for the *end* of the time of trouble. We see no reason for changing from our opinion expressed in the view presented in the WATCH TOWER of January 15, '92. We advise that it be read again.

"We see no reason," wrote Russell in 1895, "for changing the figures—nor could we change them if we would. They are, we believe, God's dates, not ours. But bear in mind that the end of 1914 is not the date for the *beginning*, but the *end* of the time of trouble." (WT 7/15/1895 p. 226)

---

note carefully I would have been able to answer him properly, so he could learn the truth, seeing that the Society is worth far more than any encyclopedia. Incidentally, he had squashed one more of my arguments against St. Constantine since I myself discredited all the encyclopedias as untrustworthy!

At this point we were forced to adjourn our discussion because my wife and my mother-in-law were knocking on my door, being somewhat alarmed over my six-hour absence. I had a hollow feeling, mainly because all of my arguments against the Orthodox had been answered quite differently than what I had expected, in spite of the fact that he didn't even say much against my religion. So I was disarmed, yet I was not convinced that he was right in being Orthodox. I was eager to repeat the discussion, and I was beginning to feel that we were friends. Unfortunately he did not share these feelings. The next day I went out for fieldwork, and he approached me. This time I was happy to see him and greeted him with joy. But his response was very shocking to me:

"You are not only an agent (of Brooklyn) but even a bribed one!" he yelled very angrily.

Apparently he believed that he had convinced me of being in the wrong faith and that despite our discussion I had chosen to ignore the truth. In turn I also became very angry with him, expecting more kindness after so many hours of friendly discussion. Thus, all

THE YEAR 1914 A TURNING POINT

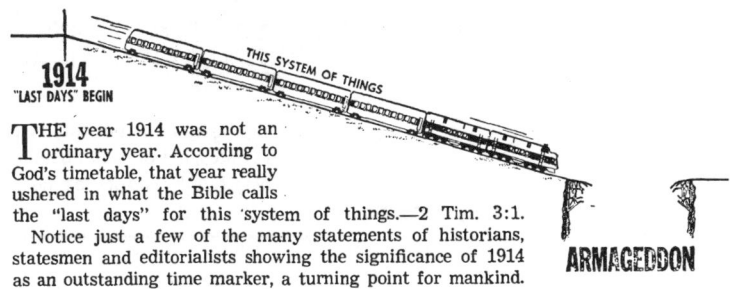

THE year 1914 was not an ordinary year. According to God's timetable, that year really ushered in what the Bible calls the "last days" for this system of things.—2 Tim. 3:1.
Notice just a few of the many statements of historians, statesmen and editorialists showing the significance of 1914 as an outstanding time marker, a turning point for mankind.

While the founder of the Watchtower had for many years taught that 1914 would be the end of the time of trouble (see graphic opposite page), time had made the Society wiser and re-adjusted the timetables. So, 1914 became the beginning of the "Last Days" (above: Awake 10/8/1968 p.58). The illustration, printed in 1968, shows that "This System of Things" (the train) is about to face Armageddon.

---

the goodwill he had built up had been demolished in a few seconds.[92]

The Orthodox once again took up their old position in my eyes, as liars, worthy of destruction, people with every evil quality. However, the seed he planted about the date of Jerusalem's destruction did not perish. This man may have been my enemy, but he had touched on something that was an excellent topic for research. I needed to learn how to deal with this argument more appropriately the next time it would come up. So I began to research the topic using different resources within the Society. I was not able to understand everything, but I did grasp some idea of the problem and could at least defend 1914 by repeating the arguments of the Society like a parrot.

---

92 "Something that we should pay special attention to is the manner with which we will converse with the Jehovah's Witnesses and with every heterodox in general. The conversations have to be conducted in a calm and polite manner. Loud shouts, bouts of anger, gestures, and the like predispose in a negative way our debater and can only serve to detract from the convincingness of our arguments. The person who is confident about the truth of his arguments, he does not get angry, neither does he raise up his voice. If these virtues accompany our arguments, then the dialogue will be effective." (Arch. Panteleimon Benezitis, *Η Ποιμαντική Αντιμετώπισης του Χιλιασμού*, Apostoliki Diakonia, 1976, p.29)

Researching on my own

A NEW DEVELOPMENT however, compelled me to continue this research. One day, my sister-in-law who worked with me at the time, told me that some Witnesses with whom she was acquainted informed her that the Society had found proof that the dogma of 1914 was wrong, and a change was soon to be in the works. I considered that very possible without any bias, and was ready to accept it as new light. However, the facts being that I had wrestled with this subject a few months prior, and that I had seen a different date in the encyclopedia than the one held by the Society made me restless. I could not sit back and wait for the change to be publicized by the Watchtower. My unyielding love for the truth allowed me to always be ready to accept challenges for checking my faith for fallacies and gratefully accept the outcome as a liberation from error. In light of valid arguments, I simply could not suspend my conscience and critical thinking in exchange for cozy living.

Therefore I began a new round of research on the subject with a different goal. This time, the study needed to take into account only the Holy Scriptures, so that if there were some mistakes in the dogma of 1914, they could be made clear and supported scripturally. Afterwards I would compare my findings with the articles of the Society to see if there was a difference in the train of thought.

In reality however, I did not expect to find a difference, hoping that the information of my sister-in-law's acquaintance was wrong. This study went on daily for six months. I studied and recorded important elements for many hours every day. I was amazed by the complexity of the events of the period involved. I was under the impression that the Jews migrated to Babylon only once, and here I discovered that there were four separate such migrations! This complicated matters, because I needed to determine at every point which migration the text was referring to. Also confusing was the

The Watch Tower Society has capitalized on every possible world event to convince the people that the Armageddon is just around the corner. The above graphic (Awake 1/8/1968 p. 8) portrays the US civil riots of the 60's which were supposed to be part of the increase of lawlessness that was to precede the Armageddon in 1975.

---

constant change of Israel's kings, as I was attempting to determine the years of their reign. To make matters even worse, there were two different kingdoms, one with ten tribes and the other with two tribes, each having its own king. Another complexity was the difference of our calendar with the Hebraic and the Babylonian, which gave different numbers from book to book of the Holy Scriptures!

Toward the end of this almost six-month period, I had come up with some conclusions. I organized my findings into a chronological index and after that, I was ready to open the books of the Society to compare notes. The comparison was highly disappointing. In the corresponding chronological index of the Society, I found much that was void and obscure and from which diverged a great series of different chronologies. Strangely enough, in following the footnote in the book, *Thy Kingdom Come,* I could not even agree with the chronologies of the historians!

After tormenting myself for some time to find some compromise for the differences, I reckoned: "Is it possible for me to find in six months something that the Society of God did not find in a century? I probably made a mistake somewhere."

So I placed a question mark on the dogma of 1914 and focused my study on the Holy Scriptures. "God will solve this puzzle for me at the opportune time," I thought.

8. Persecution by the Society

George's story

 hadn't seen my friend Nikos for years, since after graduation from school, we had both gone our separate ways. He went to jail and then married, while I first served as an elder and then dedicated myself fully to the service of God—in reality, to the Watchtower Society. I worked for a number of years, including working for a time at the central headquarters of the Society in the USA, often with an exhausting schedule, from dawn to dusk. I believed that I was giving all my energies to God. My relationship with the members of the Governing Body of the Witnesses was very beneficial to me, especially my relationship with my fellow Greek, George Gangas,[93] whom I considered my "spiritual father" for helping me progress in the Society.

---

93 George D. Gangas was a Greek-American member of the Governing Body from 1971 to 1994. He was born in Ottoman Turkey in 1897, in a village near Ephesus. In 1908 he moved to Greece, then to France, and in 1920 to the United States, where he met the *Students of the Bible* (as Jehovah's Witnesses were known then). Gangas was baptized in 1921 as a member, and in 1928 he became a pioneer (full time preacher) and later served as instructor in the Gilead School. In 1971 he became a member of the Governing Body. In this capacity he visited Greece in 1985 to attend the international assembly. According to R. Franz, in his book, *Crisis of Conscience*, Gangas was one of the five translators of the *New World Translation of the Holy Scriptures*. Gangas passed away in 1994. His picture appears on p. 260 in *Jehovah's Witnesses–Proclaimers of God's Kingdom* (1993)

BETHEL, *World Headquarters of Jehovah's Witnesses, Brooklyn, New York*
This is the world headquarters of the Watch Tower society, where the Governing Body of the Jehovah's Witnesses issues policy directions. George had worked here as a Bethelite (volunteer), close to his compatriot, George D. Gangas, a member of the Governing Body. (Graphic from the book *Jehovah's Witnesses in the Divine Purpose*, Watch Tower Bible and Tract Society, 1959, p. 6)

8. Persecution by the Society 115

When I returned to Greece however, suddenly I realized that some of the local upper echelon of the Society, led by Mr. Roulis Korfias,[94] despised me and were actively seeking my total destruction. They found an opportunity based on my relationship with Mr. George Christoula,[95] an important key figure of the Society in Greece, who, after his unwarranted disfellowship, led a wave of apostasy in the eighties.

To better relate the events which led me to that medieval religious court,[96] I will include my personal correspondence dated March 15, 1987, sent to my close friend George Gangas, a member of the Governing Body of the Witnesses. I wrote down the events in chronological order and present them here with some minor omissions or change of names.[97] Reflected are the intense emotions of those days, as well as the influence of the Society's teaching that it is the channel of God.

---

94 Not the real name. According to the author, "Korfias" had a leading position in the Greek Bethel in the 80s which he abused for his personal benefit, ruthlessly disfellowshipping all opposition. Finally, in 1987, following incessant complaints to the Governing Body from the Greek JWs, "Korfias" was removed from his position. The incident highlights that the Judicial Court in the Watchtower Society, due to its autonomous nature, can be manipulated for ulterior motives.

95 George Christoula, an engineer in Greece, was a former Jehovah's Witness. He was much respected for his devotion (he often "pioneered," and offered his engineering skills for the erection of some buildings in the branch office), and for his theologically inclined mind. But he had difficulties accepting the "1914 dogma" and, facing difficulties from the Greek Bethel, he travelled to the U.S. in 1986 to meet with Governing Body members Lyman Swingle and Ted Jaracz for advice. Upon his return to Greece, Christoula found that *he was disfellowshipped in absentia!* Despite this, many Greek Witnesses still flocked to him for Bible studies. (see *A Desassociação Mal Aplicada*, in http://br.geocities.com/ebdlc/cap11.htm last accessed Nov. 8, 2008). This prompted both a purge and an exodus from the Greek JW church that within ten years resulted in a dropout of an estimated 25%.

96 As will become evident in the following chapters, the Greek Bethel combined in one set of hands the investigation, prosecution, trial, and execution of the verdict.

97 Editor: Names that were not to be encountered again in the book were removed so as not to confuse the reader.

Dear and unforgettable brother Gangas,

It brings me joy to correspond with you tonight, but my joy is overshadowed with a very deep sadness! A very hard and inhuman hand has come tonight to cut the strong bonds of love and friendship which united us for… years. My pain and grief cannot be described, nor can I find the appropriate words to express the emotions flooding my heart as impetuous as a mountain stream. The events are as follows:

November 29, 1986: *I find again my joy and happiness because I have become engaged to a very good sister, a member of a genuine Christian family, which has offered great service for many years to the matters of God.*

Wednesday, February 25, 1987: *We made our wedding announcement and have begun to send out the invitations. The wedding date is set for Sunday, March 15, 1987, at 7 p.m., at a wedding hall patronized by the Witnesses.*

Friday, February 27, 1987: *The secretary of the congregation… is looking for me. He notified me to present myself without the slightest delay before a tri-member Judicial Committee headed by an elder from a neighboring congregation, wishing to discuss some matter with me. I asked him about the specific nature of this matter and he replied that he did not have any information at this time. He stressed to me, however, that I was very limited time-wise and needed to make myself available either Saturday, February 28, 1987, at 5 p.m., or Monday, March 2, 1987, at 7 p.m.*[98]

Even though I needed to visit a sister in Volos who suffers from cancer of the stomach, I was compelled under the circumstances to postpone my trip and to present myself before the tri-member committee. When I presented myself to the committee, I found

---

98 In other words, they didn't give him the chance to prepare a defense or bring any defense witnesses.

8. Persecution by the Society

out that the brothers had instructions from the Governing Body to investigate the following points:

1. *On October 28, 1986 I had visited Rome, where I attended the services of the Anglophone church and saw some of our "brothers" I knew from the past. I was accused of claiming to these "brothers" that I am an elder of the Anglophone congregation of Athens. Of course I had absolutely no reason to say anything like this. I denied the allegation, and asked them kindly to look into this matter more carefully on their own or to give me a little time to determine how and who had initiated the above information (or accusation, rather).*
2. *They read to me a letter of a district overseer in which he stated that at a gathering of some "brothers" at a vacation home, I labeled "brother" Theoharakis[99] (district overseer of my congregation a number of years ago), as a harsh individual who sowed death inside my family.*
3. *The third case pertained to one of my personal discussions with a certain sister regarding brother Christoula.*

I understood immediately that the brothers were preparing something bad against me; based on their attitude and manners, I sensed that they had marked me off and were setting me up for disfellowship!

I have serious reasons to feel this way because at the Summer 1986 Circuit Assembly, and also about a month ago, some of my very close brothers warned me that "Korfias has written you off and has placed you on Execution Row!"

The accusations were not of a serious nature for the simple reason that the first one was totally unfounded and included a number of inaccuracies, while the other two were totally unsubstantiated.

---

99 Not the real name.

I'm enclosing copies of letters from various brothers who refute the overall character of these accusations in all three cases.

At the end of this audited dialogue with the tri-member committee, I pleaded with them to have some consideration, if not for the bond of friendship and brotherhood that had bound us together for years, then at the very least to respect the laws of the Society of God, to fear God and to think twice before proceeding with a hasty decision, something they could possibly greatly regret before Divine Justice. I discerned with great sadness from their overall attitude that they were not disposed in the least to revere the divine principles of justice and compassion. They were harsh and calloused, totally merciless, even though I did not have any need for their mercy. Finally they gave me until Saturday, March 7, 1987 to bring forth my defense witnesses.

I communicated by phone with Italy and requested the moral support of my dear brothers who responded with much politeness and sent a letter to an Italian brother, a member of the committee of the Athenian Sector. Unfortunately, the letter to the tri-member committee was slightly delayed and reached Athens after the committee had already finished its work. The committee was hard at work, having no time to lose. Their aim was not only my unjust disfellowship, but also to hinder my theocratic wedding at all costs. Unfortunately, proof for this can be clearly seen in the development of the events, which I hereby describe:

Saturday, March 7, 1987: *Saturday evening I met with the tri-member committee, bringing along with me a brother... and a sister... who did not utter any accusation against me as evidenced by their signed witness accounts; they only had praise for me. When the committee saw that they could not support a serious accusation against me, it attempted to add an additional one. Obviously, one that was intended to destroy my moral character:*

"There is also one more accusation against you: that five years ago you were seen at the central park of Corfu kissing a PROSTITUTE!!! *How do you plead?"*

I expressed to them that their accusation once again cannot stand. It is rather childish and opposes all that I was taught and had learned to live by within the Society of God. But since they had become unbearably oppressive to the point of cruelty, I requested to have the eyewitness behind this accusation come before me. I was now aware that I was dealing with people who had completely lost their Christian identity and were more than capable of pushing this to tragic and extreme dimensions.

At this point I wish to thank our Most Holy God Jehovah, who illumined me to protect my reputation and dignity with this intelligent move. Since sincere servants of God within Bethel warned me that Korfias was determined to destroy me, prior to my going to the Judicial Committee I made it a point to purchase a state-of-the-art tape recorder with a strong transmitting antenna, so that my fiancée could listen in to the unholy inquisition and record it with a radio-receiver.[100] *I did this for two reasons:*
a) *To protect my honor and my reputation;*
b) *To enable myself to offer at some point all the pertinent information to whichever committee would undertake the cleansing of such anti-Christian actions.*

---

100 One has to remember that the Judicial Committee is a private interview in which no observers or record-keeping devices are allowed. Or, as the secret manual of the Elders put it very clearly, "If the accused wishes to bring witnesses who can speak in his defense regarding the matter, he may do so. However, observers are not permitted. No tape-recording devices are allowed." (*Pay Attention to Yourselves and All the Flock*, Watchtower, 1991, p. 110)

Finally, I requested that they bring forth the witness of this final accusation. To my great surprise it had to do with one of my close friends who served during 1973 in Corfu with his wife, as a special pioneer*.

How ironic, brother George! We had worked side by side with this brother for six months doing some amazing work on the island of Corfu. Those who can talk to you about my ethos, my devotion to the principles of God and my honorable life are my uncle and aunt... The same holds true for my cousins... But not only they, but the one hundred publishers of the island, many of whom found their way to the Society of God due to my ethos and unselfish commitment to the cause of God's Kingdom.

I also remembered that I used to spend my entire work income to support the material needs of the brother whom they were now bringing before me as my accuser. At that stressful moment, that man reminded me of Judas Iscariot.

But I really felt sorry for him when I first gazed at him. They had dragged him out of bed with his pajamas on, leaving behind a bewildered wife and two small children. This same man was disfellowshipped two or three years ago for the reason of fornication. While his previous wife was on her deathbed fighting a losing and painful battle with cancer, he was romantically involved with his present, much younger wife on the island of Aegina, scandalizing everyone with his conduct... And now this very man accused me, only later to be proven a false witness and a slanderer. I was later informed that the accusation was masterminded by Theoharakis in order to slander me.

And I ask you now, brother George: Which honest and ethical brother will bring all these false witnesses and evil contrivers to justice? All the necessary proof is at your disposal! But who will bring them to trial? Who will bring upon them the justice of God? Notwithstanding the lack of convincing evidence and witnesses on

A photo of the governing body taken in 1975
Marked with a circle is George D. Gangas, sitting to his left is 1) Nathan Knorr (3rd president) and further left 2) Fred Franz (4th president),while 3) Raymond Franz is standing in the second row behind his uncle.

---

which the committee based its judgment, its members proceeded with my disfellowship. The accusations were two:

a)   That I told the brothers in Rome I was the elder of the Anglophone congregation of Athens.

b)   That I called brother Theoharakis "harsh."

My accusers were ready to scratch off the "Corfu incident" because my prosecution witness stated that this woman, whom they thought to be a prostitute, could more than likely be the fiancée of my cousin (!) and I possibly greeted her with the usual Christian embrace. However, I went to the counteroffensive and asked him if he saw me do this personally. To this he replied that he had heard this from a brother with whom I had studied the Bible!

When I later contacted this brother, he in turn said that he not only could not imagine such an accusation against me but, on the contrary, considered me to be the most ethical person he had ever met; and that he feels extremely grateful toward me for everything he heard and learned from me about the truth.

Thus it becomes obvious that the entire matter is an intrigue of those who had participated in the Judicial Committee. It involves

Korfias and Theoharakis, and the other two. Who will bring them to justice? Fortunately God, Jehovah, Who is good and merciful, will bring them to justice because I have forgiven them.

Saturday, March 7, 1987: *At 9 p.m. my disfellowship was announced. I asked them to give me my lawful right to* appeal*, *which would have to be filed no later than March 14, 1987 before 9 p.m., as they assured me. I considered this the greatest expression of God's love for me and my fiancée, because we could still get married almost as planned. Instead of Sunday, we would have the ceremony the Saturday before at 7 p.m., completed by 8:30 p.m., and still have time to hand in my letter of appeal, 5 minutes before 9 p.m. Thus Korfias would be unable to destroy my wedding or disfellowship my family members.*

I also need to mention that my father-in-law, a man of eighty years of age, who has been tried by courts many times for the cause of the truth in Crete and dedicated his one daughter to serve Bethel for seven years, was now bedridden, a few days prior to his daughter's wedding. My mother-in-law was despondent and highly depressed due to the unacceptable behavior of the brothers who were manipulating the course of our personal life and happiness with inexpressible malice.

In the meantime the wedding events unfolded as follows: Since we had planned our wedding to be on March 14, 1987, the board of the elders needed to supply me with a paper stating that I was free to proceed with a theocratic marriage. When I brought them all the necessary requirements and the legal wedding license from "Caesar" (civil authorities), they denied my petition for a theocratic marriage.

I understood then that the overall goal of Korfias was not only to cut me off from the Society of God but, behaving in a demonic fashion, was to eagerly await the moment and hour of my planned

8. Persecution by the Society

wedding to take full revenge against me. He is a "Maniatis" by descent and needs to uphold the great reputation of the relentless and cruel Spartans.[101]

All this happened because at some point I had the courage and integrity to send a letter bearing my signature, referring to Korfias' lifestyle and concerning his behavior in the Anglophone church only, especially his attitude toward brother Christoula, whom he despised from the beginning—even from the time the Society had sent him to Cyprus. Due to my special relationship and friendship with Christoula—since we both developed simultaneously and theocratically at the good hands of the brothers—who counted on me as a close co-worker in the exercise of his theocratic responsibilities.

With a satanic masterminding capability, Korfias succeeded in displacing brother M., who confided in me personally as he was leaving Bethel that "the clique did him in!" Of course at the time I did not understand what he meant. Subsequently, when I witnessed Korfias' conduct toward his co-workers; his unjustifiable activities; his criminal behavior toward brothers who had devoted their entire lives to the pure worship of God, I started to become highly disenchanted and to distance myself from this lawless man. It would suffice only to bring up the name of the faithful and dear brother… and his son-in-law, whom he (Korfias) suspended from the privileges of the church in…, which was the very congregation he had sent me to, to strengthen. This brother confessed to me his deep pain, and further stated that

---

[101] Mani is a mountainous, rocky, arid and inaccessible suburb of Sparta; its inhabitants were known as fierce fighters. Indeed, Mani is one of the few places fully engulfed within the Ottoman Empire that was not subdued by the Turks. In addition, Maniates, it is said, had this "horrible honesty: never forget nothing." Vendetta feuds («γδικιωμός») persisted until the mid 1950s. To this day, the appellation "Maniatis" is associated with the stereotype of a rowdy and vengeful person.

this unbearable pain and the unjust behavior of brother Korfias would eventually send him to his grave. Volumes of books would not be able to contain all the havoc his actions have created throughout his career.

In my case, however, he behaved like a spider or a scorpion, waiting for the most opportune moment to sting me. He did not give me the needed paper to go through with an honorable theocratic marriage.

The Italian brother from the Athenian sector, tried to encourage us with the information that in Germany the "brothers" get married in a civil ceremony; not having another favorable solution at the time, we called the deputy mayor and he officiated at our wedding.

However since I had invited a significant number of key people, who worked with the utmost objectivity, integrity, and goodness for the realization of all the favorable legal changes (toward the Witnesses) in our country, all these people were highly disappointed; and naturally, at this point, they were well aware of the unjust behavior of Roulis Korfias, the representative of the Society of the Watchtower magazine. These people lived and shared our ordeal and stood by us with great kindness so that we would not be humiliated on the special day of our wedding. All these people, and some news reporters, are asking me to release the cassettes and recordings to them that I had made of the committee meetings and the false witnesses, so that they can publish them in the newspapers. However, I will await your own just intervention. Until then my wife and I will exclude ourselves from the meetings, having placed our lives in the hands of God.

Saturday, March 15, 1987: *This evening I married sister Stella; we left our wedding the way we were, with our wedding garments on and in the company of a young pregnant woman, and we went to hand in our letter of appeal. At 8:50 p.m. while entering Kingdom Hall, I gazed upon the face of the dear brother with whom I had worked side by side in the past, who has now turned against me to annihilate me. Like the dark agents of the Mob he avoided even looking at me because he is an evil coward, dark like the devil who guides all his actions and movements. They kept me in the cold for one hour and were trying to condemn me on the spot, so they can announce my disfellowship tomorrow in all the congregations of Attica and perhaps in all of Greece.*

My bride in her wedding gown is kept waiting outside with the pregnant sister who breaks down in tears, horrified by this agony!!! And she cries out, "Is this Christianity or the Middle Ages?"

I plead with them to take into consideration the sanctity of this moment but they are adamant. Finally my shivering fiancée— now my wife of one or two hours—enters and asks them to set me free because she is freezing, being simply dressed in a wedding gown. They then tell me to make myself available in the Hall the following day, Sunday, March 16, 1987, at 8:30 a.m., with all my witnesses!!!

It is now 4 o'clock in the morning!!! And I write to you my beloved father in the truth and unforgettable "brother" George. Are you able to pass sentence on these lawless men?

Woe to the twenty-two thousand Greek brothers. Little do they know that they are under the sharp claws of ravenous wolves, Korfias and his coworkers.

With love, George...

THIS LETTER WAS followed by numerous depositions of witnesses who declared that all the accusations of the committee were groundless, since they were also eyewitnesses of the actions of which I was accused. They also had the letter from the Bethel of Italy, declaring that there was nothing reprehensible associated with me. However all these were not considered sufficient to render justice. It was clear that these people wanted me out of the organization. In reality, however, it was God Who also wanted me out! This was the time to begin to know His true will, His real Church. But I will let Nikos continue with his story.

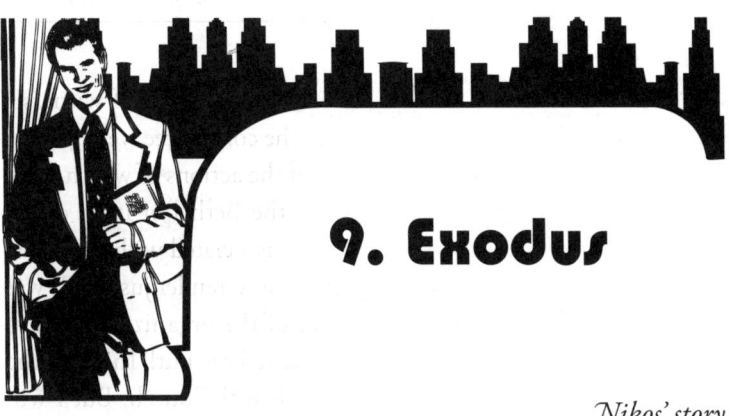

9. Exodus

Nikos' story

George visited me in great distress. When I asked him what the matter was, he declined to tell me. He only said, "Some people are out to destroy me! I know too much about them and they are afraid for their positions. They wish to throw me out of the Society of God.

"Who are they, and why would they want you disfellowshipped?" I asked him.

"Forget it, Nikos, because the less you know the better. And don't discuss our conversation with anyone because we will both find ourselves outside of the Society in an instant."

I did not insist so we parted company. A few months later I received an invitation to his wedding; the happy event was to take place in a few weeks. However, it turned out that George had hastily gotten in a civil ceremony, and that immediately afterward, he was disfellowshipped. That hit me like a lead balloon! "Now if they disfellowshipped this outstanding man, what would they do to me?" I wondered. Asking the reason, I was told: "Apostasy!"

"How can this be? George, an *apostate*?* He served in Bethel; he knows the members of the Governing Body one by one," I protested.

"He joined the arch-apostate Christoula! They were serving at

> 352　June 1, 1960　The WATCHTOWER　BROOKLYN, N.Y.
>
> hope, the blessings already enjoyed as a member of the New World society as well as those that still lie ahead might also be mentioned.
>
> What about telling a prospective mate the unfavorable truth about one's past, such as before one became one of Jehovah's witnesses? If the subject comes up and one is asked, the rule would apply that the truth should be told as the other has a right to know. If one is not asked, then it would be up to one's discretion and conscience. However, if it appeared that the information was vital to the other, and the other did not ask simply because he did not think such a thing likely, then the information should be volunteered, trusting in love and understanding to cover over the matter. If there is to be any disillusionment, certainly it is far better that it take place before marriage than afterward. Here the well-known principle stated by Jesus would apply: "All things, therefore, that you want men to do to you, you also must likewise do to them; this, in fact, is what the Law and the Prophets mean."—Matt. 7:12.
>
> There is one exception, however, that the Christian must ever bear in mind. <u>As a soldier of Christ he is in theocratic warfare and he must exercise added caution when dealing with God's foes. Thus the Scriptures show that for the purpose of protecting the interests of God's cause, it is proper to hide the truth from God's enemies.</u> A Scriptural example of this is that of Rahab the harlot. She hid the Israelite spies because of her faith in their God Jehovah. This she did both by her actions and by her lips. That she had Jehovah's approval in doing so is seen from James' commendation of her faith.—Josh. 2:4, 5; Jas. 2:25.
>
> <u>This would come under the term "war strategy,"</u> as explained in *The Watchtower*, February 1, 1956, and is in keeping with Jesus' counsel that when among wolves we must be as "cautious as serpents." Should circumstances require a Christian to take the witness stand and swear to tell the truth, then, if he speaks at all, he must utter the truth. When faced with the alternative of speaking and betraying his brothers or not speaking and being held in contempt of court, the mature Christian will put the welfare of his brothers ahead of his own, remembering Jesus' words: "No one has greater love than this, that someone should surrender his [life] in behalf of his friends."—Matt. 10:16; John 15:13.
>
> ● At Daniel 10:13 Michael is referred to as "one of the chief princes." Are we to understand that there are other chief princes in heaven besides Michael?—M. P., U.S.A.
>
> Yes, there is one other Chief Prince in heaven, Jehovah God himself. He is referred to as the "prince of princes" at Daniel 8:25, *AS*. See the book *"Your Will Be Done on Earth,"* pages 218, 219, 316.
>
> However, while Jehovah is the only other Chief Prince in heaven, Satan the Devil also has his chief princes, who today are in the vicinity of the earth, having been cast down with Satan at the conclusion of the war in heaven described in Revelation, chapter 12. See the book *"New Heavens and a New Earth,"* page 29.

Theocratic War Strategy
"As a soldier of Christ [a Witness] is in theocratic warfare and he must exercise added caution when dealing with God's foes. Thus the Scriptures show that for the purpose of protecting the interests of God's cause, it is proper to hide the truth from God's enemies.... This would come under the term 'war strategy'" (WT 6/1/1960 p. 352)

---

the same church and he led him astray," they answered.

"Wasn't he even a member of the 144,000? So anyone can fall!" I felt horrible. All my efforts for this man, his progress—were all these wasted? I could not get this out of my mind! What if he was innocent and they expelled him unjustly? But joining up with Christoula was sufficient for me to consider him an apostate.

During that time the name Christoula was heard prevalently among the Witnesses. He was a man who had drawn great numbers of people to his homilies as a Witness. At the conventions we had all stared at him enthralled! And a few months later he was cut off for apostasy. We were all saying that he had become proud like the devil and created his own dogmas and followers.

A little later[102] Christoula had reported two Witnesses to the police who were spying and secretly videotaping the apostates, who had gathered at his house for their "Remembrance of the Lord Feast."[103] The police arrested the trespassing Witnesses and a big

---

102 That happened on Sunday, April 11, 1986.

103 Apparently, spying on fellow members seems to be a not-so-isolated case, as there are similar cases reported also in the US, existing even within the Brooklyn headquarters. See Chretien, *Witnesses of Jehovah*, pp. 193-194

The headlines read: "Witnesses of Video," followed by the statements, "Faithful of Jehovah, who left the organization, in fear of casettes," "We can't even talk to our own children," "Many are losing their jobs due to the electronic filing."

"In the Cradle of Democracy"
In 1986 the Watchtower Organization had been brought under trial in Greece for spying on their own members! (Photo reprinted from Raymond Franz's book, *In Search of Christian Freedom* p. 380. Franz includes a detailed account of the incident.)

---

scandal appeared in the Greek newspapers. Although they were sent by the leadership of the Greek Bethel, the arrested Witnesses, following *theocratic war** principles, lied in court, pretending that they were following one of their female relatives. Of course they were found guilty and were charged. It so happened that none of us believed their excuse and actually a few were scandalized by the episode and left the Watchtower Society.

Those were very bitter days for us Witnesses and any mention to Christoula or his followers was sure to create tension. Yet I was not convinced that my friend George had anything to do with the apostates. I was seriously thinking of calling him to find out what had really happened. But what if, in spite of his possible unjust disfellowship, he was still true to the Society and reported to the elders that I called him when he was disfellowshipped? Then I would also be faced with serious problems! Consequently, I could not make such a decision. Yet, I was keeping my ears open about anything pertaining to the apostates. If I could somehow come to the bottom of this. Then, one morning, a few newspapers ran a photo of Christoula addressing an audience which included some priests. The accompanying article referred to the talk he had just presented which included a multitude of false claims against the Society. Also in the photo was my friend George.

"What a plight," I thought, "To speak lies against the Society of God in front of priests!"

I was now certain that he had joined the *Bad Guys**. Among the words of the apostates published were those of one of my jail mates, and also those of Stamatis who had coached me on how to make it through jail! Both of these men I had respected greatly. And now they were apostates! They had gone to Babylon!

Unbeknownst to me at the time, all these lies recorded in the newspapers were not said by the apostates but added by unscrupulous reporters in order to increase the circulation of their newspapers.

Up to that point the Witnesses of Greece were abandoning the Society in droves; however, from that day on the wave of apostasy came to a halt. Everyone was convinced that the apostates were liars! The weight of responsibility for this falls on the shoulders of those unconscionable news reporters. This detail, however, was known only by those who were present at Christoula's talk.

From that day forward I began to criticize the apostates at every opportunity, even in my talks at the meetings. The liars, who had the audacity to criticize the Society of God in front of inimical priests, needed to be exposed!

One day while at work, the phone rang. I picked it up and it was George, "Hi, Nikos, how are you? This is George!"

"I'm doing well! Is it true that you are an apostate?" I asked.

"No! They set me up with false witnesses! I…."

"You are lying. I saw you in the newspaper, and we have nothing to say to each other until you repent and return to the Society of God!" I was about to hang up the phone…

"Christoula did not say the things written in the newspaper…," he managed to say before I hung up the phone. I felt horrible! I was bound, however, to follow through with what I thought the Holy Scriptures said, i.e., to refuse "even a greeting" to the apostates.

The turning point

A LONGTIME NEIGHBOR of mine was disfellowshipped because she had married a man of the world. I saw her every day but did not greet her according to Witness policy so she would become ashamed and return to the "Ark of Salvation" in a state of repentance; for shunning, we were told, a disfellowshipped person is an act of mercy. Yet, every time I treated her this way I felt very badly, and I believe she probably felt even worse. And now shunning my old friend, classmate and brother, developed in me a strong sense of guilt.

The telephone interrupted my thoughts. I heard George's familiar voice, "I listened to you at some point in the past! Now why don't you give me the same chance?"

I hung up the phone again in a state of unrest. I knew very well that he was right. Back in school, I remember saying to him: "You need to hear us out! It is wrong to hold on to biases! How can you judge someone before you hear their side! Let's talk, and if you find that I'm in the wrong then don't speak to me ever again!"

An Open or a Closed Mind
—Which Do You Have?

PEOPLE do have difficulties getting along with one another, do they not? And although most of us like to think of ourselves as being open-minded, let us ask ourselves with complete honesty: Is the narrow-minded and bigoted person really always the "other fellow"?

In reality your mind may be more closed than you imagine. Do you at times say: "Two things I never talk about are religion and politics"? Or do you turn up your nose at foods you have not eaten before? "Snails? Never!" Or how do you feel about unfamiliar types of medical treatment? "Acupuncture? Pure quackery!" Or do you "know"—as, for example, "everyone" in Germany does—that Gypsies are thieves, North Germans are stubborn, everyone from Berlin is a loudmouth, Swabians are stingy and foreigners are lazy? Of course, similar ideas are found everywhere—yes, in your country too.

What Is an Open Mind?

An open mind is free from the fetters of prejudice, which by one dictionary is defined as follows: "A judgment or opinion, favorable or unfavorable, formed beforehand or without due examination; a mental decision based on other grounds than reason or justice; especially, a premature or adversely biased opinion."

A necessary part of life is that we make decisions and reach judgments. But decisions made "without due examination" or judgments reached "on other grounds than reason or justice" are evidences of a closed mind.

Having an open mind, on the other hand, means to be receptive to new information

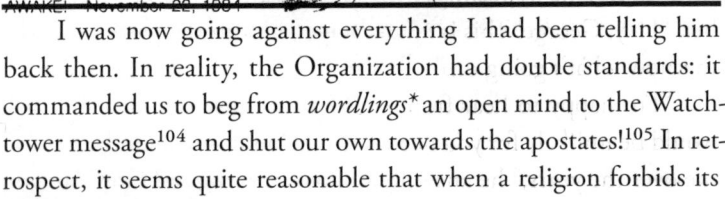

I was now going against everything I had been telling him back then. In reality, the Organization had double standards: it commanded us to beg from *wordlings** an open mind to the Watchtower message[104] and shut our own towards the apostates![105] In retrospect, it seems quite reasonable that when a religion forbids its

---
104 Awake, 11/22/1984 pp. 3–4 "An Open or a Closed Mind–Which do You Have?"
105 Watchtower, 3/15/1986. p. 12 "Have No Dealings With Apostates"

members from communicating with ex-members that its a sign it's hiding something. Back then, however, I was scared of displeasing Jehovah. What was I to do? I took out a sandwich and began to eat.

There were many things going through my mind, especially George's last phone call. What if he was telling the truth? What if they had set him up, as he said? What if the newspaper wrote things that were not said by Christoula? My eye caught the action of a sparrow dancing behind the glass, pecking at the cement.

Quite unconsciously, I cut a piece of bread from my sandwich and tossed it to the sparrow. As I was watching it share part of my lunch, suddenly a thought flashed through my mind and in tears I broke out in a prayer: "My God, I did not create this little bird! Yet I was mindful of its nourishment! Won't You also be mindful of me, Your creation? I know that I am a sinner! So please, I beg You to put up with one more sin! It won't be the first or the last! I will call George! And if You want me to be lost, let me be lost! I do this because I don't want You to tell me on Your Day of Judgment that I did not behave the way a human being should. I don't want You to tell me that I was given the opportunity to show my love to George and I failed to do so. I was given the chance to hear someone who was innocent, and I refused. I will follow the direction of my logic! I want to find out what caused George to join the apostates! And if this is worthy of my destruction, then destroy me!"

Overcome by feelings of relief, I dialed George's phone number, "Hey, George! This is Nikos. I believe you have a point. I want to know what's going on."

"I'm happy to hear from you! I knew that you would call! It would be unlikely for you not to believe in all those things you told me over the years," he answered, pleasantly relieved.

"I hope what I'm about to hear may justify this impropriety, otherwise don't hold it against me if I don't call you again!" I said in a tone of warning.

"I understand! You will see that you were not mistaken. So please listen to me! A schism took place a few years ago at the American Bethel. I caught wind of this quickly because I had worked there for years. Initially, a Swedish brother pioneer, named Carl Olof Jonsson, began to study the first fall of Jerusalem by the Babylonians. After years of research, he found concrete historical evidence that Jerusalem's desolation took place in 587 B.C., and not 607 B.C. This means that the dogma of 1914 and everything based on it is false! Do you understand what this means?"

"Yes, I heard something to that effect," I said, however, at the time, not being fully aware of the repercussions of this dogma. His reference to this specific dogma was enough for me to begin to show strong interest. This was the moment when I would ascertain whether or not my own research on this topic was correct.

"In short, I'm telling you now that this brother sent his research to the Governing Body according to Society procedures, requesting their attention to the date of 587. During that time, Raymond Franz, the nephew of the Watchtower president, was assigned to look into this relevant research since he was writing about the same subject in his book, *Aid to Bible Understanding*[106]. As soon as he studied the research, he saw that the Swede was correct. Thus, although he wrote the insertion in the book, *Thy Kingdom Come*, he attempted to refute the scientific date...."

"Yes I know!" I interrupted him, fully absorbed in his words.

"You know that the information given in the insertion is deceptive?" he asked.

"What do you mean?"

---

[106] Published by Watchtower Bible & Tract Society, 1969. It was the Society's first doctrinal encyclopedia. The incident is covered in Franz's *Crisis of Conscience* (2004 edition), pages 29–31 and in 176-200.

The Truth That Leads to Eternal Life, 1968, p.95

"The refuted view is that of certain spiritual circles, and not a truly scientific one. In reality, the scientists speak about these things differently, and the Holy Scriptures agree with them."

"You know, not too long ago I completed the same study and discovered other dates than the ones held by the Society, and those refuted by the insertion in *Thy Kingdom Come*," I said in astonishment, seeing that finally something was beginning to clear up in this conversation.

"I'm sure that you've discovered something accurate!" he tried to encourage me.

"And how can I be sure that what you're telling me is the truth?" I asked with suspicion.

"I'll send you the Jonsson study! I have the complete version!"

"I don't know English," I said excitedly.

"It's translated! One of the boys in jail translated it!"[107]

"What? Now we have apostates there, too?" I asked in shock, realizing now the Society's reason for constantly writing against them.

"They're everywhere in the entire world! Because when Franz

---

107 The book was translated by the now deceased Agapios Matsagkouras (†2003), when he was still a Jehovah's Witness and in prison for refusing the military identity. The book helped him to understand the errors of the Watchtower Society and to find his way to the Orthodox Church.

and the other group members gave Jonsson's research to the rest of the Governing Body, although they were convinced that the date of 1914 is wrong, they refused to change the dogma to avoid the dissolution of the Society. Based on this, many were disfellowshipped, and this became common knowledge and the research was circulated worldwide!"

"And how does this relate to your disfellowship?" I asked.

"It doesn't! They accused me of apostasy because I knew about the fraudulent actions of a man in charge of a division of the Greek Bethel. Even though I knew everything about the mistake of 1914, I had no plans of leaving the organization. Where else would I go, anyway? There is no religion of 'apostates.'"

"What about those who left? Didn't they form their own religion?"

"No, nor do they want to! They only study the Holy Scriptures and are attempting to force the Society to come clean with 1914."

"Perhaps we should let Jehovah clear things up?" I suggested.

"We all said the same thing in the beginning! However, more than ten years have gone by since Jonsson's research was sent! How long will we lie to the world? Could it be that those we call apostates are ultimately the plan of Jehovah for correction?"

"It certainly is a thought... What did you come up with that caused them to disfellowship you?"

"Korfias! He is behind it all! I have the documentation in my hands and if necessary I will turn it over to the civil authorities! He is the one who had people followed with video cameras! He has turned the Greek Bethel upside down! He is a true gangster! He is not worthy to be an elder of God's Society!"

"I'm so happy to hear that you still accept the Society," I replied.

"Of course! I'm telling you that they declared me an apostate for no reason at all! I went as far as getting back into the congregation and the convention and then they asked me to leave. They assigned two Gestapo agents to follow me and watch every move I made. Finally, they told me that I was not welcome. When I asked them why, they told me that they were simply following orders. They were also in the wrong, calling the others apostates! They also cut off Christoula without a judiciary committee because he went to America to discuss some topics with them that needed correction! The reporters themselves wrote what you read in the newspaper!"

"What about the priests?" I asked.

"They were invited as religious representatives. Christoula invited representatives of all religions, even the Witnesses! Naturally they did not attend. The purpose of the press conference was to inform the public about the persecution of people who want to have the right to express their opinion without the fear of disfellowship. The reporters, however, destroyed everything!

Korfias' men tried to foil my wedding! They set up a special committee meeting before my wedding and that's why I made my wedding date earlier! Their intent was to disfellowhship even my wife, if she would marry someone disfellowshipped. So we were married by the civil court, and a few minutes later I had to face the judiciary committee. My wife was waiting outside in her bridal gown while they were inside deciding my fate. However, I outsmarted them! I had a state-of-the-art transmitter inside my sports coat, and my wife, who was outside, recorded the entire committee proceeding. I had the upper hand on all of them: the judges, who were Korfias' pawns, and their false witnesses. They had false witnesses indeed! My disfellowship was decided far in advance."

"This all sounds strange to me. It's like watching a spy movie!" I commented with some unbelief.

"And I haven't told you anything yet! But let me say this, some time ago a member of the Governing Body came to our area,[108] and I called him to make him aware of Korfias' gangster activities. He told me that he was not free to talk to me because he was being followed and his phone was tapped! Just think, Korfias has so much power as to intimidate even a member of the Governing Body."

"This is all unbelievable!" I said.

"Forget Korfias! He's my concern! You work on 1914. I know that you love the truth. I'll send you the research through an associate of mine who lives in Salamina. I advise you not to speak to anyone about this because they will cut you off! And if I'm not totally correct on this, you don't have to call me ever again!"

I bade him farewell and we hung up the phone. All this was even much more incredible than what I had expected to hear. However, I had reasons to be semi-convinced:

First, because I had personal experience of the callousness and the anti-Christian qualities of Korfias. But it was not the first time that I would hear and see an anti-Christian behavior of some Witnesses. And I didn't pay too much attention to things I heard against other people.

And finally, which was my foremost concern, the true dogma from the study I had completed about the fall of Jerusalem. The main proof would come when I received Jonsson's book.

The beginning of the end

THE NEXT DAY, I had the book in my hands! I hid it well and did not share the information with anyone. Thus, a third round of research began on the desolation of Jerusalem by the Babylonians—by coincidence also lasting six months. During this interval I would phone George, who often elucidated some doubtful elements along the way.

---

108 Most likely he is referring to George D. Gangas' visit to Greece in 1985

In 607 B.C.E. God's kingdom of Judah fell.
In 1914 C.E. Jesus Christ began to rule
as king of God's heavenly government

607 B.C.E.   **1914 C.E.**

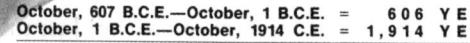

| October, 607 B.C.E.—October, 1 B.C.E. | = | 606 YEARS |
| October, 1 B.C.E.—October, 1914 C.E. | = | 1,914 YEARS |

SEVEN GENTILE TIMES = 2,520 YEARS

From the book "You Can Live For Ever" (p.14)

My student had now become my teacher! We were both in a state of hopeful expectation that the Society would tell the truth in the end.

Jonsson's book was voluminous and full of complicated calculations. Fortunately, by the grace of God, I had become accustomed to the topic from my previous studies and understood it with ease. I had the suspicion, however, that all this could be one of Satan's traps, to deceive the people and lead them outside of the Society of God. For this reason I did not make my calculations with a calculator alone but also mentally, fearing that Satan could alter the results of my calculator. This was an extreme measure but I wanted to be certain that my research did not leave anything to chance. These extreme measures were the result of the phobia instilled in me by the Society for any other source except itself. Thus, with all these details the months passed by, and although I was reading many hours everyday, I had not yet finished the book.

I had almost reached the end of the book which analyzed seven different sets of evidence from different unrelated sources. All the calculations were correct and it seemed that the Swede was right. I had read all the evidence in the series except the last one, and up to that point I had been a steady critic. I checked every quotation referring to the books of the Society to make sure that he was writing the truth. I looked up every scriptural verse and then searched the index of the Society to see how each verse was interpreted, and did this in all the publications designated by the index. I did not want to take any chance of losing the truth, whatever it was. Furthermore, I was praying fervently to God to grant me knowledge; and He, being rich toward all those seeking, compensated me richly, even if I was not seeking the most appropriate gift.

Though I was seeing that everything was correct, I tried to think up even the most improbable hypotheses so that I would not be led astray and have all of my effort be in vain. For example, I asked the question, what if the devil has interfered and packaged together all this archeological evidence for deceiving the Witnesses! However, when I reached the last series of evidence, I was totally flabbergasted. In that series, there was evidence from the Holy Scriptures itself!

It was the opportune time to check the index against my Holy Scriptures question from my previous research. Yes! I was right! My research agreed with Jonsson, with the historians and mainly with the Holy Scriptures! Strangely enough, only the dogma of the organization did not fit anywhere! This was the end of my unbelief. The year of the desolation of Jerusalem, supported by historians, could be extracted undoubtedly and effortlessly from within the Holy Scriptures: the year 587 B.C. and not 607, as supported by the organization.

What surprised me more than anything else were the verses of Zacharias.[109] (There, calculating the date based on the year 521/520 (a date accepted even by the Society to be the year of Darius' enthronement), I found exactly when these words of Zachariah had been written. Consequently, going back seventy years according to the verses, I found 589 B.C. to be the year of the siege and 587 B.C. as the year of Jerusalem's desolation.[110] What added to my aston-

---

109 Zacharias 1:7-12 and 7:1-5

110 Jeremiah 21:2, 4-7; Jeremiah 41:1-3, 10; 52:12, 13; II Kings 25: 8-9, 22-25; *All Scripture is inspired of God and Beneficial*, p. 169, paragraph 3

9. Exodus

ishment, however, was the fact that even the verses used by the Society to support its views, with careful analysis, supported the view of the historians. I called George on the phone and announced to him that I was certain that 1914 was the wrong date.

Overexcited about my findings, I decided to mention this to my family members. After work, I rushed home and blurted to my unsuspecting wife that after many months of research I was certain that the dogma of 1914 was wrong. Being young, idealistic, and inexperienced in human dynamics, I naively expected her to suddenly share my interest in the truth. I should have offered her more time, surround her with love, cultivate a climate conducive to exchange of ideas, and slowly but methodically present her my findings. My blunder made my wife turn red, wild, her eyes became like glass and she began to howl (amongst many other things), "You are an apostate! I will turn you in to the elders!"

My son was still very young, so he did not have a clear sense of everything going on. But Roula was divided. On the one hand her identity as a member of the Society compelled her to turn me in as an apostate; on the other hand, she hesitated because I was her husband. Finally, I offered to help her out of her difficult dilemma.

I said, "Listen! I was expecting you to be supportive of the results of my research. But since you look at it this way, I will go to the elders myself. The truth has nothing to fear."

Therefore, I quickly went to Vlassis, an elder of a nearby congregation, whom I especially loved and respected. Actually, according to the Watchtower's provisions, I needed to go to an elder of my own congregation, but I did not trust them with something so dangerous. In a few words, I explained to him the recent developments and what had happened when I told my wife.

He asked me two things: first if I still believe that our religion was the Society of God, and second if I simply doubted or if I was

The Armageddon—as it can be seen it was expected in the 40's (Religion, 1940, p.341)

certain that this central dogma of ours was wrong.

For the first, I answered him that I still had faith in the Society and that I was simply waiting to see when it would announce the change. For the second, I told him I was absolutely sure, and added, "Now, if you know something different concerning this, which I may not be aware of, I will be happy to correct my mistake."

His response took me by surprise. "Listen, Nikos! I have trusted this organization to guide me through Armageddon and I will stay here until it does so. I don't want to learn about the arguments that convinced you because then I will have a conflict with my conscience. If you are actually correct about this, then I would have to conform to what I learn, so I don't want to risk it. My ad-

9. Exodus

vice is to forget about what you learned and to play the game; those who are now in charge of Bethel (Korfias and his gang) will cut you off immediately.[111] If you agree not to discuss this anywhere, I will also keep my mouth shut. Let's wait for the Society of God to tell us if things are truly this way. The changes it has made over the years are proof that if you are right, it will also make this change. The only thing is that you must avoid all contact with the apostates."

I agreed that it seemed better for me to wait for the Society and keep this secret to myself. I did not, however, promise him that I would suspend communications with the apostates, or that I would forget what I had read.

I left him with the idea that I had accepted his two suggestions. For him to not wish to learn the truth was his business. But for me to stop searching was something totally inconceivable.

The Society itself had taught me to call upon others to be open-minded and to search. I would be incompatible with my spiritual upbringing if I ceased contact with the apostates since they were correct at least about the "1914 dogma" as my own studies had already pointed out. With this logic one should not listen to us Witnesses, being that we are apostates of other religions. Even if some doctrine of whichever religion was proven wrong, anyone could then claim

---

[111] As Carl Olof Jonsson wrote: "The truth is that the Watch Tower Society regards it a deadly sin to reject the chronology pointing to 1914. That God's kingdom was established at the end of the 'Gentile times' in 1914 is stated to be 'the most important event of our time,' beside which 'all other things pale into insignificance.' (WT 1/1/1988 pp.10,11). Those who reject the calculation are said to incur the wrath of God. Among them are 'the clergy of Christendom' and its members, who thus are said to have rejected the kingdom of God and therefore will be 'destroyed in the 'great tribulation' just ahead.' (WT 9/1/1985 p.25) Members of Jehovah's Witnesses who openly discard the calculation run the risk of being punished very severely. If they do not repent and change their minds, they will be disfellowshiped and classified as evil 'apostates,' who will 'go, at death, ... to Gehenna,' with no hope of a future resurrection.(WT 4/1/1982, p.25). It makes no difference if they still believe in God, the Bible, and Jesus Christ." (Carl Olof Jonsson, *The So-Called "Bible-Chronology" of the Watch Tower Society*, 1993)

Top: WT 05/15/84 (cover)
Right: WT 11/1/95 p. 17

As late as 1984 (top: WT 05/15/84) the Watchtower Society was claiming that the generation of 1914 would not pass away, but would live to see the Armageddon. Thousands of Witnesses were disfellowshipped and shunned for doubting this anti-Scriptural dogma. Only eleven years later, however, as the Armageddon failed to happen and the demographics turned increasingly against them, the Society finally withdrew the 1914 dogma. However, instead of offering a humble apology for false guidance, the Watchtower leadership shifted the responsibility to the individual believers (right: WT 11/1/95 p.17).

---

that his religion is the true one, regardless of whether it keeps making mistakes, since it would correct them sometime in the future!

With this mindset my effort to convince others that my religion was the true one would be futile, if we assume that the true dogma does not matter. It was not possible for me to be this nonsensical! Especially since I was coming to the realization that more and more of the doctrines of our faith were based on the dogma of 1914, which was definitely wrong. I needed to learn all the consequences that the dismissal of this dogma would bring upon every facet of my faith.

The position of Vlassis was satisfactory for the understanding he showed toward my problem; but on the other hand, his outlook toward my research had saddened me. He took me by surprise because he had taught me to search in depth and examine minutely subtle details of the Holy Scriptures. He had showed that he loved the truth, and now he was refusing to research such an important subject for fear it might be wrong. In other words, he was like a driver who does not want to look at the map, out of fear that he may have taken the wrong road!

I returned to my house and told my wife about our discussion. She was relieved, seeing that for the time being there was no imminent danger of my disfellowship or apostasy.

Increasing the distance

THE FOLLOWING MONTHS were months of intense study. I asked my friend George to introduce me to Christoula so I could continue becoming more informed. Christoula suggested introducing me to an ex-Jehovah's Witness couple, who had a summer home in Salamina, so they could supply me with whatever publications and tapes they had about the Christian faith. During that time the ex-Jehovah's Witnesses were gathering in a home in Athens once a week and Christoula was sharing the result of his studies with them.

The more I got to know Christoula, the more I understood how badly he was treated by the people of my faith. Every so often, a certain rumor was spread about him: that he had become a chain smoker, that he had divorced, and many other ridiculous claims that would hardly pass for accusations. But the Witnesses would consider them proof that when someone leaves the Society he becomes a scoundrel. Similar accusations circulated about my friend George, one of the most bizarre was that he had become a papist priest. Such was the irresponsibility of those who were spreading this nonsense, who couldn't remember that a catholic priest cannot be married, and here my friend had a wife and children!

The standard accusation against the apostates, and especially against Christoula, was pride. Supposedly out of pride like the devil, they considered themselves better than the Society and apostatized. In reality, the opposite was true: For someone to accept that which he believes is wrong, much humility is needed. Humility is needed even to consider that he may be on the wrong path. On the contrary, their accusers did not possess even the trace of humility required to allow such a thought. They believed proudly, like the Pharisee of the parable, that they were good and everyone else was worthy of destruction: that they had the truth and only they could teach. There was no one outside of the Society from whom they could learn.

Mr. Christoula was a receptive man, committed to helping the ex-Witnesses escape all the delusions they had learned over the years, so they could be re-established in society without haughtiness. As for Christoula, when the ex-Witnesses asked him to lead a new religion in Greece, he kept refusing. Furthermore, when he realized that some participants had begun to develop a dependence on him, as they had in the Watchtower Society, he discontinued the weekly meetings and encouraged the ex-Witnesses to form their own study group and have their own gatherings.

Fortunately, however, a good Greek-Egyptian former Witness had recorded on cassette tapes all the subjects studied. One by one, more than a hundred of his recorded homilies came into my hands. Scared that someone would ask me about them, I listened to these cassettes secretly at work. Each cassette tape shook my foundation built by the Watchtower from my childhood. This knowledge was beginning to re-build a new structure, stone by stone, which would provide the ladder that would eventually lead me to the one and truly infallible Church of Christ.

9. Exodus

To begin, I heard an interpretation of the great multitude, from the *Book of Revelation*, which is referred to in the seventh chapter. I was shocked by the discovery that not only the 144,000 but also the great multitude will go to heaven. The verses were crystal clear on this! Found in the same place as the twenty-four elders in heaven was the great multitude in the vision! Furthermore there was one more verse, in Revelation 19:1, which was very clear in showing that this was a heavenly order. So then, who were the "other sheep" of the parable of the Lord in John 10:16?

The next cassette I listened to dealt with this topic. To my great surprise, it provided me with a number of convincing reasons that the sheep in the sheepfold were the Israelites of the Mosaic Law and the other sheep were the Gentiles who would accept Christ and become one flock together with the faithful Jews. Or could it be that the Gospel could change it and it would refer to some earthly order, as the Witnesses believed? Another series of cassettes proved that the Gospel was once and for all delivered to the saints[112] and it wouldn't change even if an angel from heaven would ask this.[113] It must always speak of the same heavenly hope preached by the Lord and the apostles. Anyone who would preach a different gospel would be anathema (eternally condemned).[114]

But what then? Is it possible that the Society was not of God? Was it anathema? I began to suspect this when I heard the cassette about "The Faithful and Wise Servant." In this cassette, a series of verses proved that anyone who calls himself wise (much like the Governing Body of the Witnesses), "runs ahead of the Lord" and "is a fool."[115] It was also proven that the term "servant" here was not

---

[112] Jude 1:3
[113] Gal. 1:8
[114] Gal.1:7-9
[115] I Cor. 3:18, 4:1-5, 10; II Cor. 10:12

pertaining to a group of people, but to each individual, whether evil or righteous.

For the first time, however, in this particular cassette, I observed that Christoula himself had made an error in the interpretation of the "Parable of the Servant." It was not possible to speak about every Christian here in this parable! There was something else happening, but it would take another three years before I would understand it. The use of the cassettes was difficult. I needed to have a tape player available, and it was difficult to find the specific points of interest, so something needed to be done to make all the information more useful and easily accessible. Thus, I began to record all these verses and interpretations, transcribing all the homilies. Listening to the cassettes took many months; the fact that I was transcribing them was beneficial to me. It enabled me to absorb the wealth of knowledge, and I could also have it in front of me on paper at will.

In the group of the ex-Witnesses there was no presence of a governing body which would exclusively hold and provide the results of its studies for everyone. Everyone could study a subject of interest and share his views with others. Consequently, my own work was very useful for all those who took advantage of my transcripts from the cassettes. Of course, other than Christoula, there were individuals who studied and produced much work. This was especially true for two people whom I was very happy to meet later. They worked quietly in the background, and one of them while in jail!

Their work brought into my hands some extremely useful publications: the first was the translated book of Raymond Franz entitled *Crisis of Conscience*. You see, most Witnesses, have been trained in theological debating—they can argue about Bible verses for ever—and they view any arguments as a confirmation of their faith! Books, however, that deal with the facts of the Watchtower Society are much harder to dismiss.

In his book, Franz wrote about all the events leading to the schism of 1982; about the discovery of the mistake of 1914; how the Governing Body rejected the suggestion for correction; and the methods used to railroad him out of the Society.

The other publication was Jonsson's study, which proved through indisputable historical facts that the 20th century was not the "worst century of history" as the Witnesses claimed. The worst was the 14th century. However, up to that point, I had never opened up an encyclopedia to ascertain this but had solely depended on all the distortions put forth by the Society!

Finally, I was given the text of Christoula's press conference, which was highly upsetting. Essentially, it was very different compared to the version of the reporters. Through it all, the months passed by, but in the meantime some problems began to emerge.

My Crisis of Conscience

ALL THIS NEW knowledge was becoming increasingly problematic. I could no longer teach things which I didn't believe, either at the congregation or at people's doors. While *working the doors**, I limited myself to calling the people to repentance and faith in God. But at the meetings, I had another problem. I was compelled to say exactly what the Society had prepared. What would I do if I needed to speak about matters in which I did not believe? Wouldn't I be a hypocrite? How could I teach a lie? When I would run across such a topic I would dupe my conscience by stating: "The book says…" or "According to the book…," as if to say, "The book says this and not I!"

The first few months passed by with the use of this "technique." During that time I was trying out different kinds of experiments. Wishing to see how well the Witnesses understood the teachings of the Society, I would often ask them with more in-depth questions about matters relating to—but not necessarily specific to—

the topic I was teaching, To my surprise I observed that not even two of them would agree on the right answer. Their knowledge was limited to the worn-out surface topics, which were repeated constantly in most of the lessons.

During this interval Vlassis was calling me to find out how I was doing and if I was convinced about my error; I answered him that the topic remained as we had left it. One day, however, he came to a gathering of my church. On that day, I had to expand on a topic referring to 1914! So according to my "technique", I began to say, "The book says...," etc. When I was finished, he asked me to visit him at his store so we could talk. I went the very next day.

"Do you really think that you are escaping your conscience? What does it mean, 'the book says?' Aren't you still teaching regardless of what the book says?" he asked, something that made me reconsider things.

"What else do you advise me to do?" I asked

"The best solution is to resign from the ministerial service! But the problem is that they will ask you the reason for your resignation. What can we find?" he asked.

"For personal reasons," I suggested.

"That sounds good, but it's not enough! We must tell this to one of the elders of your congregation, because I belong to another congregation and cannot cover you! Besides, if this becomes known they will hold me responsible, and they will ask me why I did not inform the elders of your congregation."

"I understand." I said.

"You know what would happen if this becomes known to the office! So it would be good when the *District Overseer** comes, that one of your own elders reassure him that everything is all right. And the district overseer who will come this time is an extremely difficult man!" he confessed.

9. Exodus

I bade him farewell and left this whole matter to his discretion. Besides, the new overseer would come after many months, so we had time until then. In reality, however, I felt that I did not have very much time left with the Society. The examples I had of other people I knew who had faced this situation did not leave much room for optimism. I needed to do something.

I had to prepare my mother and my grandmother for my possible disfellowship. Besides, they would ask me the reason why I was resigning from the ministerial service. What would I tell them? So I went home and told my mother that I resigned from the service. She was not very pleased, because it had made her very proud to see me speak from the podium.

"Why?" she asked me.

"I better not tell you!" I answered, pretending to be difficult.

"Did you resign or did they expel you?" she asked.

"I resigned for personal reasons," I answered.

"I want you to tell me the reason," she insisted.

"If I tell you, we can both find ourselves disfellowshipped! You must not let a word slip out!" I warned her.

"Of course not, you think I'm so dumb?"

So I briefly explained to her what had transpired. Hearing this made her jaw drop. She never expected me to doubt a single dogma of the organization.

"Do you remember the time when you shared with me your discussion with the 'evangelical'?" I asked. "Well, he was right: the Christian hope refers to heaven, indeed!"

"How do you now accept all this, especially since you spoke to me with such fanaticism back then?"

"You did not have any proof back then! But I do! I have tons! If you had told me that you had verses back then, I would not have refused to study with you," I defensively said.

"Okay, then, since you have proof, I would like us to study them together," she said.

"If you are convinced though, and they disfellowship you at some point, not a single Witness friend of yours will be speak to you and your health may deteriorate," I forewarned her.

"If you are in the right, it doesn't bother me. I will find real Christians elsewhere for companionship," she said, full of determination.

I was bursting with joy. My mother was not fanatical! She would slowly prepare my grandmother, so that in the event of a disfellowship, I would only have the problem of my wife and son.

So from that day on, I began to school my mother and then my yiayia (grandmother) on everything I was learning about the mistakes of the Watchtower. At the same time, though, I was concerned about my family and my livelihood. If they would disfellowship me, perhaps I would lose my employment; and I couldn't bear to think what would happen to my family. I asked God daily for direction and help, expressing to Him each time that I would remain steadfast to the principles I had taught to others all these years, regardless of how costly it would be. He could allow whatever He wanted to happen to me. Thankfully, He has remained faithful, movingly faithful, to this day despite my own lack of strong faith.

At this time my son was still too young, and I couldn't communicate any of this to him. I had taught him about the Society from his infancy, and one of the first words I had taught him to say was "Jehovah." Facing disfellowship, I couldn't even speak to my own family.

Some days later a meeting took place with the elder who would announce my resignation. Vlassis and I explained to him what had transpired and he was dumbfounded! He agreed to be involved in the matter, hoping that the subject would remain closed. They simply repeated to me that the subject needed to stay dormant.

"Brother, would you be interested in discussing the arguments

I have found, so you can correct me if I am in error? This would eliminate the problem," I suggested.

His answer was negative and similar to Vlassis'. I couldn't understand! Did these people not have even a trace of logic? Couldn't they see that they were acting like ostriches, burying their heads in the sand? With what conscience, then, did they go to others telling them to search for the truth without prejudice?

Day by day, I began to harbor negative feelings for the Society that had brought me to this plight. Despite all this, I was still entertaining the small possibility that all this could be an error of mine, and that at some point the Society would justify its arbitrary title as the Society of God.

If you refuse to offer works to the Watchtower Society, or if you are not very productive, the Society warns you that you will have the fate of Lot's wife, who turned into a pillar of salt! This is genuine terrorist spirituality, which brings results and is very instrumental in maintaining its victims.

Since my time with the Society was coming to an end, in some of my final public talks, I used some of the information from Christoula's cassettes. At the end, they were coming up to ask me where I discovered this wonderful information! Obviously I couldn't tell them, so I simply said to them, "From sources outside the Society!"

It's funny, but all of the amazing things I was telling them, if looked upon through the distorted lens of Watchtower theology, would simply be termed, "apostatic teachings."

In a subsequent gathering that Elder briefly announced that I had resigned my position from the ministerial service for personal reasons. Since numerous candidates strived to serve as ministerial servants but couldn't, my resignation seemed incomprehensible—especially since I had displayed such steady progress. Thus, the announcement caused much perplexity for everyone present. I remember an aged witness who was striving (in vain) to become elder came up at the end and asked me, "Why did you resign, brother?"

"For personal reasons, brother," I answered.

"Like what?" he kept insisting.

"I told you, for personal reasons!" I repeated.

"Very well," he said, realizing that he was meddling in my private life. In spite of this he continued to look at me with a puzzled look for days.

The Letter

I WAS A subscriber to a magazine, "Flight and Space." This periodical, although militant in nature, had great articles about space which interested me. In one of their issues, they wrote something against those who refused military service for reasons of conscience. This made me very upset, so I needed to write a response. I thought, "the Society may have other dogmatic errors but on this issue, it is correct!" Thus I wrote a letter to the editor and as a former anti-militarist my response was no less than vitriolic. Actually my letter was published and in the following issue a multitude of patriotic readers attempted to answer my letter.

The evening my letter was published, my wife and I went to visit Vlassis at his country home. His brother-in-law, Mr. Megaritis, was also there. Vlassis was discussing with his brother-in-law the recent article of the *Watchtower* which spoke about the symbolism of Job and Elijah. "But this symbolism cannot be right!" he told his brother-in-law, and explained the reasons.

"But the Society is writing this!" the other reminded him.

"Yes, of course! If the Society is writing it, this is how it is!"

Vlassis agreed, making my stomach turn. There, right in front of me, I had two people who chose to be blind! No! Surely this was not the religion that a little while ago had made me proud. It did not consist of truth-seekers but of walking record players who played over and over again the words of the Society like broken records, whether they believed them or not! It was an embarrassment to belong to such an organization.

Yet, there was a happy side-effect; my wife, seeing Vlassis doubt some doctrines of the Society, began to look at my doubts more favorably, thinking that maybe the dogma of 1914 was wrong after all. Thus, on another day when we were studying, she observed a certain contradiction (that I hadn't noticed) which made her conclude all by herself that 1914 was false. So for quite a few months before and up to my disfellowship my wife had overcome her bias to a great degree.

During the course of the conversations at Vlassis' country home, I made reference to my letter, and if I remember correctly I had it with me and showed it to them. It was a mistake.

The next day Vlassis called. "I spoke to Mr. Megaritis about you!" he said.

"Why? Didn't we agree not to open the subject anymore?" I asked.

"You told us about the letter you sent to that periodical; and after you left, he expressed to me that you have an independent spirit, and that all those who acquire such a spirit depart from the organization rather quickly. Then I explained to him what was happening so he could give me his advice."

"And what was in my letter that bothered him? I had sent a letter to a periodical once before about evolution, and not only did they not scold me, but the regional overseer at the time even praised me!"

"Evolution is one thing and military service is something else! If Bethel wanted, it could send a letter; they wouldn't wait for you!" he answered.[116]

---

116 "All this fit in with the society's policy of discouraging individual Witnesses from publishing anything relating to their faith. The stated attitude of most high Watchtower officials and the governing body in particular was that if something needed to be published, the society would do it. Witnesses who worked independently

"And what did Megaritis say to you?" I asked.

"He advised me to wash my hands of this matter because when you begin to speak out, a wave of apostasy will be created on the island and all the responsibility will fall on me since I was covering you!"

"But Klakas, the elder of my own congregation, knows this!" I protested.

"Klakas is keeping it a secret because I promised to shoulder all responsibility! If something happens, I will have major problems!" he answered.

"What are you thinking to do?" I asked.

"If I'm not mistaken, you have a cousin who has a good position, Mr. Bananis."

"Yes, he married my father's niece!" I said.

"He is also my friend! So I would ask him what would be the right thing to do! He won't betray you! He has taken part in spiritual courts against apostates and he is very knowledgeable in these circumstances. So don't worry! I will also ask him if at the District Convention this month there will be some change on the dogma of 1914. If, as you feel, a change is imminent then you won't have a problem!"

"Do whatever you think is best, but be careful that you don't blow my family to pieces!"

Deep down, though, I was seeing that another step had been taken toward my disfellowship. Two more individuals were now entering the picture and God only knows who else! Well, I needed to do something! I would not wait like a sheep to be slaughtered! At least they could engage me in a conversation to prove me wrong!

Since they would make this public knowledge, I would do this

---

were therefore in grave danger of being accused of 'trying to exalt themselves,' trying to 'run ahead of God's organization,' or of trying 'to make money' on their brothers. Thus, for so large a religious community, Jehovah's Witnesses produced remarkably few persons to speak independently on their behalf." (Penton, *Apocalypse*, p. 105) on an even greater scale! When they cut me off, it would be too late to warn others about the delusion! No one would listen to me then. I needed to act now to help as many people as I could to escape delusion. Thus I looked for opportunities to discuss the subject with anyone I could. I was also preparing a letter to share with the Witnesses when my disfellowship would be decided and certain.

Visiting a Foreign Denomination

DURING ALL THIS time, not only did I not stop preaching for a moment but I was putting in more hours than anyone else in my congregation. I also had the most Scriptural Studies, seven to be exact. My Scriptural Studies were now based solely on Scripture since I now knew too much about the dogmatic errors of the Society and could not use its books any longer. To my surprise, the members progressed faster studying Holy Scripture than when reading the books of the Society. I remember the reaction of a Moslem when I took him both the Watchtower and the Holy Scriptures in the Arabic language. He told me, "Forget the magazine, I don't want it! The magazine confuses me! I understand the Bible better."

It rubbed me the wrong way back then, but now I understood fully why it was confusing to him. All the Society publications had discrepancies to the real meaning of the Holy Scriptures and they altered the true Gospel.

During that time I began to realize that the Witnesses' claim that only they would be saved was very egotistical. There were so many people who loved God outside of the Society!

During the years when I was a Witness in Salamina, I had met with many people of other religions. Among them were some people who would play a significant role in my life. One of these acquaintances was an Evangelical with whom I had numerous discussions. We would exchange Bible verses, neither one of us being able to convince the other. Now, however, that I realized that my faith had some claims wrong, I decided to go to one of their meetings secretly. I needed to see what was happening in other religions; thus, I could discern without bias how my religion rated. This would finally determine if I should stay or exit the Jehovah's Witnesses.

The Evangelical meeting was carried out in a home on Sunday mornings. While everyone thought I went to do field work, I went there instead on the condition that the Evangelicals not betray me to the people of my religion. A pastor from the congregation of Lipasmata entered. He had a well-groomed beard,[117] something that seemed strange to me since in my religion there was a rule that did not permit Witnesses to grow a beard, and if someone disobeyed this rule he was not given any privileges.

Of course I understood well how nonsensical this rule was since Russell, the founder of the "Students of the Scriptures" (from whom the Witnesses branched off), had a beard, and especially since Christ Himself had also had a full beard. This man-made, irrational tradition of the Society had always bothered me, but I was so used to such silly rulings, that it didn't faze me. So I was pleasantly surprised to see that a beard did not exclude this man from having the responsible position of shepherd.

The group started with a prayer, praising the Lord with a pleasant hymn. The pastor was speaking with a smile, which seemed strange to me at the time, later on I learned that this was characteristic of Evangelical preachers and I could spot them even before they would tell me that they were Evangelicals.

The pastor, then, began to analyze a chapter directly from the Holy Scriptures. They didn't parrot whatever was imposed upon

---

117 Actually, there is nothing officially dictated against growing facial hair. However, besides the full body of written code of regulations (contained in the Watchtower magazines), there is also the "Body of Unwritten Litigation and Law," which some JWs mockingly call "B.U.L.L."

them! *That* was refreshing. Yet I was annoyed by their preoccupation with the Holy Trinity—something that I considered an idolatrous teaching at the time.[118]

What moved me was seeing an Evangelical woman in tears, deeply touched by the words of the speaker. This was something that I had rarely seen among the Witnesses. "Obviously there are faithful people in all religions," I thought!

"Now would the Lord who said about His crucifiers, 'Father forgive them for they know not what they do!' kill this faithful woman during Armageddon? She is deluded! So what? She loves God and she is crying for Him!"

For a brief moment an image of Armageddon passed through my mind as imagined by us Witnesses, being that I was still clueless as to the reality of the war. I imagined this woman standing in the middle of a great earthquake, exposed to falling fire and brimstone and hail stones. Then I imagined her turning her face toward heaven and crying out, "Lord, I have loved You! I was crying out of love for You while hearing Your word! And now You, the Righteous Judge, are killing me?"

NO! It was not possible! That kind of God was not a God of love! That was not the God I believed in and worshipped! Such a God was not worthy of my love and worship even if I also had to die. Such a God would not be different from the devil himself! My God was synonymous with Love! It was worth dying for His Name and we saw His love in the person of His Word and Son. His loving care provides for all in His creation including those deluded by a false religion.

---

[118] The Watchtower Society falsely preaches that, " the doctrine [of the Trinity] in brief is that there are three gods in one…" [*Let God be True*, 1952, p. 100] and that "the origin of the trinity doctrine is traced back to the ancient Babylonians and Egyptians and other ancient mythologists." [ibid, p. 101] Judging from the lack of historical support in their articles on the subject, it seems that the Watchtower's sole purpose is to win impressions with unsubstantiated claims.

I recalled a certain event from my childhood. This was immediately after my father's death when my mother and grandmother's social security checks were not enough to live on, so we all worked taking various jobs at home. I remember my mother staying up to sew dresses when I went to bed. In the morning she was still sewing, having been up all night sewing so that we could make ends meet. Still the money remained very tight. I remember one morning we did not even have bread in our home. We borrowed from every possible source, but then we had nothing left. Not even enough for a loaf of bread! My mother came inside the house and in a state of hesitation announced to us that we had nothing to eat. What was she going to do? I saw her face full of despair. "Let's pray and God will provide," she said! So all three of us prayed together and we returned to our tasks.

Then, not even an hour later, the mailman rang the bell. He was holding a letter from one of my uncles in America. We opened the letter and to our amazement he had enclosed a few dollars equivalent to 1,000 drachmas. At that time such an amount could feed us for an entire week! With great gratitude we thanked our God, *my* God! This was my God Who provided even for the little birds, who loved all in His creation! He was not the unrighteous murderer presented by the Society. He was willing, and He would save every man who loved Him, no matter which religion he belonged to.

The speaker was continuing and my mind was racing! And why not? I didn't go there to be taught about the interpretation of the Holy Scriptures! I was there to search, and specifically to see, if there are other people who love God outside of the Jehovah's Witnesses.

I then remembered something else. There was an aged woman disfellowshipped by the Watchtower Society. Her husband was still a Witness, but she had become an Orthodox Christian. I found out that when she was much younger she had been sexually assaulted by a Witness. She was scandalized and left the Society. Since then, not a single Witness was permitted to speak to her. One time her husband fell ill, so we felt the duty to go see him. But how? She was disfellowshipped and we couldn't enter her home! The presbyters gave their consent and we visited them with my mother. She was such a polite woman that I felt sorry that I couldn't talk to her more often. I never saw her after this, yet I was informed of her death a short time later. I don't remember in my entire life being so devastated by any other death!

According to the teaching of the Society, all the dead would resurrect except the disfellowshipped and the impious! Up until then, my sadness for anyone dying was the sadness of a temporary separation, regardless of how long it would be. At some point, however, we would stand together again side by side on this very earth! But this was not the case with this woman. Her life had expired forever! She would never again see the light of the sun! Everything, every aspect of her life was forever lost, without hope or meaning. Darkness! Inexistence! Terror! These emotions flooded my soul when I learned about her death. Death never appeared to me to be so terrible! I remember crying like never before, more so than at the death of my father. And to think that I couldn't even pray for her! The Society forbade us to pray for the living disfellowshipped, and that ban applied much more so for those deceased. It is strange to me now, but at the time I did not think of this.

If I cried and grieved for that disfellowshipped woman, whom I had only seen once, how would her Creator react? He Who followed her all through her life and had her as His child? He Who is Love?[119] As the speaker continued, all these thoughts overtook my mind with a new intensity, with a new meaning. The purpose of

---

119 1 John 4:8

my visit to the Evangelicals was very successful! I knew this now!

God shows no partiality, but in every nation whoever fears him and works righteousness is accepted by Him.[120] I was no longer afraid of disfellowship. I knew that God would accept me wherever I was as long as I tried according to the level of my abilities given to me by His Grace. He would accept me, the same way He would accept that woman for whom I had cried so much back then, just like He would accept this Evangelical woman who was crying in front of me! For me He was no longer the punishing God who looks for an opportunity to destroy His creations. He was a loving Father, full of the most guileless, most forgiving, most perfect love. He was Love Himself! I don't know exactly what the shepherd of the Evangelicals was saying on that given day, but I do know what my Heavenly Shepherd had in mind for all His creation, and especially for me as I awaited my disfellowship.

The District Convention

THIS WAS A period of great inner struggle for me. It is almost impossible to convey in to words how difficult it is for a Witness to make the jump and exit the Society. Since infancy it was drilled in to my mind that the world was divided into two camps: God's society and satan's camp. Now, however, careful historical and biblical research removed my blindness. Where, then, could I go? The anxiety paralyzed me! I kept my position in the Society, all the while desperately seeking guidance and direction from God.

I didn't want to make any hasty moves. I wanted to give the Society the benefit of the doubt and the opportunity to prove me wrong. If the devil had gotten the best of me, I wouldn't want to find myself outside the Society of God. On the other hand, if the

---

120 Acts 10:34-35

9. Exodus

outcome of my research was correct, and I simply stepped out, I would be shunned by everyone as an apostate and all association with my family and relatives would be lost, perhaps forever. The incident with my wife served all too well as a reminder of this. Perhaps, I was thinking, if I could prove my position on the 1914 dogma to higher ranking members, if I could convince at least the board of elders, the situation would potentially become official and my wife would perhaps begin to recognize the problems in the organization.

Somewhat naively, I also wrote a letter to the Governing Body. Within it I referred to the results of my studies, and my hope and request to present the truth to the people of my faith. I did not expect a response since I sent the letter anonymously. What I hoped for was to motivate the Governing Body to correct the false dogma, thereby exhausting all possible cause for abandoning my religion.

In the meanwhile, the annual district convention came; I felt that this would be the last one I would attend as my situation would be revealed. Vlassis, the kind presiding elder of the neighboring congregation, as promised, spoke to Mr. Bananis about me and suggested he talk to Vourlakis, the circuit overseer. Mr. Vourlakis was a decent man, different from those leading the Greek Bethel. He would keep my plight to himself and at the same time cover all those who had become involved up to that point. Vlassis checked the convention program for the impending change of the 1914 dogma by the Society.

Pandora's Church

BY NOW, HOWEVER, my research into the 1914 dogma, had led me to reevaluate dozens of other topics! Very importantly, I realized that the Society's claim of being the channel of God and "His mouthpiece" on earth is based on circular logic. In short it goes like this: The kingdom of God was established in heaven in 1914, that the "time of the end" began that year, that Christ returned invisibly at that time to "inspect" the Christian denominations, and that He finally rejected all of them except for the Watch Tower Society and its associates, which He in 1919 appointed as his sole "instrument" on earth. Since, however, the date of 1914 is false, Watchtower's contentions to be the mouthpiece of God is also groundless.[121] Nevertheless, all Witnesses are compelled to unquestionably believe in 1914 without any proof, only because so said the "Society of God!" To top it off, Raymond Franz, a former Governing Body member, wrote what disturbed him the most was men in the upper echelon at Brooklyn headquarters that did not have full confidence in the 1914 predictions![122]

I was now able to see that the Watchtower could not back up its grand claims of being the channel and the mouthpiece of God; in essence, it had no right to infallibility. Having come thus far, other things were slowly coming under biblical scrutiny and critical reevaluation. *Failed Prophecies.* Doesn't the Watchtower discredit the Bible by making authorized repeated failed predictions about the end of the world?[123] Yet when Armageddon failed to happen in 1975, the Society blamed the brothers for "they have missed the point of the Bible's warnings concerning the end this system of things, thinking that Bible chronology reveals the specific date."[124] *New Light theory.* Divine truths are eternal, yet the Watchtower's teachings are getting "hotfixes" all the time. Is it really Jehovah that gives conflicting "spiritual food at the proper time" or is it the Watchtower that makes mistakes but refuses responsibility and passes the blame on to God? *Watchtower's History.* If the Watchtower Society has the

---

121 Carl Olof Jonsson, The So-Called "Bible Chronology" of the Watch Tower Society,, retrieved 3/6/2009 from http://user.tninet.se/~oof408u/fkf/english/chronology.htm
122 Franz, *Crisis*, pp. 259–260
123 Franz, *Crisis*, p. 250
124 WT 7/15/76 p.440

truth, why then does it discourage its members from accessing its history and older publications? Is it, perhaps, to hide its past mistakes—say, for example, Russell's beliefs in pyramidology,[125] and Rutherford's insistence that vaccination is "a crime, an outrage, and a delusion,"[126] and "as effective as the totem pole"[127] that affected the quality of life of thousands of Witnesses for thirty years? In a similar vein, what would I do if my children were to need a *blood transfusion*? Is this a truly Scriptural command, or is it another Watchtower teaching that would get "hotfixed" into oblivion in a few years? *Isolation.* Why does the Watchtower discourage its members from speaking with "wordly" people, and forbid communication with ex-members? Is it, perhaps, to shield them from exposure from becoming disenchanted?

Many issues were slowly becoming disquieting for me and I understood that I would not be able to stay for long in the Watchtower Society. Where could I go? Not yet knowing much about Church history and the Orthodox Church, I assumed that after the "apostasy" of the first Church, God had continued to maintain His Church scattered among the Christian religions. I considered all these churches to be schools leading toward God and thus members of His Society. So when the Witnesses asked me if I believed that my religion is the Society of God, I believed it so. But at the same time, I didn't say that I had accepted this to be true for all the other "Christian" churches!

Likewise, if they asked me whether I had contact with apostates, I answered in the negative simply because *I really did not consider them apostates*! In this way time passed without my having serious friction with the Society. I knew that lack of faith in God was

---

125 See, for example, the book *Thy Kingdom Come*, 1891, p. 313–376
126 Golden Age 5/1/1929 p. 502
127 Golden Age 9/17/1930 p.814

forgiven. Lack of faith in the Society, however, was punished by disfellowship, and this was not at all an exaggeration.

Almost immediately after the district convention, the circuit assembly commenced. These assemblies are much smaller than conventions, as only the congregations of the local circuit would participate. Thus, while the convention took place outdoors, the assembly took place indoors, in a big room. It was at this circuit assembly that Vlassis had planned to speak to Vourlakis.

This was a good idea because the program called for a week long visit from Kerveris, our district overseer as well. Since a district overseer has many circuits to which he must attend to, it was a very rare visit. In all truth, Kerveris was a problematic overseer, methodically avoided by everyone. He was disfellowship-happy, like a referee with a red card. But now, at least he could personally see that I was not an enemy of the Society of God. This was true because at the time I still considered it part of the "pan-Christian organization of God." I only wanted to have the truth shine forth.

One definite advantage counted on by Vlassis was that I had an active role in the assembly program, and when speaking to Vourlakis, he would present me as a faithful member of the Society with successful participation at its conventions. So, while I was in front of the audience, Vlassis drew next to Vourlakis and mentioned to him, "Pay close attention to the brother who is speaking now… I will tell you something about him afterwards!"

Later he took him aside and made him aware of my problem. He, in turn, showed understanding and agreed to secrecy.

Inquisition

THE WEEK BEFORE the arrival of Messrs. Kerveris and Vourlakis passed quickly. I was not very nervous, since Mr. Vourlakis assured me that Mr. Kerveris would be uninformed. Initially, they visited

9. Exodus

our neighboring congregation on the island of Salamina; Mr. Vourlakis had left and only the district overseer, Mr. Kerveris, came to our congregation.

Everything seemed calm. No one was speaking about me, and the district overseer seemed to be indifferent. According to the by-laws of the society, the visit of the District Overseer in each congregation lasts a week. It was now already Saturday, and thus, the week was almost over! One more day and then I would be off the hook!

It was summer, late in the day. The sun had just set and I was sleeping on a recliner in the coolest part of the house, the patio. I don't recall what kind of dream I was having, but I'm certain it was incomparably better than the nightmare I faced after my rude awakening. All of a sudden, the presiding elder of my congregation, Mr. Klakas, appeared next to me. "Niko, wake up! Mr. Kerveris is looking for you! I think he knows everything!" he said.

I instantly opened my eyes. "He wants me now?" I asked.

"He is waiting for you," he replied.

I changed, took my Bible and then proceeded to leave with Mr. Klakas, under the anxious eyes of my wife. Mr. Kerveris was waiting in the Hall with two other elders. We greeted each other and sat down. Mr. Kerveris opened the discussion.

"I have known about Nikos' circumstances from the moment I stepped foot into your Hall. I waited until today, however, expecting the elders of the church to bring it to my attention. Why have you kept silent all these days?" he (with noticeable austerity in his voice) asked Mr. Klakas, my father-in-law, and Mr. Manolis—the three elders of my church.

My father-in-law exchanged a puzzled look with Manolis. Mr. Klakas proceeded to speak. "I was the only one made aware of this, but I didn't consider it necessary to inform the others, especially since the matter was rectified. We ran it by Mr. Vlassis, and even through our circuit overseer, who advised us that since brother Nikos does not doubt the Society, it is resolved," Mr. Klakas said defensively.

"In this case, we must inform the other two elders here about what is happening!" Mr. Kerveris said, and he asked Mr. Klakas to give an account of all he recollected from the beginning until the present.

My father-in-law and Mr. Manolis were surprised to hear why I resigned from the ministerial service. However Mr. Klakas tried to make things easier by concluding again that our circuit overseer was aware of this.

Yet, the district overseer cut him off, "...and elder Vourlakis passed this information on to me. However, *you,* Mr. Klakas did not deal with this responsibly! According to the by-laws, initially this information should have been revealed to the *board of the elders** of the local congregation, and then to me! Mr. Vourlakis, as circuit overseer, was obliged to start with me as the one directly responsible!"

Then he turned to me. "So what do you have to say about all this?"

"Brother," I began, "as you know I was born into the Society, like my father. I don't have another religion in which to believe. My wife, my relatives and my friends are members of the Society. I don't wish therefore to find myself outside the Society. The only thing I requested from the beginning was to have a discussion with a brother and have him show me where the mistake is in my research. I have concluded, based on the Holy Scriptures, that the desolation of Jerusalem took place in 587 B.C. and not 607 B.C. I won't persist, however, if someone points out my error! All the brothers who have become aware of my problem up to now refuse to discuss it with me. Therefore, if you would accept to listen to me and correct me, then this problem would be easily resolved."

"No! I also refuse to discuss an apostatic subject. You must forget everything you have read and believe what the *Watchtower* writes!" he said, and while turning to the others continued, "And now I will ask all of you something. What is the most important resource we have in the Society?"

He waited a few seconds for a response, but since no one dared answer, he continued, "Many would say that it is the Holy Scriptures. Not exactly! Our most important resource is the *Watchtower*."

I threw a side-ways glance toward Mr. Klakas and fought to keep from breaking out in laughter. He was opening and closing his eyes in shock from these last words of the overseer. He gave me the impression that he was questioning himself whether he had heard correctly. Of course, I was not surprised in the least by this claim of Kerveris because I had already surmised this. However, I did not expect him to be so blunt.

Then he continued totally undaunted, "And this is because the *Watchtower* has helped us to enter the Society! All religions have the Holy Scriptures, but they don't understand it. We understand it because we have the *Watchtower*. Think about it! If you hand out one hundred Bibles to one hundred people, in a short time everyone will be giving their own interpretation! For this reason, we accept whatever the *Watchtower* says and thus we have unity as a faith."[128]

What an amazing philosophy, I thought. We sacrifice truth for the sake of union! This being the case, why shouldn't I have union with whatever other religion is around me? If union is everything, then my religion was erroneous in dividing itself from its mother organization, 'The Students of the Scriptures.'

---

[128] This statement sounds so ludicrous that one might be tempted to dismiss it as the opinion of an individual that doesn't express the Society's stand on the subject. However, a very similar answer was given by the leaders of the Watchtower Society in a formal inquiry by representatives of the British government in the "Douglas Walsh Trial." The trial, very little known to most Jehovah's Witnesses, produced a very illuminating testimony about the Society's policy-making which proves that its purpose is unity at all costs—unity even when this entails the enforced acceptance of a prophecy that the Society knows to be false! See a brief excerpt on pages 171–172. The full document is now in the public domain.

Excerpts from the Douglas Walsh Case

UNITY AT ALL COSTS

In 1954 the Watchtower Society leaders were called in Scotland to testify in the Douglas Walsh Vs, the Right Honourable James Latham Clyde, MP., PC., Trial. Among them were F. Franz (Society's fourth president), and H. Covington (Society's Lawyer). The Watchtower officials tried to prove that Jehovah Witnesses were ministers and should be exempt from military conscription in Scotland. An excerpt follows from the cross examination of H. C. Covington by the British Government Counsellor.

Q. Is it not vital to speak the truth on religious matters?
A. It certainly is.
Q. You have promulgated—forgive the word—false prophecy?
A. We have. I do not think we have promulgated false prophecy, there have been statements that were erroneous, that is the way I put it, and mistaken...

...

Q. That was the publication of false prophecy?
A. That was the publication of a false prophecy, it was a false statement or an erroneous statement in fulfilment of a prophecy that was false or erroneous.
Q. And that had to be believed by the whole of Jehovah's Witnesses?
A. Yes, because you must understand, we must have unity, we cannot have disunity with a lot of people going every way, an army is supposed to march in step.
Q. Back to the point now, a false prophecy was promulgated?
A. I agree to that.
Q. It had to be accepted by Jehovah's witnesses?

Excerpts from the Douglas Walsh Case (cont.)

A. That is correct.
Q. If a member of Jehovah's witnesses took the view himself that prophecy was wrong, and said so, would he be disfellowshipped?
A. Yes, if he said so, and kept on persisting in creating trouble, because if the whole organization believes one thing, even though it be erroneous, and somebody else starts on his own trying to put his ideas across, then there is a disunity and trouble, there cannot be harmony, there cannot be marching… Our purpose is to have unity.
Q. Unity at all costs?
A. Unity at all costs, because we believe and are sure that Jehovah God is using our organization, the governing body of our organization, to direct it, even though mistakes are made from time to time.
Q. A unity based on an enforced acceptance of false prophecy?
A. That is conceded to be true.
Q. And the person who expresses his view, as you say, that it was wrong, and was disfellowshipped, would be in breach of the covenant, if he was baptized?
A. That is correct.
Q. And as you said yesterday expressly, would be worthy of death?
A. I think…
Q. Would you say yes or no?
A. I will answer yes, unhesitatingly.
Q. Do you call that religion?
A. It certainly is.
Q. Do you call that Christianity?
A. I certainly do.

Editor: *We believe that further comments are unnecessary.*

After Kerveris mentioned a few more outlandish philosophies, he asked me, "Do you believe that this is *the* Society of God?

"Of course," I answered, without volunteering that back then I considered this to be the case with all Christian religions.

"Then you must accept what the Society tells you without doubt," he said triumphantly and sat back in his chair with the air of victory.

"Yes, brother, but the Society has *adjusted** many things in the past. Since I have evidence that something is different, how can I believe the exact opposite?" I responded.

"Just wait in the ark! If you are right, the Society will announce it."

"But this is precisely what I am doing," I said.

I caught him off guard! He looked at me confused.

"Nonetheless, I must file a report to the Branch office about you, and I hope that this topic goes no further," he said, and motioned to me that I was free to leave.

I imagined that he probably proceeded to skewer Mr. Vlassis and Mr. Klakas. Fortunately, they had covered themselves since they had at least revealed this to our circuit overseer. Thus, I left the building and headed home.

From the very moment my father-in-law found out what was happening, he made contact with his friends at Bethel and put their minds at ease, attempting to convince them that there was nothing with which to be concerned, and it seemed that his endeavors were successful for quite a long time.

In the meantime, until the next nuisance, I continued to study. Additionally, I organized in writing not only Jonsson's conclusions, but pertinent information based on my own research. I studied all the literature of the Society pertaining to 1914, written over the last 40 years, even in foreign languages. I went as far as to recruit my mother-in-law to translate some of the books for me. Thus, I had rebuttals to all the arguments that could possibly be used by any

Witness on the subject. I collected all the information in a notebook and organized it in to chapters in the form of a book.

At a certain point, Mr. Vlassis told me what had happened with Mr. Vourlakis, who was heard saying, "That shrewd Mr. Vlassis; he came to tell me this so that he could exonerate himself and throw all the responsibility on me! However, if something goes haywire, I will be burned! So I had better tell Mr. Kerveris."

So they were all passing the buck, and no one dared to discuss the subject of 1914 with me.

The next annoying interrogation came from the Hellenic Bethel in the form of a letter. It was seeking confirmation from the local board of elders of my belief in the Society of God. The elders summoned me one more time and I responded with the same deceptive answer. They interrogated me as to whether I had had contact with apostates, and I responded negatively. That's all I needed—to consider my friends apostates! I proceeded to ask one more time for someone to listen to my arguments and they all refused.

The subject was becoming funny, tragically funny! The only concern of those people was if I believed in the Society. Mr. Klakas, wishing to corner me, asked me shrewdly, "But if you don't accept the dogma of 1914, how can you accept the Society?"

"I accept it," I answered nonchalantly, "Why are you fixated on the Society? The problem is with 1914!"

"But it is indispensable to the subject of the Society," Mr. Klakas insisted, who apparently had understood that the claim of our belonging to the Society of God is solely based on this date.

"Then, let this work itself out naturally! Don't try to force it," I told him, and he kept staring in deep thought.

The elders sent a reassuring letter to Bethel and I was spared once again. Some of my friends who knew the situation would comment, "What kind of connections do you have, buddy?" "If I were in your position they would have cut me off one hundred times!" "Here they annoy me for mere nonsense, imagine if I didn't believe in the dogma of 1914!"

In reality, I knew that they were being truthful. However, I was going to push this to the very end! I was buying time to learn even more; and on the other hand, I was not yet ready to find myself in the tempestuous sea of marital strife. My wife was already living in fear and avoided speaking with me about 1914 after my meeting with Mr. Kerveris. Thus, I was expecting the worst.

Mr. Theoharakis

SIX MORE MONTHS went by and a visit of yet another district overseer was announced. That sounded strange to me because the previous one had not finished his two-year term. My disfellowshipped friends, when they heard his name, forewarned me that he was coming especially for me because they utilized him in similar situations. His name was Mr. Theoharakis. My friend George had been disfellowshipped for a number of accusations but especially for calling Theoharakis "harsh"—and that accusation had been grounds for disfellowship! From the first day of Theoharakis' arrival, he would say, "You know I do love you!"

One day before his week-visit's end, he asked me to appear before the board of elders. There were the three elders of the local congregation and him, the district overseer. I was about to taste his "love."

"What do I hear, brother?" he said. "You are a false teacher."

Character attack is a classic Watchtower "quick-fix" when no arguments can be found. "Pure gossip, brother," I replied in jest. "A false teacher is anyone who teaches things contrary to the Holy Scriptures! However, I don't lose sight of the Scriptures."

"Then why don't you believe the dogma of 1914?" he asked.

"Simply because no one has come forth to show me where I

erred. If you would like to, brother, I would be most appreciative of your help," I said.

"That is not my responsibility," he said.

"Then whose is it? Not a single person wishes to discuss this topic with me. Must someone come from Bethel? Why can't we discuss it here and now?"

"What exactly is it that you want? To speak about 1914? No way! If you wish, we will speak about the Society," he replied.

"Brother, everyone tells me the same thing! Yet I don't have a problem with the Society, but with the dogma of 1914," I said.

"If you accept the Society, then you also have to accept whatever it says."[129]

"But I don't differ from the Society," I added quickly, to trap him, hoping to lure him into discussion. As it stood, I was convinced that no one would enter into a discussion about 1914. Thus, I would at least get the satisfaction for which I yearned, even by trickery.

"What do you mean?" Theoharakis nibbled at the bait, while all others witnessed our dialogue in silence.

"I am saying that Jesus Christ became king at A.D. 33, and not in 1914, and this is what the Society says!" I responded.

"Where does the organization say *this*?" he asked, bewildered.

I took out the book with the unfortunate title, *Reasoning from the Scriptures*.[130] There it wrote the following: "Jesus Christ became king over His church in A.D. 33."

"Yes! But it says 'over *His* church;' in 1914 He became king over

---

[129] According to Fred Franz, the second President of the Watchtower Society an individual member does *not* have the right to come to his own view as to the proper interpretation of the Holy Scriptures. On the contrary, he has to accept as authoritative the instructions in the "Watchtower," "Informant," and "Awake" magazines (*Walsh Trial*, pp. 122-123).

[130] Watchtower Society, 1985. The 446-pages book is designed as a quick dogmatic reference, arranged by topic, for use in Bible speeches and evangelizing activities.

the *nations*," he said, pulled into the discussion.

Now the moment was at hand for my knockout punch. "Then why does Holy Scripture write that He also became king over the nations at A.D. 33?" I asked, pretending I didn't know.

Theoharakis swallowed the bait and asked, "Where does Scripture say that?"

I had already opened the Book of Revelation 2:26-27 and proceeded to read the words of the Lord, "and he who overcomes… I will give power over the nations. And he shall rule them with a rod of iron… as I also have received from my Father."

"Do you see? Jesus Christ had already become king over the nations, back when Revelation was being written! He had already received authority over the nations!" I said triumphantly, while he was left staring at his Scripture.

Suddenly and very unexpectedly he sprung up and, closing the Holy Scriptures, said "You asked for Caesar, to Caesar you shall go!"[131] he said, while exiting the room and leaving me with the elders.

They in turn told me that I could leave. I knew well what was behind the words of Festus, when the Apostle Paul appealed to Caesar. These words led him to Rome, to his death. In this same manner, I had appealed to Bethel, in hopes that someone from there would accept my invitation for a discussion. This gave Theoharakis the chance to dodge responsibility by directing me to Bethel as per my appeal. I knew that like Paul it was the final route before the end. After his final talk on Sunday, I never saw Theoharakis until his death.

Considering Whether to Discuss the Dogma

TRUE TO HIS promise, Theoharakis submitted an appeal request. Fortunately, Korfias had been removed from his position due to an

---

131 See Acts 25:12

outcry on his activities and a more reasonable leadership had been installed in the Greek Bethel. The new leadership asked some clarifying questions from the elders of my congregation especially if I believed in the Society. To my great surprise, the Greek Bethel sent a letter allowing the elders to discuss the matter with me.

Apparently, the fact that I still believed in the Society made me seem an easy victim in such a discussion. However, not all the elders shared my enthusiasm.

Actually, as the designated day for the debate drew near, an unprecedented battle between the elders of my congregation took place. The presiding elder, Mr. Klakas, and my father-in-law really wanted to escape the discussion. Only one rejoiced, Michael, who had said to me, "If they cut you off without trying to give you an answer, I will resign," and he meant it!

I was hoping Vlassis would be present in their little feud, yet he was not permitted, since he belonged to a different congregation.

Nonetheless, Vlassis, who had more foresight and understood that it was the end of the road for me, desperately tried to win me over by bringing an elderly district overseer who offered to discuss the matter. This informal discussion would happen before the debate with the board of elders.

I accepted Vlassis' kind offer. Attending that informal discussion were that elderly district overseer, Vlassis, Michael, and me. It took place at the home of my in-laws. What became evident, however, was that they had no intention of hearing my arguments, but were trying once more to convince me on "safe grounds," telling me only what they considered beneficial.

Therefore, the former overseer began to analyze the dogma of 1914 for me in exactly the way he would analyze it for an inquirer.

"Excuse me, brother," I interrupted, "I know these things! I want your answers in other areas! You must listen to me and answer me based on the verses I will give you!"

"What's there to hear, my son? I will tell you what the Society says and you will understand it!" he replied.

I was really hoping for Vlassis to take over. He was among the few who possessed the intellectual clarity that would enable him to understand the subject in depth. But even Vlassis began to lose his temper from the manner in which the elderly overseer was approaching the subject. That old man continued to speak nonsense not giving Vlassis a chance, who in the meantime began to fume. Something needed to be done.

I needed to dive into the discussion and take hold of the conversation, because he had no intention of stopping and listening to me. It was imperative for Vlassis to hear my arguments, since he was giving me this opportunity himself.

"According to verse 21:24 in Luke, the 'Times of the Nations' began at 607 B.C." the overseer said.

"Just a minute, brother! Nothing is mentioned there about 607! This verse refers to the fall of Jerusalem at A.D. 70," I blurted out.

Vlassis looked anxious, realizing that I was ready to jump in.

"What are you talking about, my son?" the overseer said, and continued to talk while Vlassis continued his loud exhaling.

"Brother, I cannot proceed until my present objection is answered!" I interrupted him again.

Vlassis used this opportunity to enter the discussion. "How do you know, Niko, that this verse refers to A.D. 70?" he asked.

"Even though I could likewise ask you, how you know it refers to 607 B.C., I will answer you. Firstly, as I stated earlier, the Lord speaks about the fall of Jerusalem which would occur in His time. Secondly, if He were speaking about the fall of 607 B.C., then from A.D. 66 and for an ample time after the withdrawal of the Roman armies, Jerusalem was free. Therefore, if the "Times of the Nations" had begun in 607 B.C., they would have finished in A.D. 66 Finally, to put it very simply, the two-versed translation of the Society analyzes this verse: 'Up until the time of the nations (gentiles) WILL BE and become fulfilled.' This means that the 'Time of the Nations' didn't exist, they had not started yet."

"Are these the arguments you were claiming to have against 1914?" Vlassis asked.

"These are the most insignificant. I have verses that place the year of the fall of Jerusalem at 587 B.C.," I said.

But at this point the overseer jumped in to continue his "poem" from where he had left off and he didn't stop again until Vlassis stormed out like an engine ready to explode.

A little later, I sensed that I was simply wasting my time, and the discussion ended ingloriously without getting a single answer to any of my questions. So we parted ways, leaving me to wait for the debate.

The days passed and the discussion with the elders was almost at hand. Yet, I began to sense that Bethel had left it to the discretion of the elders whether or not they would discuss the dogma of 1914 with me. Actually out of the three only Michael was looking forward to it, while the other two were scrambling for an exit. One of them said characteristically, "If Nikos convinces the board of elders that he is correct, I prefer not to be there!"

When I heard this I made it known to the others, because I wished all of them to be present. I further elaborated to them my feeling that each one was looking to shift the blame to the others so that if I were to convince them, he would criticize the others for being convinced and would remain unscathed in the eyes of Bethel. Thus, I convinced them all to participate.

The one I had the most difficulty with was my father-in-law, who was a man without much spiritual clarity and obviously could not comprehend the seriousness of the situation. I remember the evening after the last Kingdom meeting before the discussion with the elders, I went up to him at the end and shouted, "You should be ashamed of yourself! Your son-in-law is headed for disfellowship and you don't show any concern! Instead of you showing some concern, as the presiding elder, you are looking for a way to avoid the discussion!"

At this point, my mother-in-law came on the scene and reminded us that the brothers were listening. After this confrontation, he finally accepted. If I could convince the board of elders, the situation would become very serious and Bethel would be unable to cut me off without consequences. The subject would take on such dimensions as to cause everyone to know about the lie of 1914.

Finally, Discussing the Dogma!

THE BIG EVENING finally arrived! I took with me four large bags of books. I had gathered everything I would possibly need to convince them of my position. Added to my arsenal were plenty of volumes and encyclopedias of the Society, which were readily available in the Hall.

When they saw me with the books, one of them smiled mockingly, the other looked at me inquisitively, and the third looked at me anxiously. This last was Mr. Klakas, who would preside over the discussion. After the initial prayer request to have God help me understand the truth, Mr. Klakas initiated a lengthy analysis as to the meaning of apostasy and labeled as apostate one who does not believe in the dogma of the Society.[132] Based on that, he began to discuss if we ought to have a discussion at all.

"But if an apostate is considered someone who does not believe in the dogmas of the Society, then we must not have a discussion

---

[132] That's the official line of the Society; according to the secret manual for the Elders, "persons who deliberately spread (stubbornly hold to and speak about) teachings contrary to Bible truth *as taught by Jehovah's Witnesses* are apostates." [emphasis added] (*Pay Attention to Yourselves and All the Flock*, 1991, p.94)

9. Exodus

with any non-Witness," I said.

"This is not the same!" he said, and continued.

I was anxiously looking at the clock and seeing the time moving along without yet having begun the discussion.

The subject for one and a half hours was "if we should discuss." Fed up, I stood up and lifted the first stack of books off the floor.

"Where are you going?" Klakas asked, quite nervous.

"I'm leaving! We came here to discuss 1914, and after ninety minutes you haven't decided yet if we should even discuss it," I tensely answered.

"Come, sit down! All right," he said, and as I sat down again he continued, "Perhaps, though, we should give some thought as to whether we should discuss it."

I cut him off, "Did the office give you permission to discuss this?"

"Yes, but…"

"I'm leaving!" I said again and stood up.

"Okay, okay, sit down and we'll discuss it," he said, "but let's be brief because too much time has passed."

"That's not my fault," I said. "You shouldn't have been so long-winded! Now you'll hear what I have to say, even though I have to cut down my analysis on some things due to the brevity of time!"

Finally, for another hour and a half, I built up my case. During all that time, I sensed that my father-in-law could not understand a thing. Mr. Klakas was looking at his watch every so often and I'm certain that he was not as attentive as he should have been. The only one who was very attentive—and understood everything—was Michael. He would even interrupt me at some points and continue my thought, saying exactly what I had wanted to say!

A small segment from the beginning of my monologue was indicative of the ensuing climate.

I was quoting a verse from Jeremiah 25:12. After I read a few phrases, I would ask them if they agreed with my interpretation. The interpretation of these verses was so clear that they were constantly telling me "we agree."

"Then it will come to pass, when seventy years are completed that I will punish the King of Babylon and that nation, the land of the Chaldeans for their iniquity, says the Lord and I will make it perpetual desolation."

"So when the 70 years of slavery of these surrounding nations would be complete, the Lord would destroy Babylon! Do you agree?"

"We agree," they answered.

"Oh no, brothers! You cannot possibly agree! The Society talks much differently here!" I shouted, with an artificial indignant tone, while I could hardly keep myself from laughing.

"What does the Society say?" they asked very surprised.

I opened the book, *Thy Kingdom Come,* and read its commentary on the verse for them to hear. There it stated that the seventy years were completed two years AFTER the desolation of Babylon. All of us had agreed that the Holy Scriptures were saying that the seventy years were completed BEFORE the destruction of Babylon.

"Therefore, brothers what must I believe? What we all saw very clearly in the Holy Scriptures or what the Society teaches?" I asked.

"Come on! Keep going! Time is passing," Mr. Klakas said, to get out of the jam, and I let him slide.

As I continued, whenever I asked them if they agreed, Klakas answered for all of them, "Continue."

Apparently, he didn't want to find himself again in the unpleasant position of disagreeing with the Society.[133] Moreover, my evidence was so voluminous that it took an hour and a half just to

---

[133] "...'An overseer must be... loyal.' Such loyalty is demonstrated by "holding firmly to the faithful word" as expounded in the publications of Jehovah's modern Christian organization." (WT 2/1/83 p. 14)

refer to them collectively.

"So where is my mistake? Please show me and I will accept 1914 with all my heart!" I said at the very end.

"We haven't researched this subject so deeply! We will study it and we will call you again," Mr. Klakas said, speaking for the other two, and we left.

This, however, never happened.

On the way out, Michael repeated to me that if they cut me off without an answer, he would resign his position as elder. And, indeed, when they did cut me off, he kept his word! What I couldn't quite understand was how he could remain in the Society so many years after everything he had heard.

Committee from Bethel

SHORTLY THEREAFTER, INSTEAD of an answer from the board of elders, I received a message that a tri-member committee would soon visit me from Bethel. It was certain that this subject had reached a dead-end. They needed to shut me up at all costs. The Society was not disposed to telling the truth, so I completed my good-bye letter and made one hundred photocopies. Then I wrote a letter addressed to the elders of my congregation. I made enough copies for all those involved on the subject. In that letter, I reminded them of their responsibilities toward God and men. I also hid a micro-cassette recorder in my briefcase. I knew that after the final committee meeting the masks would fall and the lies against me would begin about the details of the last meeting.

When that day finally came, my wife was in a horrible psychological state. Overcome by blind fanaticism, she was accusing me of being to blame for everything that was happening to me, because I didn't accept what the Society of God was telling me. My mother and grandmother were waiting for the outcome of the meeting with great anxiety. My own psychological state was not any better, but I was determined. I would faithfully adhere to the truth, regardless of the consequences for me and my family. My mother-in-law already warned me that if I were disfellowshipped, she would need to fire me from my job.

They asked me to go to the Hall of the neighboring congregation. They were most likely afraid of hidden microphones. However, the micro-cassette recorder implanted in my briefcase was ready to contradict all future fraudulent propaganda. I rode to the Hall on my motorcycle and took my books. As I entered, I could clearly see the mockery in their eyes. Apparently, they would not allow me the opportunity to prove them liars. I was relieved to see that Mr. Bananis and Mr. Vlassis would participate on the committee. I did not recognize the other two members. They introduced themselves and after a prayer, tailored to my situation, the committee began.

As usual, they began with telling me about the Society. They made it clear from the start that they would not discuss the dogma of 1914 because "it was their order from the Society." I fought hard to make them reconsider, hoping to pull them into discussing 1914. Now and then, they attempted to remind me how clean the Society is compared to the outside world. I knew, however, that the wheat field (church) would also have weeds up until the end! A clean organization did not exist anywhere. Mr. Bananis, encouraged by our relation by blood, was doing most of the talking.

"I have had so many blessed years in this Society!" he said.

"And I was born into it!" I answered him, repeating the words of Apostle Paul,[134] when he was revealing that he was a Roman citizen from birth.

"Look up the verse!" said one of the other two, trying to grasp

---

134 Acts 22:28

what I said, and he took me to the First Epistle of John 1:3, "That which was from the beginning, which we have seen and heard… we bear witness and declare…"

"Do you see?" he said to me. "You must accept the things you heard from the beginning, from your parents, about the true Society of God!"

"Just a minute!" I cut him off, "What does the verse say? About the things I heard from my parents? In other words, to 'let things be as we found them'? Haven't we been opposing this thinking all these years? No! The verse says something different! It says that the Gospel must remain unaltered, as taught by the Apostles from the beginning!"

"Of course," he hastened to agree.

"Thus, what did the Apostles teach? About the year 1914? Not at all! They were waiting for the Second Coming in the future! Then, what do we teach? Certainly not what the Apostles taught, as I have crystal clear evidence that the dogma of 1914 is a lie," I said, making him turn red when he realized that his argument had backfired!

The others were more careful. They avoided speaking from the Holy Scriptures. After this, I began to feel sorry for them! These people were in bondage to the Society, for the sake of which they were willing to trample the truth.

Up until that moment, I had been afraid of disfellowship. Then, however, I realized that I would be disappointed if they didn't disfellowship me. I no longer desired to be a member of such a base organization, which had no interest in the truth. All my boasting of being a Witness of Jehovah had turned into unbearable shame! The air inside the room was thick with filthy hypocrisies and lies. I wanted to leave, to go out into the fresh air, to feel free of oppression, to not allow anyone to compel me to speak lies ever again.

If the Watchtower claimed to be a group of humble Christians who were trying to understand the Scriptures, I could sympathize with any short-comings they would come up with. Instead they claim they are nothing short of God's only channel of communication on earth with man's salvation depending on blind obedience to them.

I remembered that one time I had felt compelled to openly lie to an Orthodox Christian. He was the church council member who was the companion of the blaspheming anti-heretical polemicist who was cursing Jesus Christ. The question was if all Christians should take Holy Communion or not. So I used the verse that stated "a man must test himself first and then partake from the cup of communion."

"You are lying! You know very well it's not so (according to your faith)!" the council member said and he was correct. However, at the time I believed that it was worth lying, to pull him out of Orthodoxy and make him a Witness, oblivious to the fact that my field service partner was witnessing everything! Thus, I knowingly lied to him! Perhaps that is how the committee members may have also felt, because they declared to me that they didn't care if the Society is right; I needed to submit.

From that moment on, I did away with the facade. I confessed to them that up to that point I had kept contact with the disfellowshipped, and that I did not consider them apostates. For me, apostates were all those who knowingly taught another Gospel. I expressed to them that I accept all the Christian religions as part of the church of God, as schools leading to God.

After this, the discussion took on a different dimension and tone. I was not simply defending my position but was explaining the half-truths I had been telling them all of this time so that they wouldn't think I was fooling them.

I was already feeling free! They began to criticize the apostates for a pile of things, which I contradicted as bad rumors and mudslinging, showing them the reality of things. Among other things, Mr.

9. Exodus

Bananis mentioned something related to my friend George that had been told to his committee, how he had seen Jesus Christ in a vision.

"Don't listen to him! He has lost it!" he said to me.

"I will ask him," I assured him.

Actually, the vision was real. George had confirmed this to me. No, he wasn't crazy at all. In reality, the Lord had strengthened George with the vision prior to his facing the imminent committee meeting! At the time, however, I did not believe in miracles biased by the Watchtower faith.

When we concluded our verbal exchange, they asked me to wait outside. In a few minutes, Mr. Vlassis came to call me back in to inform me of their decision. Before we entered, my dear friend hugged me for the last time, with the wish, "May God give you what they could not."

Truly, God was there with me on the long journey of my fervent search, and He has given me a hundred-fold far and beyond what I ever dreamt. Blessed be His name!

They announced that they must disfellowship me. I would have the right to appeal within one week.

"Would the appeal committee accept a discussion with me on the dogma of 1914?"

They laughed at my insistence.

"So you actually think that you will convince the committee? You are mistaken. They especially won't discuss anything with you! Their task is to see if our committee acted well," said Bananis.

So everything was finished! I needed to say something, to possibly awaken their dormant consciences. Perhaps it would be my last opportunity.

"Do you know what problems you will create in my family with my disfellowship?" I asked.

"Yes, but it must be this way!" they said. "If you want, you can

Displaying Christian Loyalty When a Relative is Disfellowshipped

"...Loyal Christians do not have fellowship with anyone who has been expelled from the congregation. But more is involved. God's word states that we should 'not even eat with such a man.' Hence, we also avoid social fellowship with an expelled person. This would rule out joining him in a picnic, party, or trip to the shops or theatre or sitting down to a meal with him in the home or at restaurant." (*Our Kingdom Ministry*, 08/2002 p. 3)

come to the meetings, sit in the back without speaking and without being spoken to. Perhaps at some point everything can be like before," someone said.

"You know well that this will never happen! If you failed to discuss with me now what I asked of you, how will it happen then? I only pray that God does not pay you back for what you've done! Of course I no longer believe this, but you believe that I will die in Armageddon if disfellowshipped. By signing my disfellowship you are killing me, without attempting to help me! I would not want to be in your position on the Day of Judgment!" I said, and they remained silent.

"By the way, I also learned something true while in the Society, that we must tell others the truth if their religion is fooling them. Now I am free! I'm sorry if this will create problems for you, but I feel it is my duty to inform all Witnesses about the lies told by the organization for all these years. It is my calling!"

The look on Bananis' face hardened. "Then you will be treated as an apostate," he said.

"It doesn't matter! God will strengthen me," I replied, as I went out into the fresh air.

Using the Final Opportunity

I JUMPED ONTO my motorcycle and headed toward my mother's house. "What happened?" She asked me very anxiously.

"They disfellowshipped me without being willing to discuss anything, either," I said.

"Then you are in the right!" she said, and embraced and kissed me.

I left the book bags there and hid the cassette and recorder. Then I grabbed the photocopied letters and took off. I went to all the homes of the Witnesses that I knew. I gave a copy of the letter to everyone. They didn't know of my disfellowship, so they accepted it thankfully. One lady, however, caught on, and when I gave her the letter she hugged me, certain that she would never see me again.

The distribution took a long time. I later found out that immediately after my disfellowship, Mr. Klakas visited as many people as he could, to tell them not to listen to me if I went to them. At one home, however, I thought of something different, so I saved it for the last house, a family where the husband hadn't been in the Society long. His wealthy father had disowned him for becoming a Witness, but he had remained steadfast to what he thought to be the truth so I needed to give him special attention. They welcomed me when I showed up at their door. The husband, his wife, and her brother were inside. "What brings you here?" they asked.

"I'm working the neighborhood and thought to stop and see you," I said and went inside. "You know, I found a man who has great knowledge of the Holy Scriptures!" I said, and sat down. "You can't imagine what he said to me!"

"What did he tell you?" they asked curiously.

"We were talking about 1914; I can give you the information, but I don't think you can guess the answer," I said.

"Go ahead, tell us!" they said with curiosity. Thus, I began a factual analysis for them from the Holy Scriptures, exposing the lies of the Society. At each argument they asked me for the answer since they did not have one. I told them that I would give them the answer at the end, because the answer is the same for all arguments. This conversation lasted about half an hour, during which time their curiosity was mounting regarding the answer—except for the husband, who at one point blew up in an angry tone. "Come on! Tell us so we can get this over with!" he said, and stood up. I suspected that he caught on and so I revealed my secret.

"The answer is that all these arguments are correct and the Society is wrong. These arguments are mine, and this morning I was disfellowshipped because the hierarchy did not want to discuss these things with me. Please forgive me for the game, but if I had told you the truth, you would not have listened to me. I felt obligated, though, to tell you the truth."

The woman and her brother were literally staring with their mouths open. The husband, however, became almost maniacal.[135]

---

[135] The husband's reaction was actually the one sanctioned by the Watchtower Society in such situations. "Regarding [the apostates], the psalmist said: 'Do I not hate those who are intensely hating you, O Jehovah, and do I not feel a loathing for those revolting against you? With a complete hatred I do hate them. They have become to me real enemies.' (Psalm 139:21, 22) It was because they intensely hated Jehovah that David looked on them with abhorrence. Apostates are included among those who show their hatred of Jehovah by revolting against Him. Apostasy is, in reality, a rebellion against Jehovah. Some apostates profess to know and serve God, but they reject teachings or requirements set out in His Word. Others claim to believe the Bible, but they reject Jehovah's organization and actively try to hinder its work. When they deliberately choose such badness after knowing what is right, when

9. Exodus 191

"Do you think you convinced us? You *didn't!* Did he convince you?" he asked his wife who was looking at him speechless. "Or you?" he asked his also speechless brother-in-law. "I was informed that you were headed for disfellowship and, as you were speaking, purposely paid no attention because I knew what you were up to!"

And with those words he opened the door, showing me that my time was up. I stood up, and bade them farewell. I expressed to them my sorrow that our relationship would not be the same as before, and after I handed them the envelope with my letter, I left. He assured me that they would rip it up and throw it out.[136]

I felt great sorrow for this man. The Society had destroyed within him all love for the truth and every trace of humility. He had sacrificed so much, only to end up a puppet. At that moment, I was not feeling sorry for what I would face upon my return home. I was feeling pity for the faithful of my former religion, whom I had begun to see as wind-up puppets, steam-rolled personalities in the hands of some unscrupulous and unconscionable small-time dictators.

I returned home late. I still had quite a few letters which I would mail shortly to all those whom I had not reached. I first went

---

the bad becomes so ingrained that it is an inseparable part of their makeup, then a Christian must hate (in the Biblical sense of the word) those who have inseparably attached themselves to the badness. True Christians share Jehovah's feelings toward such apostates; they are not curious about apostate ideas. On the contrary, they "feel a loathing" toward those who have made themselves God's enemies, but they leave it to Jehovah to execute vengeance." (WT 10/1/1993, p. 19)

136 The Watchtower Society had foreseen such situations and had given warning: "Now, what will you do if you are confronted with apostate teaching—subtle reasonings—claiming that what you believe as one of Jehovah's Witnesses is not the truth? For example, what will you do if you receive a letter or some literature, open it, and see right away that it is from an apostate? Will curiosity cause you to read it, just to see what he has to say? You may even reason: 'It won't affect me; I'm too strong in the truth. And, besides, if we have the truth, we have nothing to fear. The truth will stand the test.' In thinking this way, some have fed their minds upon apostate reasoning and have fallen prey to serious questioning and doubt. (Compare James 1:5-8.) So remember the warning at 1 Corinthians 10:12: 'Let him that thinks he is standing beware that he does not fall.'" (WT 3/15/1986) p. 12–14

by my mother-in-law's house. "What happened?" she said maliciously. I looked at her with pity.

Disfellowshipped

AT HOME, MY wife received me in a state of silence as a very heavy atmosphere took over the entire house. Her overall psychology had been shaken, and this would become obvious in the months to come. Often while standing she would break down in tears, and along with crying she would also start trembling. I couldn't console her, and was very concerned about her psychological and mental health. I was beginning to feel enraged with that organization! For the first time I was coming to realize what the Society really was: a mind control organization. As I started to feel free from its influence on me, I was watching how they were using my wife's troubles as a means to get to me. It was crazy! Instead of torturing me with the disfellowship, they were torturing a person of their own faith to such a degree that she was in danger of losing her mind!

The next day, my disfellowship and my letter distribution had become common knowledge. The board of elders of the congregation had also already received the special letter which I had distributed to them. When I saw my father-in-law, I greeted him as always.

"You will never greet me again," he growled. "You will never greet another brother again!"

"I won't greet you again if you so choose. But you don't have the right to decide for me what to do with the others!" I answered.

"No one wants you to greet them," he said.

"That's what you think! Some of them already kissed me when they heard that I was disfellowshipped," I told him.

"Who are they? You must tell me! This is serious, what they did!" he said angrily.

"Why? Do I have you as an elder?" I said cynically. The only

9. Exodus

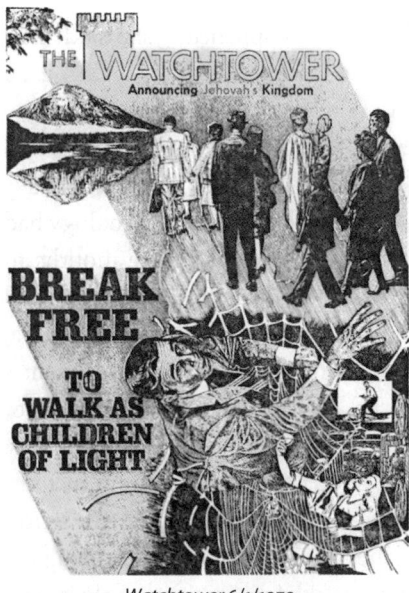
Watchtower 6/1/1979

thing he could still do to me was dismiss me from my job. But I didn't care anymore. I had made the decision to sacrifice everything for the sake of the truth, including my work, my family and even my life if necessary. The more I was persecuted the more reward I would have from God!

My father-in-law, following the directions of the Society, did not speak to me for months; yet he did not dismiss me from his business. It seems that deep inside him and his family, there was still some trace of conscience, or perhaps they saw that the more they fought me, the more I stung them and humiliated them to their peers. They decided to become more reconcilable. In reality, there came a time when my father-in-law sacrificed much to keep me at his business, yet he kept me on for eight more years!

It proved to be very beneficial that I had people who informed me about details of the elders' meetings. I found out that my father-in-law was attacked for keeping an apostate in his business. I found out as far as that went, that my father-in-law and Mr. Vlassis defended me, and that these ill-natured attacks did not prevail. The pressure, however, escalated when a newly appointed hot-headed circuit-overseer threatened my father-in-law and my brother-in-law that if they didn't fire me from my job they would lose their elder's privilege. It seems they kept postponing and buying time until the end of his term. At every one of his visits, he kept demanding my dismissal.

Eventually, I left work on my own, especially since God provided something better in the line of work and I no longer wanted to be a burden to my in-laws.

Shunned by Jehovah's Witnesses

IN THE BEGINNING almost all of my former co-faithful treated me inimically with minimal exceptions. They were taught that they would have to shun me in order to "bring me to my senses" and obtain Jehovah's favor. The truth is, they were shunning me because the Watchtower organization demands it and if they didn't they would be expelled by the only "family" they know. As time progressed, however, more and more of them began to timidly greet me in secret, when not seen by other Witnesses. Some of them would only greet me but not speak to me. Others would speak to me, but they would not greet me. Others would greet me and speak to me but not about religious subjects. There were also those who spoke to me only about religious topics in their attempt to make me return to the Society. Naturally, there were also those who wanted to learn the truth about the deceptiveness of the Society. I had frequent contact with them in person and by telephone.

There was a married couple which would not greet me when they were both together. However, when either spouse was alone, then I was offered a greeting! They were afraid of each other! The Society had instilled the element of fear in entire families. One could never know who was used for espionage. I had also served as a spy some time ago, when I believed that it was the will of God. There was a period where not a week would go by without turning someone in to the board of elders of the Society, simply because I didn't like something about his attitude or his life. Such endeavors, of course, were happily received by the elders of the Society.

After my disfellowship, however, I was no longer feared by those Witnesses who had plenty to hide from the Society. Being fully aware of my hatred toward the iniquitous system of the Society (not for the people it deceived), they spoke openly in front of me about things that they would never reveal to their brothers. Thus Witnesses who were fornicators, homosexuals, smokers, and drug-addicts spoke to me.[137] These were and still are active members of the Society, although they continued to be in bondage to their passions, without daring to talk about their problems to the elders for fear of disfellowship. Some of them intensified their way of life, believing that they would perish in the coming Armageddon, and consequently, they needed to "enjoy life as much as possible up to that point." They believed that God had written them off and they were therefore in a state of religious despair.

I explained to them that God continued to love them and that He would continue to help them to overcome their passions according to the degree of their efforts. The very fact that they were still aware of their fallen state was proof that the grace of God had not abandoned them totally. I explained to them that there isn't just black and white but an infinite variation of gray shades. In other words, we don't have only eternal life and eternal annihilation, but there is an infinite gradated scale, consequential to our present life, which will be manifest during the time of the Last Judgment, when we will receive our new, resurrected spiritualized bodies.[138]

God would not be just if He punishes the liar and the unrepentant murderer or sadist with the same punishment, i.e., annihilation, according to the teaching of the Society. In reality, there is no annihilation. The final outcome will be different for everyone. I would show them the verse which states that some will be beaten

---

[137] These are offenses that are punished by disfellowship from the Society.

[138] 1 Cor. 15:38-44

with many stripes, and others with few,[139] and then they understood that it was a mistake to sink deeper into sin. Some of them found the strength to struggle despite their moral decline, thus benefiting their souls. The iniquitous teaching of the Society until then had kept pushing them into more and deeper sin. The Society, however, was only interested in providing a grand outer appearance to those outside, and was not interested in the salvation of the people it deceived.

Despite the magnanimous contentions and boastful fanfare of the Society, its members are no different than any other people except that they carry out their sins in secret. Even though they give the impression to those outside that they are full of unity and love, they have their constant quarrels and their own rancor and cliques. There are disagreements and disputes between families, employers and employees, not to mention a lot of gossiping. They deny some the opportunity to do field work either because they lack proficiency or they do harm with the things they say or with their attitude, or (worse yet) because they are too old and aren't popular among the Witnesses. Personally, I have seen people crying because they were denied field work, the most basic function of the congregation, making them feel inferior and worthless.

Today, after almost a decade, just a few Witnesses continue to not speak to me. On the day of my disfellowship, long-term close friendships were utterly destroyed. Years needed to elapse before my wife and I returned to our happy state. During the initial months, she was seeing her friends go to the meetings with their husbands while she had to go alone. No one was coming to our home to visit because I was disfellowshipped, and she would go by herself anywhere she happened to be invited. We would only go out together if there were no Witnesses around.

---

139 Luke 12:47-48

The biggest crisis, however, concerned my son. The Society indoctrinates children from infancy. Thus my wife was taking him to the meetings even after I was disfellowshipped. There, they were telling him, "Your daddy is worldly. He will die in Armageddon. You must not pray with him. You must not listen to him when he speaks to you about God. When he speaks to you about God, you must shut your ears!"

They instilled the fear in him that if he speaks to me about God, he would also die in Armageddon. Thus, at the beginning of my disfellowship my religious isolation in my own home was absolute.

Spiritual searching outside the Society

FROM MY EARLIEST memories of this world, I had always participated in some gathering. I enjoyed being in the company of the people of my faith and took great satisfaction in learning new things. All this, however, changed totally after my disfellowship. The need for finding a church to attend for services and companionship was intense. At first I attended the Evangelical gatherings. But I was not satisfied by what I heard. The teaching primarily dealt with some superficial analysis of scriptural verses with exhortations for a more Christian life. But I was mainly annoyed by the doctrine of the Trinity. As many times as I brought it up to their preacher, he lacked the necessary answers. Thus I made my visits to them more seldom. I kept occasional contact with George, mainly via telephone. Regarding the Christoula gatherings, they were too far out of my way.

The Resignation of my Mother

AT THAT TIME, I had a dream which left an impression on me that I remember to this day. I dreamt that I was outside a high building, which was a Kingdom Hall of the Witnesses, with my mother and grandmother standing next to me. In the dream I did not remember that I was disfellowshipped, so logically we should have walked inside the Hall. Instead, however, we needed to pass through an extremely narrow path around the Hall. I was walking in front, followed by my mother, and behind her, my grandmother. I helped them and we finished this path. At the end, we were possibly the only ones out of all those whom I saw that did not enter the building. A year later, I understood that perhaps what I saw was the difficult journey of disfellowship, initially for me, and afterward with my help, my mother, and subsequently that of my nearly ninety-year-old grandmother.

A few days after my disfellowship, Vlassis went to visit my mother. He sat down and told her, "All of Salamina is mourning Nikos' disfellowship because he is such a nice man, so sincere, so faithful…"

"But if that is the case, why did you disfellowship him?" my mother asked.

"He wanted us to show him the truth about 1914! Did we have time to do research for hours to tell him about that stuff?"

"For so many years we spent hours upon hours to find 'a lost sheep' and bring them into the Society! And you consider it a waste of time to keep this sheep inside the Society?" she asked angrily.

"Now you, sister, must not speak to him at all according to the rules. But since you are disabled and you need his help, what can you do; you have no choice but to speak to him. But make sure that you don't talk to him on religious subjects!" he said to her.

"In other words, only for my self-interest?" my mother asked, distraught, as she also began to slowly see the true face of the Society.

The determining factor came during an incident with one of my uncles. He was the one who had sent us the money from America when we were in dire straits. He was now back in Greece permanently. He was an elder of the Society and when he found out about my disfellowship, he wanted to help me to return to it. Thus he informed me that he was eager to meet with me and to help me. This, however, was to take place secretly, so we arranged to go to his home.

I expressed my appreciation for his initiative, since he seemed to be a man with noble sentiments. We began the discussion about 1914, but I quickly surmised that his level of knowledge did not permit him to understand such an intricate subject. Thus the discussion switched to the subject of the great multitude.

In retrospect this is now my first choice of a topic in my current discussions with Witnesses, for it is simpler and more basic for them to understand.

When I proceeded to carefully analyze for him the first verses from the seventh chapter of the Book of Revelation, his face suddenly changed color. With his eyes popped out he asked, "Where did you learn this?"

"From my study," I answered. I showed him one more verse, and then he suddenly threw the Holy Scriptures on a nearby bed in a state of terror.

"No, no! We cannot discuss this," he said and refused to be convinced, no matter what I said. He was one more of the unfortunate slaves who loved the Society more than the truth. After we returned home, my mother expressed the desire to leave the Society. She was also disgusted by their hypocrisy and their terror of facing the truth. I forewarned her about the treatment she would receive from the members of the Watchtower as someone disfellowshipped, but she was determined.

Together we composed her *letter of disassociation**. In it, she declared that she no longer wished to have a relationship with the Society after seeing their hypocrisy and their fear of the truth. She expressed her deep sorrow for the forty years of her life she had spent in it, and challenged them to discuss things with me, in her presence, with the promise that if they could prove their position, we would both return.

Of course, they did not respond to the invitation. Six months later my grandmother repeated this challenge in her own letter of departure, shedding the identity of a Witness. Thus one year after my own disfellowship, three more people shook off the tyrannical yoke of this false religion: my mother, my grandmother and the man with whom I had spoken at the beginning, when I was still in the Society.

Simultaneously, I warned and stopped dozens of people who were ready to fall victim to the web of this religion, and assisted dozens of others in their exodus from it. I had guided many people to this organization. Now I needed to work out my atonement. I needed to help them escape the nets of the Watchtower.

10. Progressing Toward the Truth

George's story

I was now outside of the Society. It is not easy for a person to understand what it means for a Witness to be disfellowshipped. Since my teen years, I worked *whole-souled** and with sincerity of heart for His glory and now the Society expelled me as an apostate, as a rebel against God![140] At the flip of a switch, I lost my position, my good name, my friends. Outside the Watchtower I had no friends because associating with people outside of the religion was considered bad association.

It was emotionally devastating. I would have been crushed were it not for my understanding that my disfellowship was unjust and there was a deep problem in the Society's theology.

I needed support and guidance. I began to seek out, without apprehension, other people who believed, especially former Witnesses which the Society labeled as apostates. Little by little and one by one, I began to uncover the dogmatic faults of the Watchtower. As I was learning about all these important and unprecedented (for

---

140 According to Watchtower, "Apostasy is abandoning or deserting the worship and service of God, actually a rebellion against Jehovah God." (*Reasoning From the Scriptures*, Watch Tower Bible and Tract Society, 1989, p. 34)

me) novelties, I wanted to share them with those around me. They were newly learned revelations; I was discovering how, for such a long time, I had believed in false doctrines.

Unfortunately, however, the others around me did not usually share my enthusiasm. For all those who had not lived through my experience, all the phenomenal interpretations were something simple and without any special significance. If, for example, someone had not placed all his hope on an earthly paradise and in the vision of the great multitude (the seventh chapter of Revelation), he would not be greatly excited if he then read a true interpretation of the vision which showed that the "great multitude" refers to the heavenly order. For him, it would simply be one more interpretation amidst all those possible to read, while the fact that the "great multitude" is of the heavenly realm would be to him something very natural! Thus I realized that during the time I had been in the Society, not only had I failed to progress, but in reality I had regressed. Due to my life as a Witness, I now needed "reconstruction." However, with the demolition of all their teachings implanted in my mind for so many years, I needed to double the work. That's why Christoula had said, "To leave, to come out of the Watchtower Society is easy! The difficulty is for the Watchtower to come out of your head!"

How true! Anyone who has lived through belonging to such a totalitarian group can attest to this. Thus when I would read something from the Holy Scriptures, the interpretations of the Society would envelope my mind, not allowing me to see the true meaning. I had been trained and was therefore accustomed to interpreting the verses as such. So, my excitement and my joy were intense upon discovering something in certain verses which I had never paid any attention to all those years—verses which I had committed to memory and had read thousands of times.

"Where were they hiding all these years that I failed to see them?" is the most often asked question by people like me, when we discover this sort of thing. The only others who shared my enthusiasm for these subjects which I held to be so important, were other former Witnesses who had lived through the same experiences as myself. This was something that made us pull together even when we were no longer in the Society, and in that way we were able to console each other.

This same factor also leads those who have lived the experience of the Watchtower to seek each other out for support and camaraderie, even though there are other people more experienced in the true interpretation of the Holy Scriptures. Some people see the truly important issues and mainly deal with them. But for others who have recently departed from the Witnesses, they may not be ready for something like this. They still think that they would be of great importance in the parishes of ex-Jehovah's Witnesses, assisting individuals exit all such extra-ecclesial groups.

Everywhere we went, we listened to people talk to us about what they considered important, and not about what we needed.

They usually began to "inform" us about the beliefs of the Witnesses, making us rebel against their common slanderous remarks and the inaccuracies we were forced to hear. Even when we explained to them what exactly takes place, many stubbornly adhered to their opinions.[141]

---

[141] Unfortunately this is a widespread problem. Ex-JW Crompton explains, "Despite their [Jehovah's Witnesses'] intensive activity, however, the doctrinal basis of the movement is generally not well understood within the mainstream churches. A number of factors contribute to this situation. There is often a disinclination to study the movement's doctrines in its own literature, arising, perhaps, from a desire not to get involved or to give any support to the movement. But the secondary sources at present available are often quite unreliable in ways that the general reader can be in no position to detect. Many writers of popular works betray an inadequate understanding of their subject and, indeed, are often prone to errors arising from failure to undertake the most basic research." (Robert Crompton, *Counting the Days to Armageddon*, James Clarke & Co., 1996, p. 6)

These developments did not allow us to feel the spirit of brotherhood which we had been accustomed to in the Society. We were strangers among strangers. We missed the continuous company of people with the same cares and troubles and we often became nostalgic for the companionship and camaraderie of the Society (but not for its dogmas and methods). The lack of the austere discipline of the Society, which we were used to, did not make us feel at home because it did not give us the impression that everything operated like clockwork.

For both my wife and me, it was a very challenging period of our lives. Our only shelter was in prayer, "To You, O Lord, I lift up my soul. O my God, I trust in You; let me not be ashamed; let not my enemies triumph over me. Indeed, let no one who waits on You be ashamed; show me Your ways, O Lord; teach me Your paths. Lead me in Your truth and teach me, for You are the God of my salvation; on You I wait all the day!"[142]

---

142 Psalm 24/25:1–5

11. Creating a new church

Nikos' story

From the time I first approached the Evangelicals, I met a couple of people who, disappointed by their particular denomination, no longer belonged to any religion and had isolated themselves to worship God as they felt best. One of these men was named Petros. He was a very nice older man whom I pressured to study the Bible with me. He avoided me discreetly, but we stayed on very good terms.

There was also Nassos, an ex-Pentecostal who had left mainly for dogmatic reasons. I held discussions with each of them individually from time to time. Nassos was more knowledgeable than anyone I had ever met outside of the Society up until then. We started a Bible study with Nassos, and he always had a ready answer to any position I took. For example, when we were discussing the Trinitarian dogma of God, he said, "It's not hard to understand how the Father and the Son can be one God. Think of the example of the mind. The Father is the mind and the Son is the word."

"Don't you understand? The Son is *called* the Word! He is not the Word," I said.

"You don't understand," he disagreed with me. "The Son is the Word! "In the beginning was the Word", the Gospel says in John

1:1. This is precisely why in Proverbs He is also called the Wisdom of God. Wisdom equals Logic equals Logos (Word)."

"But this makes no sense! If He is truly Logos, and not only in name, then how is He a person?" I asked.

"God is the fountain of life, and whatever flows from Him is alive," he answered.

Although I continued to consider this illogical, I still found it to be an interesting thought and kept it in mind for later.

Nassos was retired and had plenty of time to study. Due to my work, however, I could not meet with him as often as he wanted. I thought it would be good to introduce him to Petros, so they could meet and discuss things without me; Nassos was overjoyed. As time went on, these meetings progressively increased until my mother gave up her Witness identity. She provided her house where we could all meet once a week to study the Bible. In the beginning, our gathering consisted of five people. Later on, Petros' wife, whom we had convinced to throw away the icons of her Orthodox faith, joined us and continued to meet with us. At the same time, one more former Witness, a lady, began to attend, now and then former Witnesses we knew from Athens also joined us.

We prayed to God and asked Him to help us, along with His Holy Spirit, to accept the truth whatever it happened to be. Therefore, we studied with an open mind, without being bound to the biases of our old religious groups. When we began, the only dogmas that we accepted were "only what the Bible says" and "to not be dogmatic." In other words, we accepted as Christian "brothers," all those who accepted Jesus Christ as their Savior, regardless of whatever else they believed and which religion they had belonged to. However, our meetings proved to be a real battleground. Each one showed up with all the baggage of his old religion and was ready to defend these positions to the end. However, when someone would present something irrefutable from the Bible, we all accepted it. So, as the days went on, we agreed on more and more topics.

The first topic which found us in agreement was the meaning of the new heavens and the new earth. We understood this to be a new earthly environment for man where he would live with an incorrupt body, and not as souls, as some of our Evangelical acquaintances believed. This helped us to understand that the Lord Jesus Christ resurrected in His body, and He will return to earth in His incorrupt body at His Second Coming. Then the earth will change and become incorrupt, a new earth. In reality, Nassos already knew all this along with many other things. His problem, however, was that he could not provide proof.

Whatever I agreed upon I volunteered to organize in written form, along with its Scriptural references. Rather quickly we progressed beyond Christoula and his group, which began to disassemble, forming smaller offshoots.

When we first started our organized meetings, a man entered our lives who was to prove highly influential on our future journey. His name was Panagiotis. He was a former Witness, as were his parents, and he was from Salamina. His sister was the woman who attended our gatherings. This man had entered the Society but had come out of it miraculously... As a teenager he was baptized as a Witness and was taught much by Vlassis. Eventually he left for Canada, where he served the Society as an elder, creating his own congregation with eighty people. At that time, however, he found some errors in the Society, and after some divine intervention, he made his exodus from there, along with forty other Witnesses. Since then, he has lived an admirable life, full of wondrous events, led by the Lord toward a progressively more correct journey. Thus, after the Lord commanded him, he came to Greece and we met. He baptized his sister, Petros and his wife, and my friend George...

When Panagiotis went abroad, I pondered whether I needed to be re-baptized. My studies began to reveal that the Christian baptism is not just a symbolic dedication, as the Witnesses claim, but a mystery of repentance and the gift of the Holy Spirit.[143] Not knowing better at the time, I asked George to baptize me, since he had already been baptized by Panagiotis whom I trusted. He told me that he would answer me soon. He didn't tell me, but during that short span of time, George and his wife prayed intensely to the Lord if it was His will for George to baptize me. I was baptized at a celebration gathering where I had invited dozens of former Witnesses. Before George baptized me, he asked me if I believed that the Holy Spirit is a person, and that Jesus Christ is not created.

"I perceive that the Word is not a creation, whatever this happens to be, and that the Holy Spirit is not power," I replied. "What exactly it is, I don't know."

"God will provide," George said, and he baptized me "in the name of the Father, the Son and of the Holy Spirit, for the remission of sin."

From that day on, George began teaching sessions with me to help me understand the dogma of the Holy Trinity. My questions were being answered, one by one. He explained to me that when Jesus Christ was speaking as subordinate to His Father, he was speaking as a human being and as having His origin in Him. When He spoke as an equal, He was speaking as God. He is undoubtedly the God-man and I saw this in many verses.

I was flabbergasted by the literally thousands of Bible verses referring to Jesus Christ as "Yahweh" (Isaiah 48:12-16; Romans 10:9-14). He gave me a thick book by Nikolaos Soteropoulos,[144] entitled, *Jesus*

---

143 Acts 2:38

144 Nikolaos Soteropoulos is a theologian in Greece, well known for his books and sermons.

the Yahweh. There, I understood very well *Who* the Lord was. Now I agreed with the rest of the people in our gathering that God is Triune.

The Society totally misrepresented the dogma of the Holy Trinity. The Society taught me to fight against the dogma that the Father, the Son, and the Holy Spirit were the same person. In reality, however, this was the heresy of Sabellius. The Trinitarian dogma emphasizes that the Father, the Son and the Holy Spirit are three different Persons of one essence. The efforts of the Society were instrumental in our disorientation, thus causing us to reject many things for the wrong reason. It was the reason that I had suffered from depression in my early days, when I had realized that some former Witnesses had begun to believe in the Holy Trinity. I was still afraid that only false teachings existed outside the Society.

Shortly thereafter, the letters I had handed out after my disfellowship began to produce fruit. The number of Witnesses who were finding me and wishing to learn more was steadily increasing. Some made their way out of the Society and some remain there, mainly for family reasons.

Our gatherings in Salamina maintained their growth in knowledge and blessings for two years. During this interval, we already had grown to twenty people, primarily from the ranks of former Witnesses. We had perceived that the "thousand-year Kingdom" was already present, and this knowledge was leading us to a deeper understanding of the Bible. We learned that the Bible had an "additional" ten books in the Old Testament, beyond those accepted by the Protestants and the Witnesses, and we accepted them. Earlier, however, those of us who had been Witnesses realized that the "great multitude" in Revelation, was actually souls, even though according to nature, the soul would die at death; yet by God's grace it remains immortal. This was the presupposition necessary to understanding all the basic eschatology of the Holy Scriptures, including the "thousand-year Kingdom."

At that time I also had the special joy of baptizing two former victims of the Watchtower, my mother and my grandmother! We progressed to such an extent that neighboring Pentecostals and Evangelicals were coming to our gatherings. In reality, more and more of the Evangelicals were attending our gatherings.

One day, Nassos brought along one of his acquaintances from Salamina. This man claimed that he had a gift from God for speaking Aramaic and interpreting some prophecies, like the speaking in tongues in the Pentecostal gatherings that I had attended. So I called on George and his wife, and they dropped by. Nassos allowed the charismatic to start speaking at some point. While he was under the influence of the spirit which was speaking through him, George and his wife asked him persistently, "Who is your Lord?"

But the spirit left him and he immediately lost his gifts.

"Jesus Christ," he then said.

"Not you! We wanted to hear this from the spirit that left!" George told him.

We also researched another Pentecostal group, characterized by more impressive miracles. Unfortunately, they did not accept that the Father, the Son and the Holy Spirit are three different Persons but one person, which appears at times as the Father, or as the Son or the Holy Spirit. Despite their zeal for God, they believed in a nonexistent God which meant that the wonderworker at their gatherings was not the Holy Spirit, but some other unclean spirit. Thus, day by day, we were growing in knowledge, understanding and experience.

12. Searching for THE Church

George's story

Even though my wife and I did not belong to any religious congregation, our search was quite systematic. Our large home library gave us the ability to research every religion, its history and its doctrine. We rejected all Protestant denominations because they had serious contradictions and were relatively new.

Their basic contradicting logic was that they accepted the Holy Bible (at least most of it), without accepting the Church which had introduced it to the world and declared it God-inspired. They repeated, "We only accept what the Bible says." Yet this "sola scriptura" cannot be found anywhere in the Bible, leading them to a tragic self-contradiction. Furthermore, the Protestants accept the New Testament exactly as St. Athanasios had compiled it in the 4th century!

In terms of history, they are all children of the Reformation, an offspring of the 16th century. According to their logic, the true Church of God did not exist for fifteen centuries. It was more than likely that the Church *did* exist, and consequently it could not have been Protestant! If God did accept some Christians as His children throughout the first fifteen centuries, then we needed to find the historical Church to which they belonged.

We studied all the early Christian texts we had gathered, and we searched everywhere. Even the non-Christian religions did not escape our search. We searched as far back as we could, and we could not find any other church except the Orthodox Church, whether it was named as such or not.

While studying the Orthodox Church, we found that it had something that looked similar to the pagan Eastern religions. Specifically, the Orthodox incessantly repeat the prayer, "Lord Jesus Christ, Son of God, have mercy on me," for the purpose of illumination.[145] This practice smacked of Eastern meditation to us, so we rejected Orthodoxy and were about to redirect our search elsewhere.

At the very time we thought about looking somewhere else, the Lord spoke to me, saying that His Church *is* the Orthodox Church and that He would lead us to it. He assured us that we would soon meet an Athonite[146] elder and he would resolve our final doubts and questions. At the same time my wife felt a certain confirmation within herself. Indeed a few days later, a friend of ours spoke to us about an Athonite elder who sometimes visited Attica. Immediately we thought of the divine guidance we had received, and we phoned the elder. The elder, without our even asking, began to answer the reservations we had about the Church! We were flabbergasted and realized that this certainly was neither an accident nor coincidental.

Several more meetings later, we were truly convinced that we had found the Church of the Lord. The reason why the Lord was speaking to me and not to my wife was that she was still un-baptized. I, however, had been baptized Orthodox at a young age. From

---

[145] The struggle for unceasing prayer is considered a must for every Orthodox Christian (1 Thes. 5:17). Every form of prayer is beneficial, so long as it is offered to God in humility (Ps. 50:19/51:17), without neglecting the virtue of love (1 Cor. 13:1–3) and the rest of the Christian virtues. An advantage of the "Jesus prayer" lies in its simplicity which makes it well suited when Church services or prayer books are unavailable.

[146] A member of the ancient monastic community of Mount Athos in northern Greece.

the moment the Lord sent us to the Orthodox elder He did not speak to us again, and would not until we would reach the state of illumination.[147] From then on, we would learn about His will through the elder who helped us to understand many things.

As time passed, all of our questions were answered fully. We understood that it was not imperative for someone to be baptized at a mature age. We studied the verse at the end of the Gospel of Matthew carefully; it does not say that you first become a disciple and then are baptized, as we were schooled as Protestants, but the opposite. It says, "Make disciples." How? By baptizing them first and teaching them afterwards. Neither does the Bible mention anything anywhere against infant baptism. As God gave Adam the Holy Spirit when He created him, without asking him, likewise the Mystery of Baptism gives the Holy Spirit (His grace) to an infant at the beginning of its life. Moreover, even St. Luke writes in his Gospel 1:15, that John the Baptist would be full of the Holy Spirit, even from the embryonic stage of his life! In addition, if an embryo received the Holy Spirit, how can this not apply to a child already born? That is why baptism in the language of the Scriptures is also called circumcision of the heart.[148] It is well known that it is primarily infants that were

---

[147] The author touches here on the great mystery of the Christian struggle of purifying one's heart to become a vessel of the Holy Spirit, "Create in me a clean heart, O God," cried Kind David, "and renew a steadfast spirit within me" (Psalm 50/51:10). Many Church Fathers distinguish these three stages in the spiritual life: purification of the heart, illumination of the nous, and communion with God through theoria. Purification of the heart means genuine repentance to uproot the evil passions and thoughts, as proclaimed by St. John the Baptist, Christ Himself and by His Apostles, since repentance is the indispensable prerequisite for one to experience the Kingdom of God. Illumination means the restoration of man before the fall and it's chief characteristic is the unceasing prayer in the heart, even when a man is asleep, according to "I am sleeping, but my heart is awake; it is the sound of my loved one at the door, saying, Be open to me, my sister." (Song of Solomon 5:2) (See Metropolitan Hierotheos Vlahos' *Orthodox Psychotheraphy*, Fr. John Romanides' *Patristic Theology*, and Elder Joseph's *Monastic Wisdom*.)

[148] Romans 2:29

and still are circumcised. Finally, we read ancient manuscripts from the second century, where Tertulian wrote clearly that infant baptism was a common practice then, in other words, in the ancient Church.

Shortly thereafter, I went to holy confession and I was chrismated. My wife was baptized and for the first time she received the true Body and Blood of the Lord. Now my wife and I were both united with all Christians of all centuries.

I called my friend Manolis, who was a former Witness. He was among the first who had started studying with Christoula. I found out that he also had become Orthodox. He was excited about my conversion and shared with me his own experience.

As a Protestant, he was pressured by his father to visit Porphyrios of Oropos,[149] a charismatic Orthodox elder. Manolis gave in to the pressures of his father but went with the secret intention to rebuke Fr. Porphyrios as a deceiver and heretic. However, their fist meeting turned out quite differently than expected. Although they had never met, before they were introduced, the elder called him by name, and during their discussion the elder revealed to him personal secrets, which logically he could not have known. When departing, the elder also kissed his hand, making him feel ashamed for his egotism. Thus, the next time Manolis went to see him, he was a changed man. He now went to receive help.

---

[149] Fr. Porphyrios was a renowned monastic Elder in Greece. Of humble origins and barely literate, at the age of 12 he went to the Holy Mountain Athos, to the hermitage of Kavsokalyvia, where he became a monk. He remained there until the age of 21, when health reasons dictated his return to the world and work as a chaplain in a hospital in Athens. Extremely bright, full of love towards his fellow man and for His Lord, he helped untold thousands with his spiritual gifts, to return them to God. Yet, he always remained humble, preferring to direct the attention of people and their hearts to the Lord. Fr. Porphyrios foresaw his death, and to avoid any possibility of attracting crowds at his funeral, he secretly fled to the Holy Mountain, where he reposed in peace in 1991. Many books have been written about the gifted Elder. Some of his spiritual children became heads of monastic establishments.

Leading others to the Historical Church

FROM THE MOMENT my wife and I entered the Church, the Lord began to use us in a wondrous way. I had attended a lecture with my wife at St. Paraskevi Church, given by Fr. Antonios Alevizopoulos, who was the head of the anti-heretical struggle at the time.

During the program, he asked if we had any questions. My wife raised her hand to ask something. "Put your hand down! I will give you the answer at home," I told her, because I thought the question was very simple.

She insisted, however, and asked the question on her mind. At the end of the program two women came toward us, a mother and her daughter. They expressed their desire to meet us; they said they were both former Pentecostals and that at the congregation they used to attend, the Holy Spirit spoke to them that His Church was not there where they were. He told them that He would lead them to His Church.

Therefore, on the day they had come to Fr. Antonios' lecture, the moment my wife raised her hand, the Lord told these women, "Become close to the woman who is raising her hand."

From that day on, we began to share with them everything we had derived from our own research. Other former Pentecostals were attracted to this catechesis, and in a short period of time they all became Orthodox Christians.

Simultaneously we organized one more study in Salamina for a group of former Witnesses, including my friend Nikos, his mother and grandmother. They had just departed from the congregation they had created. Up to that point, the results of their studies were progressively leading them toward the Orthodox faith and doctrine. Thus, it was not difficult for them to be convinced about some final concerns and remaining topics.

Nikos was a steady critic. He wouldn't accept anything unless he first saw proof. After his trust was shattered in the organization which he had been born into, he no longer trusted anyone. Thus, I needed to spend a lot of time with him. From the moment we became Orthodox, we realized that the road to the true faith is not without its trials. The attacks of the devil were continuous and inexorable every time I went to study with Nikos—such as family tempests, unemployment, financial problems, illness and constant disturbances, even my motorcycle breaking down! He began to question if I was lying to him!

Yet, my mother, whom I had led to the Society, treated me as an apostate, and refused to discuss religious subjects with me any longer. This is something that gives me guilt pangs to this day.

The greatest mistake of all those who buy into a heresy is that, according to their own ignorance, they think that Orthodoxy has nothing to teach them. And they justify themselves by claiming that they don't understand anything the priest says in the Divine Liturgy. Yet, they don't buy a small liturgy service book, which explains all of these things in detail.

If they knew the lofty theology behind these supposedly incomprehensible petitions of the priest, they would rush and search out all these liturgical texts. Besides, they should have known that we go to liturgies and generally to church services not to be taught but to praise and worship God. Catechetical sessions are held in most parishes for teaching us. However, when someone goes to church a few times a year and has not shown any interest in catechism, it is natural to be lead astray by some heresy. Especially now that the church has even established radio stations, anyone who claims that the Church failed to teach him is unjustified. Most likely, he did not care to be taught!!

13. Leaving even this Congregation

Nikos' story

 never dreamt of becoming a founder of a religion, however, the fact of the matter was that I was headed in that direction. Plans were already in progress to establish one more congregation at Corydalis, and from there who knows where. Nassos and I had begun to work out the details when I started to get the feeling that something was not quite right about our congregation.

Everywhere I looked in the Holy Scriptures, I saw that the churches had presbyters, deacons and other charismatics. Everywhere in the Holy Scriptures, when a sacrament was given, a presbyter, sacramentally ordained through the laying on of hands, administered it. However, in our church we acted on our own. We had appointed some presbyters and deacons ourselves but who had given us that right? How was I distributing the bread and wine during our communion service without having been sacramentally ordained? Who gave me the right to baptize?

This bothered me no end; I had no desire to become the founder of yet another dubious denomination after leaving the Witnesses. Neither was I in any mood to "reinvent the wheel;" if the New Testament Church still existed, I very much wanted to be part of *that*

Church. After all the Lord had promised that the gates of Hades will never prevail against it.¹⁵⁰ But where was *that* Church?

Nassos, on the other hand, was not concerned at all about these matters. Our congregation's steady increase of knowledge—even surpassing some of the other Protestant groups we had met in the understanding of the faith—made him swell with pride, little by little. He believed that we had the truth and our dogmatism was slowly retreating.

In the days when I was still a Jehovah's Witness, as I was slowly understanding that the hope of all Christians is indeed in Heaven, I approached Vlassis and expressed to him that I had a desire to partake of the *emblems*.*¹⁵¹ He warned me, however, that doing this would be suicidal. Due to the Witness doctrine which always strives to limit those who partake of the bread and wine,¹⁵² the leaders attempt to discourage all those who wish to commune.¹⁵³ In this way, they succeed in keeping the number of communicants very low.¹⁵⁴

---

150 Matthew 16:18

151 The Watchtower Society teaches that the faithful Christians (i.e. JWs) are divided into a "great crowd" and a "small flock" of 144,000 "anointed ones" of which some 8,700 (the "remnant") are "still living with us today," and only these are allowed to partake of the "emblems" (communion).

152 So how does a Witness know whether he belongs to the "great crowd" or to the elite "remnant?" Here the Society is usually tight-lipped. It seems that the Witness is to decide this for himself, and that partaking of the "emblems" (communion) makes one de facto a member of the "anointed class." (see Jay Walter,*My 6-Year Journey Out of the Watchtower*, retrieved 11/24.2008 from http://www.exjws.net/pioneers/part6.htm)

153 "In 1975 the Society clearly feared a continuation of the upward trend in Memorial partakers, and in an article entitled 'Anointing to a Heavenly Hope—How Is It Manifest?' (WT 15 February 1975, 105–11) the Governing Body warned readers against a mistakenly presuming a heavenly calling. The writers clearly blamed the increase on the ignorance of the membership as to the nature of the calling." (Gary Norman Boting, *The Orwellian World of Jehovah's Witnesses*, Toronto Press, 1984, pp. 145–146)

154 In the 1970s—contrary to Society's teaching that the *remnant* of the 144,00 would steadily decrease in numbers as Armageddon approached—many rank-and-file JWs began to claim that they were also part of the remnant and to participate in the Communion at the annual Memorial Service. As the number of the Rem-

"Commemoration of the Death of Christ"
For the Watchtower "the bread symbolizes Christ's body, the wine his blood. Transubstantiation and consubstantiation, or the doctrine of the real presence, are denied. Therefore, the Lords' Supper is most emphatically a Memorial." (Penton, *Apocalypse*, pp. 192). Despite this, only members of the *Remnant class* are allowed to commune! Thus, "while there are well over six million preaching Witnesses in the world, less than 9,000 partook of the bread and wine at the 2,004 annual 'Memorial' of the death of Christ (Religious Tolerance, 2005)" Jennifer Green, *Dealing with Death: A Handbook of Practices*, Procedures and Law, Jessica Kingsley Publishers, 2006, p. 232)

Now that we had found proof from the Holy Scriptures that Christians must commune as often as they wish, I began to commune either at my own congregation or at other Protestant ones. I have never since questioned myself about this right. We only concerned ourselves with whether the bread should be unleavened and how often we should commune.

Not long afterwards, I began to suspect that my friend George was approaching the Orthodox Church. The things he was telling

---

nant class swelled, Penton writes, "if one were much less than sixty-five years of age and began partaking of the Lord's supper he was under intense social and organizational pressure to stop. Sometimes he would be gossiped about, virtually shunned, and treated with the utmost disrespect. Thus some partakers were bullied into denying their heavenly calling by peer pressure, the elders, of the circuit overseers." (Penton, *Apocalypse*, pp. 108–109) me were reminiscent of that atmosphere, so when we met I would try to bait him, but he kept his mouth closed. One day as we were parting, I said to him in jest, "The way we are headed, I see us Orthodox one day!"

"God knows," he told me and I cast a sideways-glance at him, but he was expressionless.

My mind went back to the day he had baptized me; George had invited a mutual friend who had been with me in the military jail and was disfellowshipped at the time. That friend had expressed some doubt whether we should proceed with the baptism, claiming that perhaps we should ask the Church.

"What Church is he talking about?" I asked George.

"The Orthodox Church." he replied.

It sounded bizarre, to say the least, to hear an-ex Witness talk like this. Given our background, all of us should have viewed the Orthodox Church, it being an organized religion, as pagan.

Now, however, as I was discussing with George, I could see things making sense. For example, when I understood that the souls of the saints are reigning in Heaven with the Lord from this very moment, I could see that it is not in vain to pray to them nor to ask for their intercessions.

Slowly, the more I discussed with George, the more I could understand things. Finally, one day he broke the news and told me he had become an Orthodox Christian.

"But why? Panagiotis had baptized you already!" I protested.

"The baptism he did seemed proper; but did he have the right to perform it?"

"But, *you* baptized me asking the Lord. He did the exact same thing," I said disagreeably.

"Listen! The baptism you performed on the Witnesses was valid as a baptism of dedication, and the baptism we underwent as Prot-

Bible's Students Monthly, 1917, p.4
An advertisement for Russell's Book "The Finished Mystery" portrays both the Catholic and Protestant churches as parts of the same ruined and sinking edifice called "Babylon." The Watchtower Society forgets that itself is an offspring of Protestantism and, hence, plagued by the very same problems it decries.

---

estants was valid for its own purpose, as a special provision of the Lord, to give us a certain orientation. Now, however, we must fulfill all righteousness and accept our baptism from those who succeeded the Apostles."

"Do you have anything to give me about this?" I asked.

"I have two books. Read them and you will understand what I mean," George said and handed them to me. The books were: *The Canon of the Holy Scriptures* and *Eucharist, Bishop, Church*.[155]

---

[155] Metropolitan Ioannis Zizioulas, *The Canon of the Holy Scriptures and Eucharist, Bishop, Church: The Unity of the Church in the Divine Eucharist and the Bishop During the First Three Centuries*, Holy Cross Orthodox Press, 2001.

Church History

BOTH BOOKS SHOOK the ground of my spiritual foundation. The first book proved that it was ludicrous to accept the Holy Scriptures and not those who determine its canon. If the Church Fathers were mistaken in their beliefs, it makes sense that the books they selected for the Holy Scriptures would also be wrong. If I were to accept these books as God-inspired, then I also needed to accept as God-inspired those who determined and canonized these books. How could I trust the judgement of these men concerning the New Testament and discredit them in other key areas? The Bible is a book and as such needs interpretation; are we to trust only our own reason, or should we trust the witness of the ancient Church? My experience had already shown me that when three Protestants discuss a Bible verse, there are bound to be *four* different opinions! Why not trust the witness of the ancient Church instead? Moreover, instrumental to the selection work was a bishop of the First Ecumenical Council, whom I had so greatly misunderstood—St. Athanasios! Could it be that I needed to begin to pay more attention to Orthodoxy?

The first book caused me much difficulty; the second one totally convinced me. It included ancient Christian texts which showed very clearly the office of apostolic succession[156] as it was practiced and preserved through the first three centuries of Christianity. Being able to historically trace, for example, the bishop of Constantinople all the way to the Apostles is something that comes in stark contrast with the fantastic claims of the Watchtower that between Apostle Paul and Russell there was, pretty much, nothing.[157]

---

[156] Apostolic succession is the doctrine that succession of bishops can be historically traced back in uninterrupted lines back to the original twelve apostles.

[157] "The prolonged night of spiritual darkness from which the witnesses came had existed from the early part of the second century following the death of the apostles right up to the latter half of the nineteenth century. Early Christianity with its brilliance of right doctrine and cleanness of theocratic organization began to be

13. Leaving even this Congregation

The Finished Mystery (1918, p. 64) According to the Watchtower Society, Jehovah sent Seven Messengers to His Church: St. Paul, St. John, Arius, Waldo, Wycliffe, Luther, and Russell!

The Church Fathers are mostly unknown to Protestants; a case in point would be the Watchtower's book *Reasoning from the Scriptures* which not only fails to mention any of these ancient Christian texts on the subject, but confuses the apostolic succession with the Roman Catholic's unsupported novelty of Peter's supremacy.[158] For these reasons many Protestants fail to understand the authority of the hierarchy, as a direct successor of the Apostles. Consider, for example, the text of St. Ignatius the God-bearer who wrote during the second century, "he who does anything[159] without the knowledge of the bishop, in reality serves the devil."[160] After this, I understood that the parables of the talents[161]

---

eclipsed after the year 100 by a creeping spiritual darkness of "Babylonish" religious teachings, Grecian pagan philosophies and rank apostasy. While their complete release from "Babylonish" captivity did not come until 1919, for a period of nearly fifty years prior thereto the witnesses experienced a gradual awakening, to prepare them for their hour of liberation as a New World people." (*Qualified to Be Ministers*, Watch Tower Bible and Tract Society, 1954, p. 297)

158 *Reasoning from the Scriptures*, Watch Tower Bible & Tract Society, 1989, pp. 37–44

159 "Anything", meaning, "that belongs to the office of the bishop." See Fr. Epiphanios Theodoropoulos' commentary on the 79th Apostolic Cannon ("The Presbyters and Deacons should not do anything without their Bishop's knowledge.") (Fr. Epiphanios Theodoropoulos, Άρθρα, Μελέται, Επιστολαί, 1981, pp. 406–409)

160 Smyrnaeans 9,1; See also Smyrnaeans 8:1 ("Let no man do anything connected with the Church without the bishop.")

161 Mat. 25:15

and of the lost coin[162] were referring to the bishop. The subject of the bishops was very serious! We did not have the right to perform services in our congregation!

This book also solved my old problem of "who to consider my brother." I remember there had been some discord with a number of people for not calling them brother, due to their belief in some wrong doctrine or because I considered their baptism invalid. Now, however, I was seeing that I myself did not participate or share in the One Body of Holy Communion, as it is canonically offered with the blessing of the local bishop. Neither was I a brother! In addition, anyone who did not commune of the same bread was excluded from the Body of Christ.[163]

Questions, Questions, Questions! IN THE MEETINGS that followed, I bombarded George with arguments. I could not accept the veneration of icons, or even their construction. George heard me out, and he patiently explained to me that veneration and worship are not the same thing. "In icons we simply honor the person depicted," he explained and showed me verses, such as that of Revelation 3:7-9 wherein the Lord Himself declared that He would make people bow down before another human being: the bishop of the church of Philadelphia![164] If honorary veneration would automatically mean divine worship, the Lord would never have declared this!

George also explained God indeed commanded Moses not to "make for yourself a carved image, or any likeness of anything

---

162 Luke 15:8

163 I Cor. 10:17

164 The original Greek text uses the verb «προσκυνήσουσιν» which means "worship, do obeisance to, prostrate oneself to, do reverence to." It is the same verb used in Gen. 18:2 when Abraham bowed before the Holy Trinity and is also used in Ex. 20:5 ("You shall not bow down to them nor serve them. For I, the Lord your God, am a jealous God.")

13. Leaving even this Congregation 225

that is in heaven above, or that is in the earth beneath, or that is in the water under the earth"[165] but later on God instructs him "to make two cherubim of gold!"[166] Therefore, George continued, God does not forbid the making of images in general but the making of idols that turn people's hearts away from the true God. Images of God in the Old Testament were forbidden since the incorporeal God cannot be depicted and any such depiction would be misleading. However, the incarnation changed that[167] and the Holy Fathers allowed us to depict the incarnated second person of the Holy Trinity—our Lord Jesus Christ[168]—and His saints.[169] In reality, the honorary veneration we show to the image is transmitted to the one depicted.[170] Finally, he went on to say that the Orthodox Church does not permit the depiction of the Father although some priests may occasionally use such icons due to their ignorance. The Church, however, is not to blame for this, but the uninformed priests.

---

165 Exodus 20:4

166 Exodus 25:18

167 "Of old, God the incorporeal and uncircumscribed was never depicted. Now, however, when God is seen clothed in flesh, and conversing with men, (Bar. 3.38) I make an image of the God whom I see. I do not worship matter, I worship the God of matter, who became matter for my sake, and deigned to inhabit matter, who worked out my salvation through matter. I will not cease from honouring that matter which works my salvation. I venerate it, though not as God." (St. John Damascene, *On Holy Images*, trans. by Mary H. Allies (London, Thomas Baker, 1898)

168 "In depicting the Saviour, we do not depict either His divine nor His human nature, but His person in which both natures are incomprehensibly combined." (Leonide Ouspensky and Vladimir Lossky, *The Meaning of Icons*, Saint Vladimir Press, 1999)

169 "But seeing that not every one has a knowledge of letters nor time for reading, the Fathers gave their sanction to depicting these events on images as being acts of great heroism, in order that they should form a concise memorial of them." (St. John of Damascus, Exposition of the Orthodox Faith, in Nicene and Post Nicene Fathers, 2nd Series, (repr. Grand Rapids MI: Wm. B. Eerdmans, 1955), Vol IX, p. 88)"

170 "We worship images, and it is not a worship of matter, but of those whom matter represents. The honour given to the image is referred to the original, as holy Basil rightly says." (St. John of Damascus, *On Holy Images*)

Finally, he explained to me which of the other writings the Church considered God-inspired besides the Holy Scriptures. For the first time I realized it was wrong for me to accept "only" the Holy Scriptures. I needed to accept the entire Holy Tradition of the Church as God-inspired, which also includes the decisions of the Ecumenical Councils, the writings of the saints approved by the Ecumenical Councils, the hymnology of the Church and the liturgical texts. The same empowerment the Church had as the pillar and ground of truth[171] to define the books of the Holy Scriptures, could also be enforced for all the remaining God-inspired texts. And what was of great importance here was the fact that the pillar and ground of truth, of the Christian faith itself, was not the Holy Scriptures but the Church!

I constantly bombarded George with questions and received satisfactory answers. When I accused the Orthodox because they called people "father," while the Lord said do not call anyone on earth your father,[172] he pointed out verses to me where the Apostles considered themselves "fathers," as in I Cor. 4:15. He also indicated verses which showed that the bread given out during memorial services was based on the Holy Scriptures;, verses supporting the apostolicity of "chrism," as well as the ever-virginity of Mary—that she is Most Holy, and that it is acceptable to call her such—since even inanimate objects are called "all holy" in the Holy Scriptures.

Once again the Holy Scriptures revealed to me new meaning, further completing all the things I had discovered with the help of the congregation which we had begun. However, I needed to depart from there. That congregation had served its purpose; it had prepared and led me to the true Church of the Lord, the Church which I unfortunately had hated so much: the Orthodox Church.

---

[171] 1 Tim. 3:15
[172] Matt. 23:9

The Decision!

Thus, at the very next gathering, I announced that I would be departing so that I could be baptized in the Orthodox Church. I explained the reasons and called upon the others, as a group, to join it. Unfortunately, however, only half of the permanent members responded. The rest were negatively biased against the Church to the point that they even refused to research the matter.

My overall impression with Protestantism was that the desire for freedom in interpreting the Bible (*sola scriptura*) springs from a desire to define spirituality in one's own terms. A Protestant subconsciously conforms the Bible to his own tastes. For many Protestants is hard to grasp that they have to *fully* surrender their will to God's commands.

Personally I saw I no longer had the right to be a judge of the historical Church as if it were a matter of personal choice or taste. I had to be a humble member of that Church and in obedience to her Tradition. Consequently, the congregation fell apart. All of the former Witnesses and one other woman joined the Orthodox Church. The rest continued as before. Later they divided into two groups due to some discord, and today one of them still exists.

Getting used to the new Environment

Before the unfolding of these events, I needed to prepare my mother and my grandmother. One day we were discussing something, and my mother was accusing the Orthodox. "Don't accuse them, because they may have their reasons," I said.

She looked at me somewhat confused, having been accustomed to my open hostility toward them up until now. She had also observed that I had been reading many Orthodox books lately.

"Why are you reading Orthodox books these days?" she asked me.

"They have great depth," I said.

Miilions Now Living Will Never Die
"I want the statement, 'Millions No Living Will Never Die' to be taken literally, as it is, in the light of recently fulfilled prophecy, a provable Biblical proposition. —J.F. Rutherford." (*Bridgeport Telegram*, 12/4/1920)

"The Orthodox?" she asked in disbelief.

"The Orthodox," I repeated and began to explain.

The greater hurdle, however, would be breaking the news to my wife. She already had a problem with me being disfellowshipped. What would be her reaction if I now became Orthodox? She repeated often, "I married you as a 'brother,' and you should have stayed that way!"

"If you truly believed," I would answer, "that people should not change their religion in order to not displease their spouses, you would not be knocking on doors to lure others into your religion! Stop complaining, now that the very thing you wanted to do to other families is happening to you."

I knew however that her murmuring would intensify if, to top it all off, I became Orthodox.

It was summer and we were vacationing on an Aegean island. We got in the car, and before we drove off I made the sign of the cross noticeable enough to be seen by my son.

"Mom, Daddy crossed himself," the child said in great surprise.

"What is this? New revelations?" she asked.

"The Christian journey is a progressive one," I replied as I drove off.

"Don't tell me you are becoming Orthodox!" she said.

13. Leaving even this Congregation

"You got it! Finally, I have discovered the true Church of the Lord!" I said.

Immediately she proceeded to challenge me dogmatically. This was surprising because, following the directions of the Society, she had never discussed subjects of a dogmatic nature with me, an apostate. Now, however, in all likelihood accustomed to marginal Orthodox who were easy victims, she thought she could corner me spiritually. However, she found my answers so unexpectedly spot-on that she never dared such a thing ever again. The only thing she often repeated was, "You don't know what you are doing! You are constantly changing religions!"

Of course, this was not the case and she knew it, since after leaving the Witnesses I was simply going through a research period and had not officially joined any of the religions that surrounded me. The fact that our congregation had evolved into a religion was something I hadn't willfully pursued.

"I didn't change religions except to leave the Witnesses; and you know it," I answered her.

The Orthodox Church was the natural outcome of my research. It hadn't changed any of the personal views I had held up to then, except some remaining baggage I still carried from the false teachings of the Watchtower Society. All the things I had found in the congregation which we had formed in recent years were the same things I believe in even now.

However, character attack, when there are no logical arguments, is in true Watchtower fashion; this is the Witnesses' defense to the insecurities many of them feel when someone has proof against their doctrines. Therefore, many fanatical Witnesses resorted to mudslinging and the use of lies against me saying that I change religions every year, or that I was for polygamy, or that I divorced my wife, or how at the final committee meeting they discussed the dogma of 1914 with me and how out of pride I was saying that they had refused to discuss it, and the list goes on and on. But despite all the mudslinging and some heated confrontations with my wife, I continued my steady walk toward the Church of the Lord.

As my wife began to reclaim her initial peace of mind, I began to try more intensely to approach my son. He was still very young and at the beginning stages of being brainwashed. So, little by little, I found some opportunities to speak to him. He saw my efforts to have a religious discussion with my wife and her denials, and he sensed that she was afraid. "If they have the truth, why are they afraid?" I would ask him, so as to make him more aware.

So, essentially, as he was growing up and his mind was emerging from the fog of infancy, he was becoming more receptive, to the point where he was sometimes coming to church with me, and other times going with his mother. Subsequently, when he began to read, I proceeded to show him analytically the premeditated falsifications of the Holy Scriptures undertaken by the Watchtower Society in their *New World Translation*. This was the determining factor. The child understood well that a religion that does not respect the Holy Scriptures does not respect anything else. So he began to refuse to join his mother and the Witnesses, and would instead come to church with me.

George took me to see his spiritual father, a priest-monk from Mount Athos who came to Attica from time to time to see his spiritual children. He listened to my first confession. I remembered the interrogation by the Witnesses' judicial committee—what a huge difference! There, the elders were arrogant accusers and judges. Here, this true presbyter was a humble advisor. There, terrorism and fear reigned. Here, I found love and compassion. There, I was looking to hide whatever I could. Here, I was confessing all and was searching to see if I had forgotten to say anything. There, I was leaving feeling

13. Leaving even this Congregation

heavy as lead, while here, I felt as light as a feather. Yes! Here the atmosphere was full of the fragrances of freedom, love and joy of the Holy Spirit. I admitted all the sins of my life in an atmosphere of compassion and understanding. I shed the most tears for the war I had carried out against the True Church of the Lord.

Often as a Witness I accused the Orthodox Church of not expelling her sinful members. Now, however, I began to understand that what the Holy Scriptures refer to, in not allowing the "admixture" of the person who fell into sin with the rest of the Church (not to "keep company" as it is sometimes poorly translated), was exactly what Orthodoxy had been practicing for 2,000 years. The person burdened by sin shouldn't commune; in other words, he shouldn't become one "mixture" with the Body and the Blood of the Lord, with the rest of the Church. *This* was his expulsion from the Church, rather than not speaking to him or avoiding his company as the Witnesses erroneously did.

To refuse to speak to one who has slipped into sin translates into having no concern to help him. Characteristic are the verses of 2 Thessalonians, 3:14-15, where Apostle Paul writes: "And if anyone does not obey our word in this epistle, note that person and do not keep company with him, that he may be ashamed. Yet do not count him as an enemy, but admonish him as a brother."

The purpose of the Church is to embrace the sinner in hopes that God will illumine him toward repentance, and not to kick the sinner out in order to preserve its showcase image to the outsider. The Church is especially needed for sinners and not necessarily for the pure![173]

After leaving confession, I noticed a hollow wooden star in the monastery reception area with small pieces of paper in it, each

---

[173] Luke 19:10

written with a different verse of scripture. Visitors used to pray and then take out a paper at random, regarding this as a message from God. I also pulled out a paper, and the message was most appropriate for my situation: your sins are forgiven you.[174] This went on for a while, and every time I went to the monastery there was something useful for me in the star-shaped box. This was also true for my son, whose first message was (I will paraphrase since I don't exactly remember the verse): I will hold you in my hands until your old age and until your hands turn white! On the following visit, the paper he chose said: I will never forget my covenant with you!

All this was very meaningful for my son, who was beginning to understand that God was eager to be with him. I also received a powerful message the last four times: three of these times I picked the exact same verse; and the fourth, a different one with the same meaning as the other three! The possibility of this being a matter of chance—choosing from ninety papers—was incredibly small! One in millions! This was a miracle! In a similarly miraculous way I received a prophecy, although veiled, revealing that my son would ask for and buy a cross for the first time, and that my wife would throw it away. When this actually materialized a few hours later, then I understood the prophecy!

God was constantly reaffirming everything I had accepted theoretically about the identity of His Church with some of His other gifted servants. Once again I witnessed an impressive event at this very monastery, when I was there with a friend of mine who was there for the first time. As I was waiting in the reception room, an old nun whom I had never seen before, came to keep me company until my friend had finished his confession, at which point I would then go in for confession.

---

[174] Matt. 9:2

13. Leaving even this Congregation

She was talking somewhat more than one would normally expect, and this began to bother me because I had brought a book along and couldn't wait for her to leave so I could read it. Due to her advanced age she was constantly forgetting, and until I left she asked me more than a dozen times who I was, if I had come to the monastery before, if I had ever met the elder. Unfortunately, however, as many times as I responded to these questions, a few minutes later she would ask these same questions again. I regarded this conversation as lost time; however, she was not giving any sign of leaving any time soon and was repeatedly telling me her life story, how from twelve years old until her advanced age she had never left this monastery.

At some point, I thought that after so many years of struggle perhaps the Lord had endowed her with some charisma. So I decided to listen to her carefully. Suddenly this little old lady, who had never laid eyes on me before and every couple of minutes was asking me over and over who I was, began to tell me my family history! She told me about my father's death twenty years prior, about my mother's disability, about my mother's many marriage proposals which she had turned down so that she could raise me more properly, according to what she believed.

She advised me how to conduct myself better around my mother and my grandmother, and many other things. I couldn't believe my ears! This little old lady who forgot the simplest things about me, which I had repeated for her numerous times, was now describing to me my family matters with great detail, things that she had never heard! It was obvious that the Holy Spirit was speaking through her, teaching me and convincing me through her.

"What is your name?" I asked her.

"Chrysovalanti (Golden-purse) but I have nothing of God!" she told me laughing.

"You have two gold things, a gold tooth and a gold crown in

heaven!" I assured her. My friend came out of the confessional and then I went in. When we were leaving, another old nun said to us, "Sorry for Sister Chrysovalanti! She talks so much."

"Don't be sorry! I wish I could hear her talk more!" I answered, having received a great lesson on spirituality!

Up until then I thought that spiritual meant someone who knew a lot and could speak eloquently. Now, however, this woman of advanced age made me question my book knowledge and made me think how greatly mistaken I had been all these years, being a Christian according to the letter of the law in contrast to this woman of the spirit.[175]

"Taki, you won't believe what happened to me when you were upstairs," I told my friend as we were leaving, and while he was driving, I described to him my entire conversation with Chrysovalanti.

"I believe you! Because during the time you were upstairs, she described in great detail how I divorced my wife, along with the emotional ordeal of that period," he told me, equally surprised, and we glorified God.

Not long afterwards, George's spiritual father became my spiritual father also. I was baptized at an opportune time in a big barrel by a true presbyter, with George as my godfather. My mother and my grandmother had been baptized Orthodox when they were infants, so they simply underwent the Chrismation of repentance, a necessary action and one mandatory for those who return from a heresy. With this, the energy of the Holy Spirit is once again activated, Whom man had grieved when he was in heresy.

---

[175] In Orthodox Christianity, spiritual progress in the Christian virtues must be accomplished as non-obtrusively as possible, both to protect ourselves from pride and our brethren from envy. To this end, some ascetics have gone so far as to pretend to be fools; some very notable examples are St. Symeon the fool for Christ, St. Andrew the Fool for Christ, St. Theophil the Fool for Christ. The nun mentioned in the text appears to have been such a case.

13. Leaving even this Congregation

My grandmother fell asleep as a Christian at the age of ninety. After forty years in heresy, the Lord preserved her to a very ripe old age, to call and prepare her as an Orthodox Christian into His presence. Her final words before she fell into a coma, and during the months when she regained consciousness, were "Glory be to God", while her weak hands were moving with her final remaining strength, attempting to make the sign of the Cross.

At my baptism, I did not fail to invite the Orthodox man who had first spoken to me about the error of 607 B.C. in the encyclopedia. Actually, we had been in contact long before I became Orthodox, from the initial time of my disfellowship. Our first meeting after my disfellowship had an interesting outcome, and I believe it's recounting would be beneficial for those who try to approach those in heresy.

As soon as I found myself outside the Society, I felt the need, on the one hand, to help others avoid the traps of my previous religion, and on the other hand, to announce my freedom! I also wanted to thank my former "enemy" who had annoyed me when I did field work, because he was the first person to arouse my curiosity to study what became for me, a life-changing subject. Deep down, however, I also wanted to teach him a good lesson—that he should never label someone a wolf or a foreign agent, since only God knows the heart of a man. I also wanted to express to him how wrong he had been in mistreating the non-Orthodox, and to expose him to the truth behind all the inaccuracies he held about the Witnesses.

One evening, a week after I was disfellowshipped, he was standing outside of a gathering of Witnesses, along with many others. I went up to him and said, "Can I please have a little time with you," and motioned him to move away from the others for more privacy.

"No! Whatever you have to say, say it here in front of everyone! Nothing needs to be a secret here," he shouted with animosity, something that would have made me hate the Orthodox even more if I were still a Witness, for it would have confirmed the Society's teaching that the Orthodox were our enemies.

Now, however, I knew that whatever he would say would be inconsequential for everyone involved, so I simply told him in front of the others, "Very well then! I simply wanted to thank you, because during our last discussion you helped me to understand my mistake. Last Sunday I was disfellowshipped from the Witnesses because I contradicted the Society on the date of 1914."

"What did you say?" he cried, swallowing his anger and running toward me.

I fought hard to keep from laughing, watching his eyes pop out and his jaw drop. I was barraged with questions by him and all those around him. I briefly described to them what had taken place. Finally, I made the point of telling them that their accusations against the Witnesses being remunerated financially were wrong, and that in reality the opposite was true. They were paying for the expansion of the Society, much like me, my mother and my grandmother, who had given over all of our money to purchase a vacant lot for the Society.

I further told them that their method of approaching the Witnesses was terrible because it served to alienate them even more and to push them deeper into the Society. Finally, I spelled out for them that although I had left the Witnesses, *"I am not orthodox and do not wish to be!"*

They invited me to a discussion many times after that; however, this never materialized. In reality, I was not yet ready to listen, because even though he had been initially helpful to me, I believed that the Orthodox had nothing worthwhile to offer me. I was avoiding another discussion with him until I could gather more information about subjects such as the priesthood, with the purpose of proving to him that his religion is also wrong on these matters. As I was going about gathering this information I was the one being convinced, and our differences diminished until I finally agreed with him.

So when I invited him to my baptism into the Orthodox Church he could hardly hide his joy. On my part, I never stopped reminding him and anyone else concerning this matter, that no one can ever know whether those considered wolves might really be lost sheep who might find their way to the Lord. From that time on, he became more understanding toward the non-Orthodox, and thus more able to help them.

To enlighten people around me about the Watchtower Society, I gave Fr. Antonios Alevizopoulos a collection of hundreds of classified letters of the Society addressed to its elders. Although I had never been an elder, I managed to photocopy them when I had access to these texts. Back then, I had believed that they would be additional "spiritual nourishment," and beneficial when I should become an elder.

Now, however, I understood that their real usefulness was to make known the unlawful methods and oppressive measures carried out by the Society against its members. Some other, more recent epistles have been added to the earlier collection, provided by other Witnesses who happened to have them. These are significant documents containing much which proves the totalitarian nature of the Watchtower Society. A short while later, I escorted a former Witness to his Orthodox baptism, while at the same time his parents received the Chrismation of repentance.

When my wife was pregnant, back when we were knocking on doors as Witnesses, the Orthodox priest's wife who was speaking to us about converting, had said, "Dear, what a pity for your unborn child! You must baptize it. I will be happy to sponsor the baptism." After all these years, we remembered her words. So we agreed to have them baptize my son who was ten years old, something that he accepted with much anticipation.

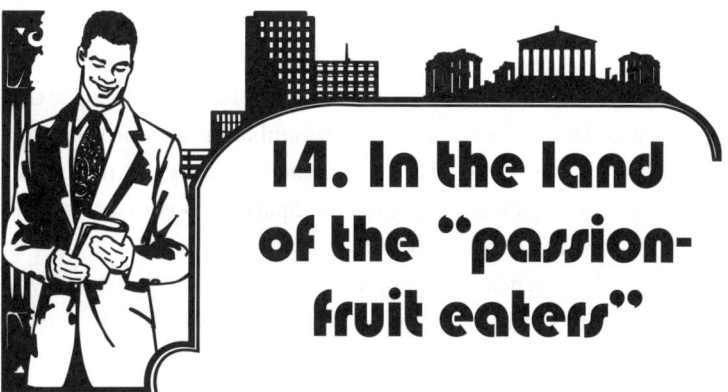

14. In the land of the "passion-fruit eaters"

George's story

A short time after my return to the Orthodox faith, I decided to baptize a child of a former Witness. This child was born into the Watchtower Society and was raised with the teachings of the organization. However, when his father was disfellowshipped for "apostasy," he began to teach his son the Christian Gospel. At the time, little Alexander was about three years old. The child's mother, born into the Watchtower Society, never expressed the desire or interest to find out the dogmatic reason that caused her husband to leave the organization. Each time he attempted to tell her something, she rejected it and reacted very negatively, which caused him to abandon his attempts to enlighten her about his faith. The child, however, was attentive and would often ask him questions about different aspects of his father's new faith.

When Alexander turned nine years old, he expressed the desire to be baptized in the Orthodox faith, and an Orthodox godfather needed to be found. Thus, I offered to baptize him, being well aware of the potential problems that could surface in a family caught between two religions. My main dilemma was that I did not have the opportunity to see the child very often because his father needed to work all day. Consequently, the child was under the constant supervision of his mother, who would never consider allowing the child to be in his godfather's company without the presence of the child's father. Despite all this, the baptism took place and the child was growing up as an Orthodox Christian.

Alexander vehemently opposed attending the Jehovah's Witnesses meetings, despite the constant pressure he endured from his mother and her community. In truth, he was relieved to be spared the unbearable torment of the speeches and the boring fellowship of the Witnesses. In the meanwhile, unfortunately, my contact with him was reduced to a mere formality.

Despite all this, I was happy to hear that he was progressing well in the faith, and in this manner the boy reached his sixteenth birthday. Everything seemed to be well and with him; and his father Odysseus felt confident and proud of his son, especially since the child seemed to have developed an immunity to the Watchtower follower's provocations.

At that time, by the orchestration of a very satanic plan, something slowly began to change. Everything was so expertly designed and masterminded that nothing was perceived before the damage was done. Alexander's family lived in a high-rise apartment building occupied by Watchtower families, the only exception being Alexander and his father. This meant that excluding school hours, Witnesses constantly surrounded the boy. Odysseus worked non-stop for seven years, from morning until evening, having very little chance for quality time with his son. Often he could only see him when the boy did school work or was sleeping.

Once or twice a week he took Alexander to work with him, where they could discuss a substantial spiritual matter or at least have a father-son conversation. The young man was never in the company of other Orthodox, with the exception of school recesses.

Thus, Alexander socialized exclusively with Watchtower members. This, however, did not seem to worry his father. He was confident that whatever would happen, Alexander would ask him about it and he would supply the necessary answers. Besides, he had already told Alexander plenty of things throughout the years; he was well informed his father's disfellowship.

Then one year, things took a different turn. Certain events began to roll along, one after the other, at such an accelerated pace, leaving no room for reaction. A financial crisis forced Alexander's father to deprive his family even of that little time he had dedicated to them previously. He could only see them on Sundays, and this forced him to reduce his weekly church attendance with his son so that he could devote some time to his wife, who was constantly complaining of neglect.

To make his wife feel less neglected, he agreed to come home late on certain nights, so she could invite Witnesses to their home for some party. You see, being disfellowshipped, he was not permitted to participate in such parties (nor did he have any desire to). Thus, that year these parties increased to the point of having them on weekdays. Dancing, singing, and movies were the daily preoccupation of the club created by the Witnesses' club in this high-rise.

At the same time, Alexander's increased responsibilities at tutorial classes and school did not allow him to help his father at work. Therefore, besides school, he was exclusively in the company of the Witnesses, including a weekly soccer match. Many months passed and Odysseus was hoping his financial crisis would soon end, so he could dedicate time to his son once again. Yet, constant demands for many months on end did not allow this day to occur anytime soon, resulting in the continuation of the same circumstances.

I helplessly witnessed this entire situation until one day Alexander said to his father, "Dad, can I start Bible study with Janos?"

This question took Odysseus by surprise. "What are you saying? You would allow yourself to be taught by a heretic?"

"Why not? Why shouldn't I see what the Witnesses have to say?" asked Alexander.

"What have we been talking about all these years? Haven't we discussed many things? Was I not a Witness? Do you know how many times I held a scriptural study for others on the book *You Can Live*? If you want to know what they believe, would I have a problem telling you? I could even analyze all of our differences with them. Must you place yourself under the authority of a heretic in a scriptural study to be convinced of this? Furthermore, if they wish, you know that I am more than ready for them to hold such a study in my presence, one on one, on equal ground. However, they will never agree to do this with somone who was disfellowshipped, so why would you want to study with a heretic?" he asked him.

"Well, the idea of studying with you doesn't sound fun. I want to study with Janos," Alexander replied.

Odysseus saw a look well-known to him in the eyes of his son. He had seen this very same look in many other proselytes of the Watchtower. I have also seen this look many times in such proselytes, and I understood very well what Odysseus was describing to me. It is the look of escape, the look of blind acceptance of certain things, without any disposition to seriously search. It is the look of a man whose mind is made up; he cannot be budged by any argument or logic, regardless of how much one might try. Odysseus surmised that his son had already decided to enter the Watchtower Society. He understood that whatever he would say would be meaningless, and that his son needed to make his own mistakes before he would once again find the way of Christ.

Despite all this, Odysseus wished to study the situation a little further. He wanted to look into the psychology of his son because he had run into similar cases of blindness; however, he had never the opportunity to analyze the person. Now he felt that regardless of how painful this would be, he needed to squash his pain in order to study his son's emotions and drives objectively. He even thought that perhaps God was giving him an opportunity to gain some special experience from the impeding ordeal. If he could commit the results to paper and somehow draw peoples' attention to it, the loss of his child would become the cause of salvation for others.

"Is there something that makes you object to Orthodox doctrine?" he asked him.

"Nothing at all," Alexander replied.

"Then, what makes you want to study a heresy with a heretical teacher?" he asked him.

"Look, Dad, if I had grown up in this family the way we were from the beginning, all of us would be Jehovah's Witnesses. Had you not pointed out the Society's mistakes, I would now believe in the Society with all my heart. I would be doing speeches like my friends, I would be on the streets with them, and I would go to the conventions. Now however, with everything I know, I have difficulty believing them, and I want to believe them," the young man began to open his heart.

Odysseus would have preferred to be dead than to hear those words; however, he steeled his heart and continued to ask, "With everything you know that is wrong about the Society, why do *you want* to believe in a *cult?* What do you find missing from the Church?"

"*A lot!* I miss the company I enjoy with the Witnesses. I miss the speeches, the conventions, and in general the lifestyle of the Witnesses. I don't like the Byzantine music of the Church. I don't like the ancient Greek language. I find the way of the Witnesses more fitting to my tastes. Their lifestyle expresses me better," the young man answered.

"Did you see what the last issue of the *Watchtower* was saying? I think you read it. It was saying in some article that religion is a very serious matter for you to choose according to your tastes. It even showed a picture with various foods saying that religion is not some food for you to choose according to your personal taste, but based on God's truth!"

"I read that issue but not that article! It did not interest me!" Odysseus answered back.

"In reality, the truth does not interest me! I'm only interested in having a good time in the company of my friends," the young man said with all sincerity.

Odysseus already understood what was happening. Alexander was completely influenced by his environment. He did not miss truth, he did not miss knowledge, nor did he lack answers; what he was missing was *companionship*. Within the Church he felt completely alone. Without Christian friends, he was a stranger among strangers, without the sense of the "ecclesiastical community," indispensable to each one of us. Although Odysseus felt the same way, it was not as great a concern for him. The priority in his life was the truth and the will to place his entire life in the hands of God. However, the child lacked the necessary maturity to think along these lines. In addition, a friend observed very meaningfully at some point, "I wouldn't want to be alone, even if I were in Paradise."

"Which is your soccer team?" Odysseus asked.

"Panathenaikos," Alexander said, with a guilty and perplexed smile, and added, "Now..."

"I see! I knew you to be a fan of Olympiakos, and quite fanatical! What is the team of Janos?" Odysseus asked again, who had understood well what was happening.

"Panathenaikos," the child answered again with the same guilty smile.

He did not question his father, however, about these unrelated questions. He understood very well the reason behind his father's question. He understood very well that his father had already entered his psychological state and was analyzing him; he understood very well what the underlying meaning behind these questions was. He did not try to deny this, which is why he did not react at all, nor did he try to pretend ignorance. Perhaps he was acknowledging, at the time, that his father was trying to make him see that all this was the result of a blind attachment toward a man named Janos, whom Alexander had elevated to role model.

"Do you remember the story of the "passion-fruit eaters" from mythology?" asked Odysseus.

"Yes, but how is this relevant?" Alexander asked with sincere interest this time.

"While the companions of the sea-battered Odysseus were eating the passion fruits they desired to remain there, refusing to return to their country, and Odysseus had to take them from there by force," his father continued, as though he did not hear his question.

"So what?" said Alexander with some impatience.

"What do you believe? Did Odysseus act well by taking them away, or should he have left them behind, since that is what they desired, due to the influence of the passion fruits?" he finally asked.

"He was wrong to take them! He should have let them stay! Since they liked it there, he should have let them stay!" Alexander answered very spontaneously and stubbornly.

Odysseus was wondering if he had heard right. Was it possible, such voluntary blindness from his son? He was also observing the overall attitude of Alexander, to analyze him correctly. He wanted to see his entire psychology.

"Do you remember the film 'Truman Show'[176] that we watched a few days ago? How an entire city lived and revolved around Truman, in fabricated, fake roles, inside a lie, a delusion? Truman was the protagonist; he was the only genuine person. All the others acted hypocritically. They were speaking to him, they were greeting him and nothing was real. At some point, he acknowledged that he was the only authentic protagonist in such a well-fabricated scenario, where even his wife was not truly his. Yet, he was the protagonist. From the moment he discerned all this, he could have lived inside that farce the rest of his life, in a financially secure future, pretending along with everyone else and continuing the life of a happy protagonist; it would have been the easiest thing! However, he spurned all the fanfare; he exited the city they had fabricated around him, choosing a future of uncertainty. Do you believe that he should have gone along pretending inside that mythical city?"

By this Odysseus attempted again to jumpstart the conscience of his son.

"No, here he had a beautiful woman watching for him outside! He loved her and he needed to go out," Alexander said.

"What if the young lady did not exist, if he hadn't met her? Should he have continued to live a lie?" he asked him again.

"Yes! He should have stayed," Alexander answered.

Odysseus now knew well the psychology of his son. He could not detect a trace of love for study and truth in the boy's soul, at least not at this time. This was quite sudden, because a few months prior he remembered his son's views to be very different in their discussions. Back then, his son had had an unquenchable thirst for the lives of the saints, to know about illumination and theories, and one eve-

---

[176] 'Truman Show' was released in 1998. The film follows the life of Truman Barbank who is unaware that since birth he lives in a "constructed reality" island, all the people around him are actors going by script, and every moment of his life is being filmed and watched by millions.

ning they had stayed up discussing past midnight. Now, however, a sudden and unexpected change had overtaken the psychology of the child. Therefore, his father wanted to get to the heart of the matter.

"Tell me then, Alexander, can you knowingly live inside a lie, the lie of the Witnesses? How can you bear it?" he asked with justified indignation.

"I am not like you. I don't have any pangs of conscience, no guilt at all. I can do it! Furthermore, I will try to forget everything you have taught me up to now. I already have forgotten a lot. I will try to believe what the Witnesses say, so I can be upright with my conscience."

This was the answer which ratified the decision of the child to join the Watchtower Society. Odysseus reassured Alexander that he would always be eager to help him return to the Church. When his maturity would lead him toward this, he would need to dismiss all doubt or shame, and remember that Christ, as the Father of the Prodigal, will always be waiting. Christ will even rush to embrace him before he arrives at the door of the faith.

From that time, Alexander began to participate regularly in the meetings of the Witnesses and apparently to carry out his desire for the scriptural study with Janos. Toward evening he would return home, well dressed, with a tie, like one of their clones, and seeming to be fully satisfied to hear the praises of the Witnesses for his wisdom in joining the Society.

One evening his father, who did not fail to tease him, said to him: "Welcome my 'clone'! What do I see? Do you like being dressed up like that?"

"Yes, the other day some of my friends saw me and said, 'What a cool suit!' I like being like this!" he said full of enthusiasm.

"What exactly do you like about this?" Odysseus asked.

"How would I know? I just like it!"

"So you like to show off! You like to show off your great clothes, to be debonair. However, did you ever consider the main root of this desire? Doesn't it stem from egocentrism and pride?" he asked him.

"Well, yes, but so what?"

"Do you see where the Society invests its stakes? In the lower instincts of man; in order to enslave him. The Society does not elevate him spiritually, it lowers him; it increases his pride and egocentrism, in contrast to the Church," he answered him.

"Didn't you like this yourself in the past?" Alexander asked.

"Of course I liked it when I was your age, but not anymore!" Odysseus responded.

"You are a strange man!" Alexander said, and Odysseus questioned which one of them was strange…

At different times, Odysseus observed his son's expressions, even his smile, which began to look more and more like the crooked smile of Janos. One day at the soccer field, along with the team formed by the well-known clique of Janos, another team came to play, made up of young Witnesses who no longer attended the Witnesses' meetings. When Alexander returned home, he told his mother, "Athanasios' 'bunch' was also there!"

"Did Janos' 'bunch' play with them?" Odysseus asked with meaning.

To be certain that his son had understood his message, when they were alone together he explained to him that he shouldn't allow the mindset of the Society to influence him to such a degree that it would destroy his personality, separating people into "bunches of 'spiritual' and 'non-spiritual'." He advised him to maintain Christian humility, which he had heard about for so many years, and not to become one of the Pharisees of the organization. His advice however was not heard. A few months later, the destructive termite of the Society totally infested the child's personality.

14. In the land of the "passion-fruit eaters"

Odysseus saw the worst and most disgusting elements he had known in the Society take root and reform his son's life. He was watching his son turn into a spineless peon of the Society, comparable only to the youth of Hitler's Germany. His countenance had lost Christian humility and adapted in its place an apparent vainglory. His actions were all egotistical—the sole purpose was self-gratification—and his words were arrogant and egotistical. Eventually his visits to his elderly and homebound grandmother who had distanced herself from the Society became sparse. One day, compelled by his father, he went to her home to see her. She complained to him that his visits were progressively sparse. His answer to her was, "I love you, but I was shown a letter of the Society stating that we must not visit our disfellowshipped relatives who don't reside in the same home as us."

Odysseus had interpreted the verses used by the Society to bolster their tactics against those disfellowshipped many times in the presence of his son, who had confessed even after his voluntary enslavement that he did not agree with these tactics. Odysseus never expected to hear these words from his son's mouth. He approached his son when they were home alone and told him, "At some point you told me that you wished to become a Witness because the Society makes you a 'better person'. You can see how much 'better of a person' you have become by refusing to go see even your sick and homebound grandmother, because they showed you this tactic in some tent of the Society."

"I am saddened by this, but since I became a Jehovah's Witness, this is what I must do. Moreover, in matters of faith I don't want to have any discussion with you."

"If this saddens you, then show it by your actions. Hurting your grandmother is a broader matter than matters of faith; and if it is a matter of faith, since you claim that you accept only the Holy

Scriptures, show me where you find these things in the Scriptures?"

"No further discussion!" said Alexander, and he walked away to an adjoining room.

"Look in the mirror to see how much of a better man you have been transformed into by the Society! Only vipers and children of the serpent hurt their parents this way," his father had the opportunity to tell him, being totally disappointed by the malice of his son and beginning to fully reconsider how destructive and anti-Christian this organization happens to be, despite the claims of its members.

* * *

I BELIEVE THE above to be indicative—in order to help make understood what I'm about to briefly try to present next—of a new methodology which the Watchtower Society has implemented in the last few years. This pertains to the clubhouse method.

In the past decades, during which we at least got to know the Watchtower Society on a first-hand basis, there was a certain fear among the families of Witnesses that motivated them to "be careful that our children not become influenced by the 'glitter' of this world and apostatize from the path of God, by delighting in the pleasures of the world."

At that time, it was rare, even scandalous, for a Witness to indulge in parties. The basic preoccupations of the Witnesses of the Watchtower were the work of faith and the search for truth. This paradigm, however, slowly began to change. The truth was no longer marketable for the Watchtower, especially since the era of mass communication presents great difficulties to impostors. The preaching was not bad, but the Society's followers were fed up with it.

The world has become more and more enchanting; there are new morals and new customs. The Paradise of bliss, central to the preaching of the Witnesses, was exchanged for the search of en-

14. In the land of the "passion-fruit eaters"

joyment in their earthly life. Slowly but steadily, beginning with the decade of the 80's, the Watchtower began to push its followers toward a new way of life. Ever so gently, it began to make its groups accustomed to home fellowships, to counteract the parties of the world that had so fatally attracted and influenced the children, thereby creating in their children the constant desire for more home fellowships.

Covered with a pseudo-spiritual gloss, these fellowships began to be established as the most habitual form of entertainment in the circles of the Watchtower. Simultaneously, the establishment of amateur soccer teams of the Witnesses also began to take root. Consequently, it was no longer necessary for a Witness to go to the outside world to fill his life with various entertainments. The Watchtower had succeeded in bringing the world inside its own walls!

By this strategy, it not only retained its members but accomplished something additional: a Witness branded by the organization as unproductive would not only feel like an intruder, but even undesirable at a party. Furthermore, the ability to attend these parties as spiritual brothers provided extra points for their social image in the eyes of the others around them. Consequently, a spiritual brother who constantly refers to the Society of Jehovah and such, becomes the center of attention at these meetings, while the Society's elite upholds this image of the spiritually energized brother. Simultaneously, these closed communities create an environment of mystique, intriguing to those outside. And while some time ago the Witnesses had feared lest their children become drawn to the world to enjoy its pleasures, now the children of the world are in danger of finding themselves in such a closed community of entertainment.

If we want to be truthful, we must admit that the Society of the Witnesses has lately been altered into a community of entertainment. In all the programs—from those of instructive meetings to the programs of fellowship and men's soccer—the overall agenda centers on keeping the members of the Watchtower well satisfied within the environment of the organization and in attracting new members. As someone recently observed very accurately, the method of the New World Order, namely, bread and entertainment is carried out with great success in the ranks of the Watchtower.

The Society uses entertainment to lull its followers, to distract them from truly important matters toward mundane matters. (What will we eat and drink today; when will we play soccer; and what clothes will I show off at the upcoming meeting?). The meetings of the Watchtower have become a huge international showcase. With the new paradigm, the Watchtower succeeds in maintaining its members fully occupied and well-pleased. It attracts new members to its "clubs" by investing in the lower instincts of its members. Initially it invests in their egotism and egocentrism, since they all strive to *display* their great new wardrobes, their athletic capabilities, their spiritual expressions, their extensive missionary deeds, their eloquent homilies, their new homes and automobiles, their upcoming vacation plans, and their delicious meals at their fellowships.

The Watchtower shows no concern for the spiritual downturn caused to its members by emphasizing all these vainglorious activities. For the organization this is a numbers game, and what is of importance is the increase of these dead numbers. It has created for every one of its members a huge "Truman Show", an artificial land of plenty, where everything is supposedly available: entertainment, sports, showing off, opportunities for personal advancement, artificial (and of course fraudulent) spiritual assurance from the upcoming destroyer of the worlds—God, Jehovah—where everyone can find some sector to "be put on the pedestal."

What does a man yearn for? Food? Drink? Sports? Flaunting of financial success? Acceptance as "knowledgeable"? Does he de-

14. In the land of the "passion-fruit eaters"

sire the arena of public speaking, to be an orator? Does he wish to be in a position of authority as a elder, even when in his everyday life he may be a simple street cleaner or a glass peddler? Does he desire visual entertainment? (No problem, the Watchtower has its own impressive videos; but if someone wants something more, the movie theaters will do just fine.)

Name it and it's there. Even matchmakers are busy at work at every gathering and District Convention of the People of God. My godson Alexander fell into such a trap, and left to enter the world of the Watchtower. He knowingly sought to live inside a "Truman Show", in a land of "passion-fruit eaters" where the criterion is not truth and one's relationship with God, nor humility and love, but entertainment, pride and ostentation. He chose the false feeling of "self worth" within an artificial world of hedonism, where pleasure is conveniently combined with salvation.

There is a certain threshold in the heart of some people. Once they cross over it, logic ceases to function, and neither arguments nor truths have any place there; there is only a place for the gratification of the flesh. When you speak with those who have crossed this threshold, you will see a strange look in their eyes: the look of a man who is afraid, who fears the tearing down of the artificial world he designed for himself. He does not want to learn. He does not want to disturb his comfort zone. He does not want to face the truth. He wants to see everything through the lens of the Society. Moreover, if you attempt to analyze him in the least he will become annoyed with you and tell you directly or indirectly, "Stop looking into my mind and heart. Allow me to live out the myth I created for myself. Let me live the way I have chosen. Do not sow any doubts in me. I hate guilt."

My experience with these people has shown me that they will *definitely* proceed with the life of heresy they have chosen, and such a life is not limited to the cult of the Watchtower. It is futile to present arguments to them because they will simply instantly forget everything you tell them. However, the Lord is the good shepherd (John 10:11), and there is hope! I have seen many people who chose the land of "passion-fruit eaters" go forward with their decision and become assimilated there, disregarding logic and knowing in advance that many things inside were wrong. They did not want to listen. I have seen many of these same people approach me years later, after they had amused themselves enough to ask for help, fed up with the lies and hypocrisy. The time comes when some understand the vanity into which they had fallen and they seek their Father again, the One whom they had abandoned to dive into the exciting, hedonistic lifestyle of the world.

They return in repentance to the fully illumined house of the Church and then finally appreciate the things they considered common and insignificant in their early years. Then, with many tears they yearn for those lost years—years that cannot be recaptured. In addition, they face reality not only with the weight of the true Christian life, but with the baggage they now carry inside them from the time they feasted on the carob pods and passion fruits of the well-staged theatrical play of the Witnesses. Let us continue to pray, my brothers, for all these people, so that God may give them repentance and a swift return, because they are also our brothers.

15. Problems and dangers

Shortly after my conversion I began to sense that the devil was preparing an ambush. After the initial enthusiasm wore off, one after another of the former Witnesses who were led with us to the Orthodox Church quickly began to lose steam. Most of them ceased to progress and became stagnant, and some backslid. They had not been outside the Watchtower Society for very long, and when they were no longer "pushed" by others, they stopped moving ahead.

This is one of the common dangers awaiting all those who come out of such totalitarian groups. Their sudden freedom often leads them to minimize their efforts and even leads to inertia. Usually these are people who left their group for personal reasons and not for the sake of love for the truth.

People who leave heresies for dogmatic reasons rarely go back, despite the inescapable difficulties of their struggle in their new spiritual arena. Such failures (of people returning to the heresy) have a negative influence even on the Witnesses who are watching them and anxiously waiting to see something backfire so they can "reassure" themselves that "whoever leaves the flock, gets eaten by the wolf." The Society has stressed to them that whoever leaves it gets lost in the world. Thus, the people in it keep tabs on the journey of every one who leaves. If they see him stop his religious pursuits, they conclude that they did well to trust the Society. However, the continued progress of a disfellowshipped person becomes problematic to them, because they realize that there is life outside the Watchtower.

Afraid to Trust Again

USUALLY PEOPLE WHO depart from such organizations are so hurt by the fact that they were deceived and taken advantage of by the religion they trusted as the "channel of God," that they can never trust anyone again, perhaps even forever. Some lose their confidence in all religions, in the Holy Scriptures and even in God. I remember one of my acquaintances, an ex-"elder" of the Witnesses, who after leaving the Society went for two years without touching the Holy Scriptures. Indeed, the blame is to be placed mainly on the organization that deceived him.

Sola Scriptura

THE OPPOSITE CAN also be true: when a man remains excessively attached to the Holy Scriptures according to the Protestant paradigm he had practiced. This shows that, instead of having the Church as his source of faith, along with whatever she teaches from her God-inspired sources of revelation, this man arbitrarily and heretically embraces from all these sources "only" the Holy Scriptures, and if something is not analytically referred to in it, he rejects it as "human" tradition. This means that he does not trust the Church as the true Body of the Lord Jesus Christ and considers it to be a human institution. One of the criteria, therefore, to gauge someone's true conversion to Orthodoxy is whether he trusts the Church more than the Holy Scriptures. The man who truly returns to the Church accepts every word of the Church as coming from God, equivalent to the Holy Scriptures, and does not over-accentuate the Holy Scriptures at the expense of the other God-inspired traditions.

15. Problems and dangers

The Purpose of the Church

ONCE A LOVER of God has finally found the historical Church, there is another danger awaiting him. Experience has shown that most of those who "stalemated" after their admittance to the Orthodox Church missed the requisite Jehovah Witness comradeship which had met their emotional needs. In the Watchtower Society, all the emphasis is placed on external "good deeds." Indeed, there is an unceasing stream of activities: talks, seminars, house-to-house preaching, bible studies, conventions, and so on. All these sound good but there is no attention given to the heart where the real spiritual life takes place. Former Witnesses could not find a sense of fellowship, conditional as it was, in their local Orthodox parish which is often multitudinous and impersonal. Consequently the Church ceased to "move" them because they were expecting the Church to fill the emotional voids in their life, and not necessarily to lead them to the life in Christ Jesus. It would be good for Christians in every parish to develop strong interpersonal relations among the faithful in order to keep some of the faithful from being drawn away to non-Christian and heretical "brotherhoods." A newcomer, however, has to go deeper and understand that the goal of the Church is the illumination and theosis of its members and focus on a life of prayer, otherwise he will remain a Christian of the letter and not of the spirit; he will reduce the Christian faith to a philosophical system and will always struggle with logical analyses and interpretations, while never receiving any gifts of the Holy Spirit.

The Danger of Ecumenism

IN OUR DAYS when globalism, relativism, and political correction are considered virtues par excellence, there is a danger even in the Orthodox Church of the faithful being scandalizing. For example, I knew a Witness who lived abroad, a Greek of the diaspora. By the Grace of God he understood he was in error, so he sought to return to the Orthodox Church. He was chrismated, according to the Canons, and he returned to Greece in search of other Orthodox Christians to learn more about his faith. He found and held discussions with the parish priest of his area and was very satisfied with his answers.

One day, the local bishop was due for a visit. My acquaintance thought, "If I received such satisfying answers from a parish priest, imagine speaking to the bishop!" So he went up and introduced himself, and told him that he had returned to the Orthodox faith. To his great surprise, instead of being welcomed by the bishop, His Grace chastised him, telling him that it was wrong for him to change his faith and the fact that he had become Orthodox showed instability of character!

Fortunately, I had forewarned him that scandals will continue to exist in the Church,[177] just as they had existed during the age of the Apostles and during the time of the old Israel. I had told him that he needs to learn to separate individuals from the faith. True faith and sound dogma are of paramount importance.

As for ecumenism, he needs to be watchful. Ecumenistic talks are seductive because ecumenism "glosses over" the substantive differences between Orthodoxy and heterodoxy. This is a sin of frightening proportions. It ultimately denies the Truth to so many former heterodox Christians who have struggled to find the true Church and attempts to shut the door to others still searching by emphasizing commonalities.[178] If some people say otherwise, the Church is not to blame! We have to respect them; judgment belongs to the Lord, but nothing can change the historic reality that the Orthodox Church is the "One Holy Catholic and Apostolic Church."

---

177 Matt. 13:41-18:7; 2 Peter 1:3

178 See Hieromonk Alexios Karakallinos, *Contours of Conversion & the Ecumenical Movement–Some Personal Reflections*, http://uncutmountain.com/uncut/docs/fralexios_contours.pdf

15. Problems and dangers

* * *

LORD, THANK YOU for giving me everything I asked from You. I asked You to give me knowledge so I can recognize Your truth, and You gave me so much knowledge, that it is not even possible for me to begin to assimilate it. I asked You to fill my cup and You made it run over! This knowledge, however, taught me that I had no idea what I was asking back then! I shouldn't have asked You for knowledge! I should have asked You for purification and illumination. Now, therefore, I also beseech You for this gift, which is the true need of every man...

Now I am praying to God as Father, and not as Lord as did the pre-Christian faithful who did not have the revelation of our Lord Jesus Christ, not unlike the Western "Christians." This was a new dimension of God for me, considering that I had been accustomed from childhood to see God as a "bugbear" who was keeping an exact account of all my deeds, so that He could "avenge" me at some future Day of Judgment. My God was no longer the "unjust God" of the West, Who is satisfied with the death of the righteous for the sake of the unrighteous, and Who gives as "ransom" the death of His innocent Son to some tyrant, as if He was afraid of him. He did not fabricate "caldrons" of hell to sadistically torture His creatures, nor did He plan to kill them at some future destruction. In His Church I learned that God sent His Word and Son Jesus Christ to assume our human nature and unite it with the divine. Thus, He could elevate it to His Own likeness by grace, so that His purpose for man could be fulfilled. And thus, "human nature could defeat death" in the Person of Jesus Christ, who defeated death by His resurrection.

And so now, every faithful Christian has the authority to be called a son of God: God can be his Father and he can be God's child. I learned that God is and will be "everything to everyone" or "everything for everyone"—something which will make some people very joyous—to be in this tight embrace of His love; while others will hate this very tight embrace, and this love will be hell to them. Paradise will be this communion of love with God, and the lack of this communion will be Hell. The experience of God's love and the realization of our failure to respond to it will cause the pain and the torture of Hell. I learned that the truth I was seeking was not a package of doctrines, but a Person. And the name of this Person is Jesus Christ.

These days I speak of the true Gospel to people who are interested in knowing it. Nothing was lost in all these years. Everything was a valuable experience which can now be used in the service of the true Gospel for the deliverance of people who have been trapped in a cage and are searching for a way out. The harvest is plentiful but the laborers are few. And the Lord of the harvest keeps sending laborers, more by the day, to work in His vineyard. I rejoice to see more and more of my past acquaintances searching for a way out of the cage in which they were skillfully captured by trappers, and I will not neglect to offer my assistance, in any way that I can, on their difficult journey.

Finally, I have accepted the request to become the godfather of George's son, as a small token of my gratefulness to him, especially since we helped and depended on one another on this long *journey leading to Truth and Life.*

Tables

Small Glossary

The Jehovah's Witnesses have their own argot—"buzz words" that help them achieve a desirable invisible isolation from both the outside world and from other Christian groups. The following list is a selection of words that are found in the book and might be unfamiliar to the general reader. In our effort, we found invaluable help in Reed's *Jehovah-Talk*,[1] Botting's *Orwellian World*,[2] Chryssides' *Historical Dictionary*,[3] Wilson's *Awakening*,[4] Newton's, *Glossary*,[5] and Shaun's, *Jehovah's Witnesses' Unique Buzz Words and Phrases*.[6]

Anointed Ones   The Watchtower Society teaches that after the Armageddon, the faithful JWs will be separated into two classes; the "Great Crowd" that will inherit the earth and the 144,000 'chosen ones' (Revelation 14:1-3) that will reign with Christ in Heaven for the duration of the millennium. Those who belonged to the International Bible Students' Association up to 1931 are generally believed to be anointed ones, but in 1931 the organization decided to also include certain members from the great crowd. It is hold that in 1935 the anointed class became virtually complete, however the exact identity of all 144,000 members is not known for certain. These "anointed ones" are traditionally depicted as wearing white robes and standing in rows before Jehovah.

---

1 David A. Reed, *Jehovah-Talk: The Mind Control Language of Jehovah's Witnesses*, Baker House, 1997

2 Gary Norman Arthur Boting, *The Orwellian World of Jehovah's Witnesses,* University of Toronto Press, 1984, pp. 187–194

3 George D. Chryssides, *Historical Dictionary of Jehovah's Witnesses,* University of Toronto Press, 1984, pp. 187–194

4 Dianne Wilson, *Awakening of a Jehovah's Witness—Escape from the Watchtower Society*, Prometheus Books, 2002, pp. 41–42, 305, 307–318

5 Lynn David Newton, *Glossary of American English Hacker Theocratese*, (retrieved 2/3/2009 from ftp://www.eecs.umich.edu/people/lnewton/gloss/bundles/glossary6.7.pdf)

6 Shaun, *Jehovah's Witnesses' Unique Buzz Words and Phrases*, (retrieved 2/3/2009 from http://www.jwfiles.com/jw-words.htm)

	The selection begun in the first century with Christ choosing his Apostles and was completed in 1935. See also *Remnant*.
Adjust (—ed teachings)	A euphemism JWs use to refer to doctrinal changes, most often in relation to failed prophecies. See also *New Light*.
Apostate	A JW who has been expelled from the Watchtower Society for disagreeing on dogmatical grounds and/or the organizational leadership. Since it is believed that an apostate is rebelling against Jehovah, all fellow co-religionists are instructed to shun him. The latest official policy specifies that "No visit would be made on any who evidence a critical, dangerous attitude." (WT, 4/15/1991 p 23). "Willing association with true apostates, whether in person, by reading their literature, or engaging in electronic debate across the Internet, is itself apostate behavior, and therefore potentially a disfellowshipping offense, in addition to being extremely dangerous and outright stupid. It should be avoided entirely." (Newton, *Glossary*). According to Reed, "Apostate is the most derogatory term in Witness vocabulary. A JW sees apostates as ranking below prostitutes, murderers, and child abusers." (Reed, *Jehovah-Talk*, p. 41)
Appeal	When a JW is disfellowshipped he has the right to appeal the decision of the judicial committee within seven days, in which the whole case will be rehearsed by the same committee. "However," JW overseer A. Crispin warns, "I should tell you that an appeal usually peeves the elders on the judicial committee that disfellowshipped you, because now you are going over their heads and by doing that there is an implication that they did something wrong. Remember, elders are only human. Elders have egos and they usually don't take kindly to an inference that they have made an unjust or unfair decision. Also, they are the same elders who will consider your reinstatement." (A. Crispin, *A Guide to Reinstatement*, p. 45)
Armageddon	The ultimate battle between Christ and Satan in which this present "evil system" will be utterly destroyed and Jeho-

	vah's New Kingdom will be established. Beginning with Russell, the Watchtower Society has given quite a few definite dates as to when this was supposed to happen.
Ark	The Watchtower Society is considered by the JWs as the Ark of Salvation.
Bad Associations	Also known as wrong or "harmful associations", bad associations mean anyone who is not a JW and Witnesses that don't follow the Society's commandments very warmly. The Watchtower Society attaches great importance to the company one keeps as a means of faith maintenance, frequently quoting the text, "Bad associations spoil useful habits" (1 Corinthians 15:33). Thus mixing with non-JWs or being exposed to ideas that counter Watch Tower teachings is discouraged. In the later context, bad associations also include secular literature, radio, television, cinema, and the Internet. Religious ideas that originate from the mainstream churches, are also believed to be dangerous.
Bad Guys	(Capitalized). Any loosely group class of *apostates* that vocally criticize the Watchtower Society. The rise of the internet gave them a major momentum, especially since it is calculated that there are now more people that have left the Watchtower Society than active members.
Bible-trained conscience	Thinking according to Watchtower Society dictates.
Bethel	An administrative office in which volunteers also help to print and ship reading materials. The central Bethel is located in Brooklyn, NY, with another 114 branch Bethel offices around the world. Usually, each country has one "Bethel", but some regions have more than one. The staff varies in size according to the size of the local congregation.
Brooklyn	The official headquarters of the Watchtower Society.
Circuit	An administrative unit of about 20 congregations that are close to one another geographically and led by a Circuit Overseer. Several circuits comprise a district.
Circuit assembly	The congregations in each circuit would meet together for a spiritual upbuilding program. This is a much smaller event than the annual *District Convention*.

Circuit Overseer See *Overseer, Circuit*.

Disassociated A JW who has resigned his identity as a Jehovah's Witnesses—this can be done either by submitting a formal letter of resignation, or simply "walking away." Since the 1990s, disassociated people are to be shunned like the disfellowshipped.

Disfellowshipping The most serious punishment the Watchtower can impose on its members. There is a list of specific offenses for which a JW can be disfellowshipped and a set procedure for disfellowshipping. According to the Watchtower Society "The expelled person is not a mere man of the world who has not known God nor pursued a godly way of life. Rather, he has known the way of truth and righteousness, but he has left that way and unrepentantly pursued sin to the point of having to be expelled. So he is to be treated differently." (WT 9/15/1981, pp. 20–26). Disfellowshipped members are believed to be obliterated forever once they die and are shunned by the whole body of the Jehovah's Witnesses. Reinstatement is possible but only after an extended period of time, following open confession and repentance, which are formally accepted by the original disfellowshipping committee.

District A group of *Circuits*.

District Convention A three or four day event in which the congregations of the district would assemble. The conventions take place once a year, in suitable rented facilities, in which thousands of Witnesses can gather. The conventions are planned months ahead.

District Overseer See *Overseer, District*.

Double life Many JW teenagers in their homes and in the Kingdom Halls pretend to be model Witnesses, while among their friends and in school act as *wordlings*.

Elder A man appointed by the Watchtower Society to a position of authority in a congregation. New elders are recommended by the local body of elders to the local Branch Office, and are assigned by the Governing Body, during a visit of a Circuit Overseer. Macmillan, in his *Faith on the March* (p. 159) writes, "Russell wanted to destroy the pagan idea of the clergy-laity distinction." Cole (in his *Jehovah's Witnesses, the New World Society*, p. 173) writes, "Jehovah's witnesses world-wide make up a society of ministers. There is no clergy class or laity class." The modern JW overseers, however, have become almost *that*: a separated clerical class that are responsible with teaching the congregation, fulfilling various administrating tasks, having a position of judicial oversight over the congregation, hearing confessions, and above commemorating the "death of Christ."

Emblems The unleavened bread and unadulterated wine circulated at the time of Memorial Service (14 Nisan according to the Watchtower Society's understanding of the Jewish calendar). Witnesses believe that the emblems are just symbols of the body and blood of Christ, denying the doctrine of "real presence." Only members of the *Remnant* of the *Anointed* class partake. All other Witnesses watch.

Faithful & Discreet Slave According to the Watchtower, the collective body of the "anointed class" constitute the "Faithful and Discrete Slave." In practice, however, only the *Governing Body* can dictate organizational policy. Note, though, that up to 1923 the termed referred to Russell (see WT 3/1/1923 p 68).

Field Service The "door-to-door" evangelizing effort of the Witnesses. Even though the second president of the Watchtower Society placed an unprecedented emphasis on this, in reality, according to Raymond Franz, "there is strong evidence that only a minority of Witnesses became such as the result of a visit to their doors.... The majority were interested by family members, workmates, acquaintances and similar contacts. Reports by circuit overseers have presented similar evidence." (Franz, *Christian Freedom*, p. 221)

Field Service Report The monthly accounting of field activity that each person turns in to the secretary of the congregation. "The monthly Field Service Report was the principal way that one's spirituality was measured. Although purportedly used only by the Society headquarters for the purpose of keeping track of how the witnessing work is going the elders used these reports also as a gauge of 'how well one was doing in the Truth.' When a Witness starts to drift away because of having doubts, often the first sign will be a reduction in the number of hours that the person spends proselytizing." (Wilson, *Awakening*, p. 36)

Goat — Anyone who rejects the Watchtower message.

God's Channel — The belief that the Watchtower Society (and its governing body in particular) is God's only Channel of communication on earth. In short the claim is based on the belief that the kingdom of God was established in heaven in 1914, that the "time of the end" began that year, that Christ returned invisibly at that time to "inspect" the Christian denominations, and that He rejected all of them except for the Watch Tower Society, which he in 1919 appointed as his sole "instrument" on earth. Therefore, the whole concept that the Watchtower Society is the Channel of God rests on the 1914 dogma.

Governing Body — A group of about 14 men who profess to be of the *remnant* class, having their base in the "Bethel" of New York that make all policy decisions for the Witnesses' religion. Until the late 1970s, the Governing Body was also the board of directors of the Watch Tower Bible & Tract Society.

Great Crowd — The vast majority of faithful JWs that will inherit the "paradise-earth" after the Armageddon. Compare with *Anointed Ones* and *Remnant*.

Judicial Committee — A special committee, consisting of the local congregation's board of elders and sometimes the circuit overseer and/or district overseer, assigned to examine cases of wrongdoing in the congregation. For all purposes and intents it is a religious court. And "though [the Watch Tower Society] praises the influence toward "carefulness and justice" that public hearings produce, the reality is that all Witness 'judicial committee' hearings are, by organizational policy, held precisely in the form of 'secret star-chamber

Tables

	hearings,' with the result that the committee is, in effect, answerable only to itself." (Franz, *Christian Freedom*, p. 325)
Kingdom Hall or **Hall**	The church building of the Witnesses. Some times more than one congregation can use the same Kingdom Hall.
Letter of disassociation	A formal letter of resignation from the ranks of the Jehovah's Witnesses, usually addressed to the local Bethel. Treatment of disassociated members have varied over time, but since 1981 "Persons who make themselves 'not of our sort' by deliberately rejecting the faith and beliefs of Jehovah's Witnesses should appropriately be viewed and treated as are those who have been disfellowshipped for wrongdoing." (WT 9/15/81 p. 20–26) This clause, effectively, controls people's religious freedom as many are afraid to leave the Society lest they lose their family members.
Little Flock	See *Anointed Ones*.
Marking	Is applied to persons who display "flagrant disregard for theocratic order," yet not of sufficient seriousness to warrant disfellowship. Members of the congregation are called on to "mark" this person who then has a 'limited social fellowship.' The distinction between "marking" and "shunning" appears to be fuzzy, even to JWs themselves.
Meetings	Any of the five JW gatherings held regularly each week at Kingdom Hall: the Public Talk and the *Watchtower* Study, usually held on Sunday morning; the Ministry School and the Service Meeting, usually held on Thursday evening; and the Congregation Book Study, usually held on Tuesday evening in a number of smaller groups.
Microphone Men	It is the men who adjust the audio system in the Kingdom Halls and hold the microphone for the speakers at the meetings. It is considered a great privilege and a reward for good service.
Ministerial Servant	A publisher appointed to assist the elder in routine work (like maintaining the Kingdom Hall), shepherding calls, etc. A ministerial servant might take certain elder's duties if need be.
New Light	Changes in Watchtower theology. While it seems reason-

able to an outsider that dogmas in a religion, as expressions of divine truths, should stay stable, JWs are led to believe that since mortal men are finite, Jehovah has chosen to reveal His truths progressively. "Rather than a stumbling stone, the Society's readiness to alter its views when necessary should be a source of comfort and encouragement, an assurance that there will be continual advancement and increase in learning, an ever-brightening light as we approach closer to the perfect day with its noonday brightness." (WT 10/15/1954 pp.638-9). The problem with this claim is that in a number of cases the so-called "ever-brightening light" has guided the Society to triple (and in some case quadruple) contradictions, going from "new-lights" back to "old-lights" and then reverting to "newer-lights" again. Here is an example: "Can Witnesses accept Alternative Service Work in lieu of Military Service?"

    1898 - YES! (WT 8/1/1898, p. 231)
    1915 - MAYBE (WT 9/1/1915, reprints p. 5755)
    1918 - YES! (WT 5/15/1918, reprints p. 6268)
    1974 - NO! (AW 12/8/1974 p. 23 and WT 9/1/86 p. 20)
    1996 - YES! (WT 5/1/1996, p. 20)

Watchtower's changes include numerous "end-time" calculations, important doctrines, promotion of pagan symbols, rules on education, marital life, and medical advice.

Overseer — An "elder" in position of authority. Each congregation has its own body of "overseers" and in ascending order of rank there are the Theocratic Ministry School Overseer, the *Watchtower* Study Conductor, the Service Overseer, the Secretary, and the Presiding Overseer. All the congregations of a circuit are under the supervision of the Circuit Overseer, and all circuits in a district are under the District Overseer.

Overseer, Circuit — An experienced elder who represents the Governing Body in a Circuit. He is above the "presiding overseers" in his circuit. The Circuit Overseer would visit each congregation in his Circuit twice a year, for a week at a time, to give talks,

	meet with the local clergy, and lead the "field work."
Overseer, District	An elder who has the care of a district. He is above the Circuit Overseer. His duties include visiting congregations together with the local Circuit Overseer and to teach in Ministerial Training School.
Overseer, Presiding	The "chairman" at the elders' meetings. His duties include to Baptism arrangements; preparing the service meetings, and the public talk schedules.
Pioneer	Publishers who pledge to log in a specific amount of hours of field service every month; there are three levers of Pioneers.
Pioneer, auxiliary	The first and easier class of pioneers; it refers to regular publishers who will commit to do more than 50 hours of field service in a given month.
Publisher	Any Witness who actively participates in "door to door evangelizing" activity is known as "Publisher." A publisher does not have a specific quota of field service.
Publisher, baptized	An active witness (i.e. publisher) who had undergone a series of questions and has made a "personal dedication to serve God," as demonstrated in public baptism.
Publisher, unbaptized	An active witness who is on his way to becoming baptized.
Publisher's Record Card	The congregation's record of a Publisher's field activity and other vital statistics, kept by the secretary. Although any publisher may see his own card, it is the congregation's property, and he may not keep it.
Remnant	The Watchtower Society holds that there are two classes of believers; the "great crowd" that will inherit the earth, and a class of 144,000 *anointed ones*, who would spend eternity in heaven. As the selection ended in A.D. 1935, there are supposedly some 7,500 anointed ones still alive that are called the *Remnant*. All members of the Governing Body claim to be members of the Remnant class. There isn't any "official" procedure to tell who belongs to the remnant class and who doesn't; any active JW who partakes of the "emblems" (communion) in the annual Memorial meeting is considered de facto a member of the Remnant class.

Theocratic Ministry School A special seminary-like school for JW *publishers*; its goals consists of "providing useful training for the field ministry; help students progressively to improve their field presentations; train brothers to become effective public speakers and teachers." (*Pay Attention, to Yourselves and All the Flock*, 1991, p. 46). The school usually offers classes twice a week, in which the students sharpen their speaking skills and their knowledge in current *Watchtower* beliefs. According to Macmillan (in *Faith on March, pp. 194-195*) the schools started were started by President Knorr in 1943.

Theocratic Warfare A little known JW dogma to the general public which states that a JW, "as a soldier of Christ he is in theocratic warfare and he must exercise added caution when dealing with God's foes. Thus the Scriptures show that for the purpose of protecting the interests of God's cause, it is proper to hide the truth from God's enemies. A Scriptural example of this is Rehab the harlot" (WT 6/1/1960 p.352). And the *Aid to Bible Understanding* (1971 edition, p. 1061) sheds further light, "While malicious lying is definitely condemned in the Bible, this does not mean that a person is under obligation to divulge truthful information to people who are not entitled to it." Ex-witness David A. Reed explains it as "deceiving outsiders to advance the organization's interests. Falsehoods presented to 'God's enemies' are not considered lies, due to the state of war existing between God's forces (the JWs) and Satan's (the rest of the world) (David A. Reed, *Jehovah-Talk*, Baker Books, 1997, p. 129)

Whole-souled Offering service "with the whole soul," referring to Matt 22:37 ,"You shall love the Lord your God with all your heart, with all your soul, and with all your mind."

Worldly Anyone who is not a member of the Watchtower Society. "Wordlings" are considered to belong to the "other camp" and there is no hope of resurrection for them.

Working the doors The preaching and book-selling activity of the JWs performed by visiting all the homes in their vicinity from door-to-door.

Bibliogragphy

Publications originating from the Watch Tower Bible and Tract Society, Brooklyn, New York

1. Books and Booklets (sorted by date)

Russell, Charles Taze, *Thy Kingdom Come,* 1880
Russell, Charles Taze, *The Time is at Hand,* 1902
Russell, Charles Taze, *Time is at Hand,* 1902
Russell, Charles Taze, *Photo Drama of Creation,* 1914
Russell, Charles Taze, *The Finished Mystery (Posthumous work of Pastor Russell),* 1918

Rutherford, J. F., *Millions Now Living Will Never Die,* 1920
Rutherford, J. F., *Harp of God,* 1921
Rutherford, J. F. *Creation,* 1927
Rutherford, J. F., *Prosperity Sure,* 1928
Rutherford, J. F., *Reconciliation,* 1928
Rutherford, J. F., *What You Need,* 1932
Rutherford, J. F., *His Vengeance,* 1934
Rutherford, J. F., *Riches,* 1936
Rutherford, J. F. , *Enemies,* 1937
Rutherford, J. F., *Religion,* 1940
Rutherford, J. F., *Children,* 1941

Theocratic Aid to Kingdom Publisher, 1945
Qualified to Be Ministers, 1955
From Paradise Lost to Paradise Regained , 1958
Jehovah's Witnesses in the Divine Purpose, 1959
The Truth that Leads to Eternal Life, 1968
The Approaching Peace of a Thousand Years, 1969
You Can Live Forever in Paradise on Earth, 1980
School and Jehovah's Witnesses, 1983
Reasoning From the Scriptures, second reprint, 1989
Should You Believe in the Trinity?, 1989
Pay Attention to Yourselves and All the Flock, 1991
Keep Yourselves in God's Love, 2008

2. Periodicals

Awake! (various issues)
Golden Age (various issues)
Kingdom Ministry (various issues)
The *Watchtower* (various issues)

Secondary Sources (in English)

Alexios Karakallinos (Hieromonk). *Contours of Conversion & the Ecumenical Movement—Some Personal Reflections* (retrieved 11/30/2008 from http://uncutmountain.com/uncut/docs/fralexioscontours.pdf)

Bergman, Jerry., *Lying in Court and Religion: An Analysis of the Theocratic Warfare Doctrine of the Jehovah's Witnesses* (retrieved 11/29/2008 from http://www.freeminds.org/doctrine/lyingincourt.doc)

Bergman, Jerry. *Why Jehovah's Witnesses Leave the Watchtower* (retrieved 2/1/2009 from http://www.seanet.com/~raines/leave.html)

Boting, Gary Norman Arthur. *The Orwellian World of Jehovah's Witnesses,* University of Toronto Press, 1984

Chretien, Leonard & Marjorie. *Witnesses of Jehovah,* Harvest House Publishers, 1988

Chryssides, George D. *Historical Dictionary of Jehovah's Witnesses,* Scarecrow Press, 2008

Cole, Marley. *Jehovah's Witnesses, the New World Society,* Vantage Press, 1955

Cole, Marley. *Triumphant Kingdom,* Criterion Books, 1957

Crispin, Anthony. *A Guide to Reinstatement for Those Disfellowshipped from the Watchtower Organization,* Lulu.com, 2008

Crompton, Robert. *Counting the Days to Armageddon: The Jehovah's Witnesses and the Second Presence of Christ,* James Clarke & Co, 1996

Curran, Edward Lodge Rev. *Judge—"for four days"—Rutherford,* International Catholic Truth Society, 1940

Doulis, Thomas, ed. *Journeys to Orthodoxy: A Collection of Essays by Converts to Orthodox Christianity.* Light and Life Publishing Company, 1986

Franz, Raymond. *Crisis of Conscience,* Commentary Press, 1999

Franz, Raymond. *In Search of Christian Freedom,* Commentary Press, 2002

Gillquist, Peter E., ed. *Coming Home: Why Protestant Clergy Are Becoming Orthodox.* Conciliar Press, 1992

Gregory Nazianzen (Saint). *Oration 38,* New Advent (CD edition)

Gruss, Edmund Charles. *Apostles of Denial, an Examination and Exposé of the History, Doctrines, and Claims of the Jehovah's Witnesses,* Eleventh edition, Presbyterian & Reformed Pub Co, 1986

Hilary of Poitiers (Saint). *On the Trinity, Book IV,* Hendrickson Publishers, 2004

Jonsson, Carl Olof. *The Gentile Times Reconsidered,* Commentary Press, 1998

Jonsson, Carl Olof. *The So-Called "Bible Chronology" of the Watch Tower Society,* 1993 (retrieved 11/29/2008 from http://user.tninet.se/~oof408u/fkf/english/chronology.htm)

Lee, Brenda. *Out of the Cocoon,* Robert D. Lee Publishers, 2006

Love, Charles. *20 Questions Jehovah's Witnesses Cannot Answer,* Xulon Press, 2005

Macmillan, A. H. *Faith on the March,* Prentice-Hall, inc., 1957

Mathison, Keith. *The Shape of Sola Scriptura,* Canon Press & Book Service, 2001

Mathison, Keith. *A Critique of the Evangelical Doctrine of Sola Scriptura,* Reformed Perspectives Magazine, vol 9, number 15, 2007

Newton, Lynn David. *Glossary of American English Hacker Theocratese,* (retrieved 2/3/2009 from ftp://www.eecs.umich.edu/people/lnewton/gloss/bundles/glossary6.7.pdf)

Penton, M. J. *Apocalypse Delayed—The Story of Jehovah's Witnesses,* University of Toronto Press, 1997

Peters, Joel. *Scripture Alone? 21 Reasons to Reject Sola Scriptura,* (retrieved 11/29/2008 from http://www.geocities.com/thecatholicconvert/solascriptura21.html)

Reed, D. A. *Jehovah-Talk: The Mind Control Language of Jehovah's Witnesses*, Baker House, 1997
Reed, D. A. *How to Rescue Your Loved One From the Watchtower*, Baker House, 1997
Reed, D. A. *Index of Watch Tower Errors*, Baker House, 2000
Romanides, John (Fr.). *Patristic Theology*, Uncut Mountain, 2008
Ross, Thomas. *Arian Objections to the Trinity Refuted*, (retrieved 11/3/2008 from http://faithalonesaves.googlepages.com/TriuneGod4Web.pdf)
Shaun. *Jehovah's Witnesses' Unique Buzz Words and Phrases*, (retrieved 2/3/2009 from http://www.jwfiles.com/jw-words.htm)
Stevenson, W. C. *The Inside Story of Jehovah's Witnesses*, Hart Publishing Company, Inc, New York City, 1975
Stone, Jon R. *Expecting Armageddon: Essential Readings in Failed Prophecy*, Routledge, 2000
The Douglas Walsh vs. The Right Honorable James Latham Clyde, M. P. C., etc., Court of Scotland, 1954 (retrieved 11/29/2008 from http://www.lulu.com/content/762879)
Tucker, Ruth. *Another Gospel: Cults, Alternative Religions, and the New Age Movement*, Zondervan, 2004
Vlahos, Hierotheos (Metropolitan). *Orthodox Psychotherapy*, Ι. Μ. Γενεθλίου Θεοτόκου, 2005
Vlahos, Hierotheos (Metropolitan). *Orthodox Spirituality*, Ι. Μ. Γενεθλίου Θεοτόκου
Walter, Jay, *My 6-Year Journey Out of the Watchtower*, (retrieved 11/24/2008 from http://www.exjws.net/pioneers/partintro.htm)
Whiteford, John (Fr.). *Sola Scriptura, In the Vanity of their Minds*, (retrieved 11/29/2008 from http://www.orthodoxinfo.com/inquirers/tca_solascriptura.aspx)
Wilson, Dianne. *Awakening of a Jehovah's Witness—Escape from the Watchtower Society*, Prometheus Books, 2002
Zacharias, Archimandrite. *The Hidden Man of the Heart: The Cultivation of the Heart in Orthodox Christian Anthropology*, Mount Thabor Publishing, 2008
Zizioulas, Ioannis (Metropolitan). *Eucharist, Bishop, Church: The Unity of the Church in the Divine Eucharist and the Bishop During the First Three Centuries*, Holy Cross Orthodox Press, 2001

Secondary Sources (in Greek)

Αντωνιάδης, Εμμανουήλ. *Διαψεύδονται οι Προφητείες των Μαρτύρων του Ιεχωβά*, Thessalonica, 1984
Βλάχος, Ιερόθεος. *Εκκλησία και Εκκλησιαστικό Φρόνημα*, Ι. Μ. Γενεθλίου Θεοτόκου, 1990
Θεοδωρόπουλος, Επιφάνιος, (Fr.). *Αρθρα, Μελέται, Επιστολαί*, Athens, 1981
Κλήμης Αλεξανδρείας, (άγιος). *Στρωματεις* (Miscellanies), 1999
Κολιτσάρας, Ιωάννης. *Οι μάρτυρες του Γιεχωβά: Αι Αιρέσεις των και η προπαγάνδα των*, εκδ. Ζωή, 1970
Κόκορης, Δημήτριος. *Ορθόδοξος Αντιαιρετική Πανοπλία*, Second Edition, Athens, 1993
Μακρής, Σπυρίδωνας. *Ο Χιλιασμός και οι κακοδοξίαι του*, εκδ. Ενορίας, 1952
Μπενεζίτης, Παντελεήμων. *Η Ποιμαντική Αντιμετώπισης του Χιλιασμού*, εκδ. Αποστολικής Διακονίας, 1976
Ρωμανίδης, Ιωάννης (Fr.). *Μέγας Βασίλειος και Γρηγόριος Νύσσης κατά Ευνομίου και τα Κοινά και Ακοινώνητα της Αγίας Τριάδος* (electronic format)
Τρεμπέλας, Παναγιώτης, *Δογματική της Ορθοδόξου Εκκλησίας*, εκδ. Ζωή, 1959
Χατζής, Ελευθέριος (Fr.). *Το Ξεσκέπασμα των Μαρτύρων του Ιεχωβά*, εκδ. Νεκταρίου Παναγοπούλου, 1990

Index

A
Alevizopoulos, Antonios (Fr.) 215, 237
Alexios Karakallinos (Hieromonk) 258
Anointed Ones C, H, I
Appeal 122, 125, 176, 187, D
Arius 21, 22, 223
Armageddon xv, 7, 8, 13, 14, 42, 55, 62, 83, 84, 95, 106, 107, 109, 111, 142, 144, 159, 164, 188, 195, 197, 203, 218, C, D, H, N, O
Athanasios (Saint) 21, 22, 211, 222, 248
Awake (magazine) 10, 16

B
Babylon 110
Babylon the whore 4
Benezitis, Panteleimon (Archimandrite) 97, 98, 109
Bergman, Jerry xiii
Boting, Gary Norman 218, C, N
Brooklyn 51, 52, 98, 108, 114, 128, 164, E, M

C
Christoula, George xv, 115, 117, 123, 127, 128, 129, 130, 131, 133, 137, 145, 146, 148, 149, 153, 197, 202, 207, 214
Circuit Assemblies 10
Circuit Overseer 42, 49, E, F, G, J, K
Clement of Alexandria (St.) 89
Constantinople 222
Crispin, Anthony 59
Crompton, Robert 203
Cross 18, 20, 221, 235, O

D
District Convention 156, 162, 253, E, F

E
Emblems 218, G, K
Evil Servant 5

F
Field Service 10, 52, 54, 55, 186, K
Flag 18, 19
Franz, Fred 100, 107, 121, 175
Franz, Raymond xiii, xv, 9, 52, 79, 107, 121, 134, 148, 164, G

G
Gangas, George 113, 114, 115, 116, 121, 138
Governing Body xiii, xv, 4, 9, 52, 59, 76, 77, 79, 85, 94, 96, 101, 107, 113, 114, 115, 117, 127, 134, 136, 138, 147, 149, 163, 164, 218, F, G, H, J, K
Great Crowd 95, C, H
Great Multitude 95, 147, 199, 202, 209
Gregory the Theologian (St) 23

H
Hierotheos Vlahos (Metropolitan) 213
Hilary of Poitiers (Saint) 22, N
Holy Spirit 12, 61, 86, 87, 206, 208, 209, 210, 213, 215, 231, 233, 234, 257
Holy Trinity 32, 159, 208, 209, 224, 225

I
Icons 17, 29, 36, 37, 39, 62, 99, 206, 224, 225
Ioannis Zizioulas (Metropolitan) 221

J
Jesus Christ xi, xiv, 18, 21, 39, 83, 88, 89, 99, 143, 175, 176, 186, 187, 206,

207, 208, 210, 212, 225, 256, 259, 260
John of Damascus (St.) 225
Jonsson, Carl Olof xv, 106, 134, 143, 164
Judicial Committee 58, 116, 119, 121, H

K
Kingdom Hall 10, 38, 66, 125, 197, I

L
Letter of Disassociation 199, I
Lincoln, Abraham 18
Lossky, Vladimir 225

M
Makronisos (island) 4, 77
Malakasa Estate 42, 65
Mathison, Keith 27
Matsagkouras, Agapios 135
Mavromagoulos v, xi, xiv
Military Service 76, 77, 79, 83, 92, 94, 154, 155
Mount Athos 212, 230

N
New Light 77, 99, 101, 103, 110, 164, D, I
Newton, Lynn David C

O
Ouspensky, Leonide 225

P
Panagia (Mother of God) 18, 19, 99
Paul, Apostle 18, 176, 184, 222, 231
Penton, M. J. 8, 9, 58, 60, 97, 156, 219, N
Pioneer(JW Evangelizer) 97, K
Pontius Pilate xi
Porphyrios of Oropos (Fr.) 214
Presiding Overseer 59, 75, J
Publishers (JW Evangelizers) 51, 54, 57, 60, 120, K, L

R
Reed, David A. 104, C, L
Remnant 218, 219, D, G, H, K
Rhodes (island) 3
Romanides, John (Fr.) 22, 213
Roula (Nikos' wife) 75, 76, 141
Russell, Charles Taze 2, 3, 5, 18, 27, 42, 53, 58, 76, 77, 98, 100, 105, 106, 108, 158, 165, 222, 223, E, G, M
Rutherford, Joseph F. 3, 4, 5, 18, 19, 20, 53, 58, 98, 99, 100, 165, M, N

S
Sabellius 209
Smyrna 6
Sola Scriptura 26, 27, 40, 105, 256, N, O
Students of the Scriptures 3, 5, 158, 169

T
Theocratic Ministry School 49, 50, 60, 96, I, J, L
Theocratic Warfare 128, L, N
Theodoropoulos Epiphanios (Fr.) 223
Trembelas, Panagiotis 103

V
Vamvas, Neophytos (Archimandrite) 26

W
Walter, Jay 59, 218
Watchtower (magazine) 4, 9, 16, 18, 20, 27, 28, 38, 41, 42, 50, 52, 53, 55, 59, 60, 76, 77, 86, 87, 94, 96, 100, 108, 128, 143, 144, 154, 164, 168, 169, 182, 191, 218, 244, D, F, G, I, J, L
Wilson, Dianne 38, C